The Professional Developments Series

These eight books provide you with a wealth of insight into all aspects of nursing practice. The series is essential reading for qualified, practising nurses who need to keep up-to-date with new developments, evaluate their clinical practice, and develop and extend their clinical management and teaching skills. Through reading these books, students of nursing will gain an insight into what the essence of nursing is and the wide range of skills which are daily employed in improving patient care. Up-to-date, referenced and appropriately illustrated, The Professional Developments Series brings together the work of well over 200 nurses.

Other titles in The Professional Developments Series:

Dunne **How Many Nurses Do I Need: A Guide** 1 870065 24 7
on Resource Management Issues
This book provides valuable advice and information for all nurses facing the challenge of taking direct responsibility for managing human resources and planning, providing quality assurance and managing financial resources.

Garrett **Healthy Ageing: Some Nursing Perspectives** 1 870065 22 0
This book puts healthy ageing into the context of a growing, healthy elderly population and looks at care aspects of daily living, health problems in old age, and working with older people.

Glasper **Child Care: Some Nursing Perspectives** 1 870065 23 9
In three sections, this book covers many pertinent issues that are associated with caring for babies, young children and adolescents, in hospital and community settings.

Horne **Patient Education Plus** 1 870065 11 5
This book helps to develop nurses' teaching roles, and covers an extensive range of clinical topics. Each chapter contains a useful handout which can be freely photocopied or adapted for use with clients.

Horne **Practice Check!** 1 870065 10 7
Each Practice Check presents a brief description of situations which may arise in practice together with open-ended questions and discussion to enable problems to be explored and effective solutions to be found.

Horne and Cowan **Staff Nurse's Survival Guide 2nd edn** 07234 18063
Relevant to recently qualified and experienced nurses working in all healthcare settings, this brings together chapters on a wide range of clinical and non-clinical issues in patient care.

Horne and Cowan **Ward Sister's Survival Guide 2nd edn** 07234 18071
This book is essential reading and a valuable reference for all nurses with direct clinical management responsibility.

Contents

Health Education

Loss and Bereavement

Psychotherapy

Introduction

Nursing is essentially about teamwork – working in cooperation with other nurses and healthcare professionals as part of a multidisciplinary team and in partnership with the patient or client. Effective communication is undeniably central to this process. By developing a close relationship with patients and clients, nurses can help prepare them for treatment, offer support in times of acute anxiety, or simply be someone who is prepared to listen. It is a short step from here to acting as the patient's advocate to the rest of the multidisciplinary team.

This new edition of *Effective Communication* does not aim to offer a comprehensive analysis of the theory of communication, but provides practical and useful examples of how nurses can develop and apply communication skills. The book begins by examining the role of communication in nursing, and shows the variety of settings and ways in which it can be applied. It proceeds to focus on health education, and concludes with an overview of loss and bereavement and counselling. All chapters were first published in *Professional Nurse* magazine, and have been revised and updated for this new edition; they are relevant to nurses working in both hospital and community settings. I hope you and your colleagues will find them useful in your own practice and professional development.

Tracy Cowan
Assistant Editor, *Professional Nurse*
London, March 1992

Developing Communication Skills

1

Empathy: the key to understanding

Philip Burnard, PhD, MSc, RGN, RMN, DipN, Cert Ed, RNT
Director of Postgraduate Nursing Studies, University of Wales College of Medicine, Cardiff

To fully understand another person seems a worthy aim in most aspects of nursing. The literature on the development of empathy as a vital prerequisite of skilled nursing is growing (Anthony and Carkhuff, 1976; Pluckhan, 1978). This chapter looks at practical methods of developing empathy, those which may be used by individuals working alone, or in pairs or groups – perhaps in training settings. This variety of approaches may be used as they stand, or adapted for use in basic nurse education or on counselling and other interpersonal skills training courses in continuing nurse education.

The problems and methods described here are relevant to both clinical and tutorial staff. The training guidelines can be used in both clinical and education settings.

True understanding

Empathy is the ability to see the world as another person sees it: to enter another's 'frame of reference'. We all view the world according to our own cultural background, educational experiences, belief and value systems and personal experiences. What happens to us as we grow up colours the way we perceive the world. To empathise is to attempt to set aside our *own* perception of things and attempt to think the way the other person thinks, or feel the way he feels. It is a very different quality or skill to sympathy. Sympathy involves 'feeling sorry' for the other person – or, perhaps, it involves our imagining how *we* would feel like if *we* were experiencing what is happening to him. With empathy, we try to image what it is like *being* the other person and experiencing things as he does. Sympathy is rarely as valuable a quality as empathy.

Empathy is the basis for truly understanding another person. It is the basis of any interpersonal relationship and has many implications for nursing. Until nurses can empathise with others they cannot attempt to understand what hospitalisation means to patients. Empathising can help nurses to appreciate other people's pain or distress, indeed most aspects of nursing can probably be aided by its development.

It does, of course, have its limits. In the end, it is impossible to *completely* enter someone else's frame of reference: to *exactly* experience the world as they do. It is important, though, that nurses try: if not, they will assume that other people's experience is similar to their own, and lose sight of the fact that other people live different lives, believe different things and feel different feelings. Nurses' attention should focus on understanding others: empathy can help to do this.

Individual development of empathy

The development of empathy is therefore important in all branches of nursing. Empathy training may be introduced into introductory blocks developed throughout training and continued into further education programmes. So how can individuals develop the ability to empathise?

The main method for individual development can become a way of life. It involves the ability to fully focus one's senses on the other person and to resist the temptation to rush to 'interpret' what the other person says or does. Thus the nurse must sit and fully observe the other person. She must listen to the patient, observe his nonverbal behaviour and register all this without any attempt at judging or categorising what he says or does.

This is different to 'normal' conversation, where one usually checks constantly to see whether or not what the other person says or does fits in with one's own belief or value system. Usually, too, one is rehearsing what one is about to say, and thus not fully attending to the other person. The method being described here suggests that it is valuable merely to sit and absorb all aspects of the other person while suspending judgement upon them. In doing so, one enters the other person's perceptual world, forgetting temporarily one's own viewpoint.

Clearing a space

This ability to fully focus on the other person is not easy. It is particularly difficult if the nurse is under pressure to think, or do, other things. When she is busy or distracted by her own problems, the ability to give her attention fully to the other person is reduced. With practice, however, it is possible to set aside her own pressures and problems in order to create the right conditions for true attention. Gendlin (1981) describes this well and calls it 'clearing a space'.

Briefly stated, 'clearing a space' involves an individual quietly reflecting upon the distractions that are going through her mind, and then finding ways of setting aside each of those distractions in turn until she is able to focus attention clearly on the other person. Some people find it useful to imagine each 'distraction' being packaged up in some way and temporarily being put to one side. This is not to say that this process somehow 'cures' the problems or distractions the aim, is merely to pull away from them for a while to give attention to others. Clearing a space and offering full attention in this way can be developed by a nurse working on her own.

Focusing attention Focusing attention fully on the other person involves a conscious decision. We have to decide that, for the next few minutes, we will give our time totally to the other person. This conscious element of the skill allows us to train ourselves. Because it is a conscious effort, we can *decide* to engage in it or not to engage in it, as the case may be. This process has been called 'conscious use of self' (Heron, 1977) and is listed as a skill in the 1982 Syllabus of Training for Psychiatric Nurses (ENB, 1982).

Training ourselves to give others our attention in this way can enhance our listening ability, make us more accurate as communicators and is the basic requirement for the development of empathy. If we are not truly concentrating on the other person, we cannot empathise with them.

Working in pairs

An elaboration of the self-training described above is empathy training in pairs. This method may be used as a training tool in a variety of nurse education settings.

The simplest two-way exercise involves two people, A and B, sitting opposite each other. A talks to B for five minutes while B listens and does not comment. After five minutes, the roles are reversed and B talks to A while A listens passively. The aim of this exercise is to develop the concentration. The exercise is *not* a conversation but an attempt at exploring, fully, the process of completely attending to another person. When both A and B have taken turns as talkers and listeners, they can discuss the process of the exercise. Pertinent questions here are: 'What was it like to really listen?' and 'What was it like to be listened to?'

An elaboration of this exercise involves A listening to B and then offering B a paraphrase of what she has just said. This is a difficult exercise – what we *hear* and what we *think* we hear are often two different things. Once A has accurately paraphrased B's talk (to B's satisfaction), the roles are again reversed.

Reflection A third exercise in empathy building for use in pairs uses the same format. A talks to B who uses only reflection as a response in the conversation. Reflection is a counselling intervention skill described by Egan (1982), Burnard (1985) and others and involves repeating the last few words of an utterance back to the talker. Alternatively, the response may be a brief paraphrase of what the person has just said. The following conversation demonstrates the use of reflection:

A: "When I first came into hospital, I felt completely alone and that nobody would come and see me."
B: "You thought that no one would come and see you..."
A: "Well, I knew my husband would, but I wasn't so sure about the rest of the family – particularly my older children."
B: "You weren't too sure about the family..."

A: "We've quite a large family and they mostly live a long way away..."

In this example, the use of reflection allows the nurse to try to enter the perceptual frame of the client without imposing other ideas and without adding anything to what the client says. So, in this exercise B responds to A by using only reflection and thus practises the process of developing empathy. One drawback to this exercise is that both A and B are 'in the know' about the use of reflection, and sometimes the exercise can feel rather contrived. It is worth saying, however, that if this contrivance is acknowledged, many people find that 'practising' in this way is a useful aid to developing the skill of reflection (and thus empathy development) in real life.

It is not suggested that reflection is the *only* method of response to a client's conversation, nor that it is the *only* method of displaying empathy. It is one among many further empathic interventions described in the counselling literature (Nelson-Jones, 1981).

Group method

There is also a method of training in empathy development that may be used by groups of about five to 15. Fewer than this can make the exercise too easy and thus insufficiently challenging: numbers greater than this can lead to the development of subgroups or 'groups within groups'. If larger groups are to attempt this exercise it is useful to break them up and run a number of smaller groups concurrently.

This exercise is one that Carl Rogers used in empathy development as part of his counselling skills training courses (Kirshenbaum, 1979). It involves running a group discussion on any topic with one 'ground rule': that once someone has spoken, the next person to speak must summarise the last contribution to the satisfaction of that person before she offers her own contribution. Thus the exercise is an elaboration of the one described earlier for use in pairs. It requires the group members to listen closely to each other. The facilitator running the group should ensure that the 'ground rule' is adhered to and that the summary made satisfies the person who last contributed.

It is useful to run such an exercise for a set period of time, say 45 minutes, and then hold a discussion for 30 minutes about what the experience was like. It is important that this discussion focuses on *what the experience was like* and does not become an extension of the topic discussed in the exercise. It is sometimes important, too, for the facilitator to point out that the ground rule need not apply to the discussion.

These practical exercises may each be used to enhance empathy. All three may be combined for use in nurse education. The individual focus is useful as an ongoing discipline for the nurse in training. The pairs exercises are valuable as introductory exercises in human relations training, and the group activity is useful as a means of developing empathy towards a number of people. It is particularly effective for nurses who, as part of their job, run groups of any sorts. Many other exercises are available and the reader is recommended to explore the literature (Canfield and Wells, 1976; Francis and Young, 1979).

Problems in empathy training

What are some of the problems that may arise in empathy training? The first is, perhaps, the reticence of some nurses to take part in these activities at all. It is important that any such participation is voluntary and, paradoxically, the more freedom people are given to 'sit out' on these exercises, the more readily they usually join in! It is important, then, that any abstentions are respected. It is also important that any empathy-building exercises used are clearly set up and that an accurate rationale for their use is offered to those taking part.

A second problem that sometimes arises is that people find the exercises artificial. This point has been dealt with to some degree already. It is important to acknowledge the criticism but, equally, it is important to acknowledge the *value* of this skills training. It may be analogous to learning how to give an injection: this is often taught using inanimate objects to represent the person, so the basic techniques are learned and can then be transferred to the 'real' situation. So it is with empathy training. The initial steps are 'tried out' in the educational setting: the basic skills learned can then be used in 'real life'.

It is important to note that skills training of this sort is *not* role play, but a form of direct experiential learning. Role play invites people to act out roles other than their real-life one. In skills training of the above sort, all participants remain 'themselves': they are *not* acting out a role.

A third potential problem is that of time. As with all forms of experiential learning, the activities described above (if they are done properly) take considerable time. It is particularly important that the follow-up discussions after the activities are lengthy. This is the time when new perceptions are being formed and new learning takes place. It is of little use to merely undertake the exercise without considerable reflection upon it afterwards. It is recommended that only *one* exercise is tackled in a session of at least two hours.

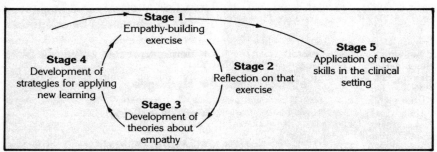

Figure 1. The experiential learning cycle.

Learning gained from empathy-building sessions can be incorporated readily into everyday nursing practice. Figure 1 outlines the experiential learning cycle (Burnard, 1985) which identifies the stages involved in learning through the exercises described here. In stage one, the exercise is undertaken by the individual, pair or group. In stage two, reflection upon that experience can lead to the third stage – that of developing theories about how empathy 'works'. In stage four, new strategies are designed so that the new learning may be applied, and in stage five, the nurse uses her new skills in the clinical situation.

A lifelong process

Empathy development is a lifelong process. It does not start, or finish with a selection of exercises. However, training does enable the issues of empathy to be addressed and enhances the nurse's natural empathic ability.

This natural ability is of prime importance. Skills training cannot give people sensitivity or respect for others, but, based as it is on the individual nurse's experience, it can do much to develop those qualities. One cannot leave the ability to empathise to chance, nor imagine that it will somehow develop throughout a course of training.

It is important that empathy training is not seen only as the concern of the nurse education unit. The training methods described here can be used by those working in the clinical setting – whether ward- or community-based. For example, it is possible for the exercises described here to be used as the basis of a series of clinical seminars. In this way, the learning gained has direct application. There need be no gap between 'theory' and practice. The skills are both *learned* and *used* in the clinical setting. The nurse needs empathy to fire the relationship between her and the patient, so it would seem valuable to learn the art and skill of empathising as close to the patient as possible.

References

Anthony, W.C. and Carkhuff, R.R. (1976) The Art of Health Care: A Handbook of Psychological First Aid Skills. Human Resource Development Press, Massachusetts.

Burnard, P. (1985) Learning Human Skills: A Guide for Nurses. Heinemann, London.

Canfield J. and Wells, H.C. (1976) 100 Ways to Enhance Self-Concept in the Classroom. Prentice-Hall, New Jersey.

Egan, G. (1982) The Skilled Helper (2nd edn). Brooks/Cole, Monterery.

ENB (1982) Syllabus of Training: Professional Register: Part 3 (Registered Mental Nurse). ENB, London.

Francis, D. and Young, D. (1979) Improving Work Groups: A Practical Manual for Team Building. University Associates, San Diego, California.

Gendlin, E. (1981) Focussing, Basic Books, New York.

Heron J. (1977) Behaviour Analysis in Education and Training: Human Potential Research Project. University of Surrey, Guildford.

Kirschenbaum, H. (1979) On Becoming Carl Rogers. Dell, New York.

Le Shan, L. (1974) How to Meditate. Turnstone Press, Wellingborough.

Nelson-Jones, R. (1981) The Theory and Practice of Counselling Psychology. Holt, Rinehart and Winston, London.

Pluckhan, M.L. (1978) Human Communication: The Matrix of Nursing. McGraw Hill, New York.

2

Developing skills as a group facilitator

Philip Burnard, PhD, MSc, RGN, RMN, DipN, Cert Ed, RNT
Director of Postgraduate Nursing Studies, University of Wales College of Medicine, Cardiff

Nurses are frequently called upon to run groups of various sorts. In general hospitals they may organise and run case conferences, teaching sessions and quality circles, and in psychiatric and mental handicap hospitals they may be active participants in group therapy as well as being engaged in educational activities of various sorts. Group facilitation calls for the exercise of particular and specific skills. As well as needing a thorough knowledge of group processes and dynamics, the nurse is required to use a variety of verbal interventions to keep the group going.

This chapter identifies three sets of facilitator behaviour that will enable the nurse to choose the appropriate type of verbal intervention for the particular group at a particular moment. The sets are based on the behaviour analyses of John Heron (1977) and Rackham and Morgan (1977). Group dynamics, group activities or procedure are not discussed. The aim is to offer a practical framework that the nurse may use while conducting groups of various sorts. Some ideas are offered of the types of group interventions available which can be developed further by the group facilitation training offered by many colleges and university departments. Such training is increasingly becoming part of basic and continuing nurse education.

Framework

The framework offers three groups of possible verbal interventions focusing on three different aspects of time: recent past, present and future. The headings of those groups are:
- clarifying recent talk;
- developing current talk;
- initiating further talk.

By an appropriate mix of the three types of intervention, the nurse can facilitate a group discussion that is continuous, dynamic and lively — not that such interventions can be learned by rote. The particular words chosen are dependent upon a variety of things, including, at least: the context, the nurse's own background and personality and the particular needs of the group at the time. The headings and the examples that follow are, therefore, guidelines to verbal behaviour — they suggest methods of making interventions: they are not examples of specific verbal statements. Each of the three groups will now be broken down into examples of methods.

Clarifying recent talk

Here, the nurse uses interventions to enable the group to be clear about what is and what is not under discussion. Some of the methods that may be used to clarify are:

Summary   Offering a summing up of the group discussion so far, and a clear and accurate statement of the main threads and issues of the preceding talk.

Inter-relate   Indicating how various points under discussion link together to form a cohesive whole.

Disagree   Suggesting a reasoned alternative to what has gone before as a means of clarifying and leading on to further discussion.

These are three methods the nurse may use to clarify recent talk within the group. Such interventions may be used periodically throughout the group meeting or whenever there seems to be misunderstanding.

Developing current talk

Interventions are used to further draw out group members on the subject under discussion. They are similar in nature to the sorts of interventions used in non-directive or client centred counselling. Some of the methods the nurse may use here are:

Reflection   Repeating the last few words said by a group member to enable that person to further develop what they have said. Alternatively, the nurse may paraphrase the last few statements to similar effect. This is sometimes known as 'echoing' or 'mirroring'.

Checking for understanding   Rephrasing something a group member has said and checking whether or not that restatement represents a clearer version of what was meant. Alternatively, the nurse asks the direct question: ''are you saying that . . .?''

Support   Agreeing with or encouraging the statement made by a group member in order to promote further discussion.

These are basic methods that may be used throughout a group meeting. They are encouraging and promote the development of group cohesion.

Initiate further talk

Interventions are used to encourage the group to move on and to develop further. Some of the methods that may be used here are:

Propose   Suggesting a new direction for a new topic for consideration by the group. The group is then free to adopt or reject the proposal as it chooses. Alternatively, the nurse may wish to consult the group first about a plan of action and then make a proposal arising out of that consultation: a 'consult, then propose' format.

Question A variety of open questions are posed to encourage movement within the group. Generally speaking, questions that begin with 'why' are best avoided. 'Why' questions tend to sound interrogative; they can sound moralistic and they can lead to sterile theoretical discussion that only impede group development.

Disclose As facilitator, the nurse offers the group personal thoughts, feelings or experiences. Disclosure begets disclosure. The nurse who reveals something about herself sets an example to the group of openness which may encourage further disclosure on the part of group members.

These methods may be used to encourage the group to develop, to stretch itself and to move into new areas. They need to be timed accurately paying regard to the atmosphere at the time. If they are used too often or too quickly they may not be well received. On the other hand, if they are used deftly, they can ensure that the group continues to develop.

Conscious use of self

Other group interventions that do not easily fit within the three groups above may be identified. The nurse may, for instance, bring in a group member who contributes little by asking for their thoughts or feelings on a particular matter. On the other hand, the nurse may gently shut out the over-talkative member who may tend to lionise the group. Both these interventions need to be used with tact and sensitivity.

Sometimes the nurse will offer specific information. Again, 'information giving' needs to be well timed. We have all experienced facilitators, teachers and chairpeople who offer too much information. Group facilitation should be concerned more with *sharing* ideas than with dispensing information.

Interventions so far described may be practised through conscious use within a particular group. In other words the nurse monitors herself and chooses only to use these sorts of interventions. Such self monitoring takes concentration and practice. It is a form of what Heron (1977) calls 'conscious use of self' and such use of self is now defined as a skill in the psychiatric nursing student's syllabus of training (ENB, 1982).

Such conscious use of self is an important aspect of group facilitation. It suggests that the group facilitator pays close attention to what is said and done while the group is running. Thus, group facilitation becomes a task of greater precision — little is left to chance. Group facilitation is, after all, a skilled task — it is not something that needs to be regarded as 'coming naturally to some and not to others'. We would not say this of other nursing skills, nor need we say it of the interpersonal aspects of nursing.

Theoretical assumptions

Other aspects of group facilitation that may be considered by the nurse include: coping with silences; dealing with decision making; opening and closing groups; dealing with 'difficult' members and so forth. Again, such aspects of group work can be learned through training courses and through the experience of working with groups.

Anyone who runs a group does so from a particular theoretical position — they have a theory about how people act in groups. This may be clearly thought out or it may be something of which the nurse is only dimly aware. It pays considerable dividends to explore these underlying theoretical assumptions before setting out to organise and run a group. One method is to write down in note form a series of assumptions, followed by an attempt to justify those assumptions. The process of doing this can help to clarify values, beliefs and assumptions about people in groups, some of which will have been adopted through nurse training. Psychiatric nurses, for instance, will probably tend to hold a number of assumptions about 'group psychology' based within one or more of the three broad categories: behavioural, psychodynamic or humanistic. It is worth clarifying these before group work is undertaken.

Awareness and skill

The framework offered here may be used as a typography of verbal behaviours for use in research. It can be used in quantitative research for categorising types of observed behaviour in group activities, and it also has applications in more qualitative work to explore group processes in participant-observer studies.

Nurses working with groups need a sound theoretical basis for the work, a thorough grounding in practical facilitation skills and an awareness of research into groups. After experience as group facilitators, they may then add to the body of knowledge by conducting their own research. In this way, nurse facilitation can develop both as a dynamic science and as an art.

Example of the group at work

The group is a small number of student nurses in the nurse education centre. The facilitator is a newly qualified nurse who is using a facilitative approach to discussing the concept of counselling.

As the session unfolds Jane continues to use facilitative interventions only and thus allows the group to explore *their own* thoughts and feelings without offering direct suggestions or prescriptions of her own. Notice, too, that Jane's *own* disclosure prompted the disclosure of others.

This, then, is one application of the framework — to *consciously* use interventions from the three categories. After a while the categories are internalised and the need to make such conscious decisions becomes less important. By this time, the facilitative style has become the person's natural style.

Group Discussion	Example from the framework
Jane (tutor) "Do you think nurses *should* be trained as counsellors?	Initiating further talk (question).
Samantha (student) "No, not really!"	
Jane "You don't feel they should?"	Developing current talk (reflection)
Samantha "It should be left to people trained as counsellors . . ."	
Peter (student) "But we are trained as counsellors."	
Samantha "Not enough, though . . . . not to do it properly . . ."	
Jane "So . . . one of you thinks nurses should counsel and you're not so sure.	Clarifying recent talk (summary)
Jane "What are other people's views?	Initiating further talk (question)
Silence	
Jane "I feel slightly uncomfortable . . . I'd hoped that you'd all have something to say . . ."	Initiating further talk (self-disclosure)
Ruth (student): "I think that counselling is important as long as we all know what we are doing . . . you know . . . properly trained"	
Samantha: "Do you know all about it then?	
Ruth "No, but I'm learning.	
Peter to Samantha: "You're very aggressive today! Why are you so negative?"	
Samantha: "I just think we've got to be clear, that's all . . . I didn't mean to sound negative . . . I only hope we get more practical work on counselling.	

References

ENB (1982) Syllabus of training: Part 3 Registered Mental Nurse.
Heron, J. (1977) Behaviour Analysis in Education and Training: Human Potential Research Project. University of Surrey, Guildford.
Rackham, R. and Morgan, J. (1977) Behaviour Analysis in Training. McGraw Hill, London.

Bibliography

Berger, G. and Berger, P. (1972) Group Training Techniques. Gower, Aldershot.
  This offers an overview of group training processes and practical activities for group skills development.
Bion, W. (1961) Experiences in Groups. Tavistock, London.
  A classic work on the psychodynamic view of group development.
Burnard, P. (1985) Learning Human Skills: A Guide for Nurses. Heinemann, London.
  A practical handbook containing the theory of self-awareness and experiential learning. It also offers a range of exercises for counselling and group facilitation skills development.
Cartwright, D. and Zander, A. (1968) Group Dynamics: Research and Theory. 3rd Edition. Tavistock, London.
  A comprehensive volume of almost all aspects of group dynamics and processes.
Francis, D. and Young, D. (1979) Improving Work Groups: A Practical Manual for Team Building. University Associates, California.
  A useful compendium of activities for developing group skills.
Heron, J. (1977) Dimensions of Facilitator Style: Human Potential Research Project. University of Surrey, Guildford. Contains a presentation of six dimensions of group facilitation.
  A useful guide to both the theory and the practice of group facilitation.
Schulman, E.D. (1982) Intervention in Human Services: A Guide to Skills and Knowledge. 3rd Edition. C.V. Mosby, Toronto.
  A comprehensive account of various approaches to interpersonal skills training.
Smith, P.B. (1980) Group Process and Personal Changes. Harper and Row, London.
  A very thorough review of the literature on groups and group dynamics. Not always easy reading but very useful!

3

Teamwork: an equal partnership?

Gill Garrett, BA, RGN, RCNT, DN(London), CertEd(FE), RNT, FPCert
Freelance Lecturer, Bristol

From being one of the fundamental tenets in the care of groups such as elderly people and those with mental handicaps, the vital nature of the team approach has become recognised and accepted in all areas of nursing. Many patients have a multiplicity of needs – medical, nursing, therapeutic, social – which no one discipline can hope to meet; only by close collaboration and cooperation can different practitioners bring their skills into concert to attempt to meet them.

Increasingly in recent years, the validity of this contention has been appreciated by both hospital and community workers, and the gospel has been preached. But how effective has the concept been in practice? While no doubt in many parts of the country teams are working efficiently and harmoniously together to the benefit of all concerned, it would seem that in others there are areas of concern which demand urgent consideration and action if the concept is not to prove a meaningless cliché. With this in mind, this chapter considers the prerequisites for effective teamwork, points out a few of the common problems which may arise and offers some suggestions as to how these problems may be ameliorated.

Who makes up the team?
One very basic question to ask before considering the work of the team is who makes up the team? On multiple choice papers, students will indicate the doctor, nurse, therapists, dietitians – all the professional partners in the venture. But integral to every team must be the people most meaningful to the individual patient: her family if she has any, her supportive neighbour, or whoever. If our aim is to rehabilitate the patient or to maintain her at her maximum level of functioning, these are people we neglect at our peril – and much more importantly, at the patient's peril. As professionals we must learn that we do not have a monopoly on care, nor do we have a dominant role in an unequal partnership. The contribution of relatives or friends, as agreeable to the patient, is vital – whether discussing assessments, setting goals or reviewing progress; their non-contribution, if excluded from active participation, may indeed frustrate all professional efforts. Although most of this

chapter concentrates on those professionals who are conventionally seen as team members (primarily because of the space available), this point cannot be overstressed.

Why are teams necessary?

Perhaps an even more basic question is, why does the team exist? It is easy to lose sight of the fact that its sole *raison d'être* is the patient and her need. An old adage runs, "The patient is the centre of the medical universe around which all our works revolve, towards which all our efforts trend". In economic terms we are quite used to this concept of 'consumer sovereignty', but in our health and social services management at present, all too often our consumer exists more to be 'done to' rather than canvassed for her opinion, offered options and helped to make choices. A thorny question often raised about the multidisciplinary team is, which professional should lead it? An equally important one not so often posed is, who should be the 'director' of team activity? If we recognise the patient as an autonomous, independent person (albeit with varying degrees of support), surely we must have the humility to acknowledge that this directing role falls inevitably to her. For patients with mental or other serious impairment, of course, the question of advocacy then arises – again an issue subject to much current debate.

Having allocated the role of director to the patient, the team leader then becomes the facilitator of action. It has been said that, "Fundamental to the concept of teamwork is . . . division of labour, coordination and task sharing, each member making a different contribution, but (one) of equal value, towards the common goal of patient care" (Ross, 1986). What do these elements demand? To make for efficient division of labour there has to be an accurate assessment of a situation and the input needed to deal with it, a recognition of who is the best person for which part of the job, and the carrying through of the appropriate allocation. Coordination demands the ability to see the overall, the sum of all the individual parts, and to recognise their relative weightings in various circumstances; it needs effective communication skills and the ability to use feedback to take adjustive action as required. Task-sharing demands that team members have an understanding of different roles and their effect upon one another, that they recognise areas of overlap and are prepared to shoulder one another's problems should the need arise. Such demands are not light; they require considerable training and practice to perfect.

Status and power within the team

Consideration of the second part of the Ross quotation brings us to one of the common problems experienced in multidisciplinary teamwork: ". . . of equal value towards the common goal of patient care". Is that how all team members view their own contribution or that of their partners? Status and power imbalances can make for great difficulties in team functioning; tradition accords high status and consequent power to the medical establishment, for example, with much affection but little standing to nurses. But if nurses have been seen as lacking in power and status, even lower on the rungs of the ladder comes the patient; in general, society grants a very low status to ill and disabled people, and institutional care strips all vestiges of power from inhabitants.

For workers who see themselves as being the juniors in teams, the presence and influence of more powerful members may prove intimidating, and consequently they may make only tentative and limited contributions to discussions and meetings. It is important that they realise that, however 'junior', they have a right to contribute, indeed a duty to do so, if they have what has been described as the "authority of relevance" (Webb and Hobdell, 1975) – if they have knowledge relevant to the patient's own feelings of need or wellbeing which must be brought to the team's attention. So often it is those members who spend more time in close proximity to the patient who possess such authority, rather than the senior medical personnel who may visit her only on a weekly basis.

'Follow my leader' A second problem may arise out of the power and status imbalance, especially when team members have become used to suppressing their views or do not recognise their authority of relevance – regression into the 'follow my leader' phenomenon. There may be the tendency to leave all the thinking to another group member who is perceived as being more prestigious or simply more articulate, often the consultant. His thinking and directions are seen as definitive, with team members abdicating their own professional responsibility to think and speak for themselves and for their patient from their own vantage points. Except in the unlikely event of the team leader being qualified in a multidisciplinary capacity, this obviously acts to the detriment of patient care – we can none of us prescribe or wholly substitute for each other's contributions. A variation on this 'follow my leader' phenomenon is sometimes seen where two leaders emerge from subgroups in a team, each with his or her own following. In addition to the drawbacks already mentioned, the results in situations like this are invariably divisive too.

'Groupthink' This is the name that has been given to another possible problem in teamwork; it is generally seen in well-established, long-lived teams whose members over time have grown very used to working with each other. Team meetings are always amicable and 'cosy', there is no bickering or dissension and everyone gets on terribly well with everyone else. The group gives the appearance of having its own internal strength, with a marked sense of loyalty and supportiveness. But this denies that disagreement and conflict are facts of life and often signs of constructive enquiry and growth; all too often such teams ". . . become rigid, committed to the status quo . . . less open to input and feedback. Hierarchies become established and bureaucratic qualities emerge which resist questioning and change" (Brill, 1976).

Patient confusion   In case this should all seem a little esoteric, consider for a moment one last very basic possible problem in multidisciplinary teamwork – potential confusion for the patient. Unless each member of the team extends to her the courtesy of an introduction to their personal role, with an explanation of how this fits in with the overall individual plan of care, especially in the acute phase of an illness, the patient (particularly if elderly) may well find so many professionals overwhelming and muddling. If she is to feel in any degree in control of the situation and if any confusion is to be lessened, time must be taken to be sure a personal approach, with all care being presented as part of a concerted whole, and with common goals identified towards which all the team are working.

This last problem, then, is usually amenable to a common courtesy and common sense solution. But what about the others? The problems associated with status and 'follow my leader' have a more deep-seated origin and, although rectifiable in the short term in individual teams, in the longer term they demand a close scrutiny of, and changes in, professional education. 'Groupthink' demands flexibility of individuals and a system which encourages and permits a regular turnover of personnel to maintain healthy group dynamics.

Common core training?

If in effective teams there is no room for professional superiorities or jealousies, what is needed is an open, trusting relationship based on knowledge of, and respect for, one another's professional expertise. But this demands in turn an insight into other trainings and backgrounds to understand one another's terms of reference – the differences in emphasis we have in relation to patient care. While individual effort and inservice training programmes can go some way towards this, the difficulties with late attitudinal change are only too well known. Most of our basic feelings about our own profession and those with which we work are formed during our initial training period. Nursing is widely introducing training programmes based on Project 2000, with a common core foundation programme for all nurse practitioners. Is it not time we were much more adventurous, and explored avenues of common core training for all health professionals? Certain knowledge, skills and attitudes are prerequisites whether we are to be doctors, nurses, therapists or social workers – if we learned them together how much easier it would be to practise them together. The intention of such common training would not be to reduce all teaching to the lowest common denominator, but rather to look at areas of mutual concern, highlighting the unique contribution of each professional, and the bearing this has on the work of the other team members.

Value of difference

Educational change may also help us to recognise the value of 'difference' and the constructive use to which conflict may be put, so that 'groupthink' becomes a less likely problem. Better training in interpersonal skills – including assertiveness – should help the creation of a climate in which there is freedom to differ, to look more dispassionately at dissent, while acknowledging the areas of basic trust and agreement that do exist and can be built upon. The need for turnover in team membership has to be balanced, of course, by the need for reasonable stability over a period of time. Change every five minutes for the sake of it helps no one, but there must be recognition that long-term team stagnation (however well camouflaged) is beneficial neither to the group nor to the professionals within it – and certainly not to the patient and her family.

Realism

This chapter provides only a brief overview of a very important area. Readers' personal experiences may differ considerably from the scenarios which have been outlined. It would seem, however, that most experienced nurses have had the experience of needing to temper idealism in striving for effective teamwork with realism, given the situations in which they work. But recognition of this is in itself a step forward; we must have in mind that "under the aegis of teamwork, strange bedfellows are discovering, in time, that they must *learn* to work together before they *can* work together . . . teamwork is not an easy process to understand or to practise" (Brill, 1976).

References
Brill, N.I. (1976) Teamwork: Working together in the Human Services. Lippincott, New York.
Ross, F.M. (1986) Nursing old people in the community. In: Redfern, S. (ed) Nursing Elderly People. Churchill Livingstone, Edinburgh.
Webb, A.L. and Hobdell, M. (1975) Coordination between health and personal social services: a question of quality. In: Interaction of social welfare and health personnel in the delivery of services: Implications for training. Eurosound Report No. 4, Vienna.

4

Effective use of health education skills

Jill Macleod-Clark, PhD, BSc, SRN
Professor of Nursing Studies, King's College, University of London

Sally Kendall, PhD, BSc, RGN, HV
Senior Lecturer in Nursing Studies, Buckinghamshire College

Sheila Haverty, BA, RGN
Formerly Research Officer, Department of Nursing Studies, King's College, University of London

The importance of developing the nurse health education role is now well recognised. The need for a shift in emphasis has been accepted by the profession (UKCC,1986). Project 2000 proposals, for restructuring nurse education reflect this acceptance by recommending that health concepts and issues underpin the first eighteen months of nurse education programmes (UKCC, 1986). Similar recommendations have also been made in the Judge Report (1985), the Cumberlege Report (1986) and the Royal College of Nursing (1990).

There is thus a growing awareness in nursing of the need to move away from the medical model and ensure that the focus of care directed towards enhancing health. This conflict of philosophies often makes it difficult for nurses to be health educators – they are trained to care for the sick and dying by following doctors' orders not to take on a more autonomous role based on promoting or maximising health.

Previous work has shown that nurses need to develop both their knowledge and their interpersonal skills in order to become effective health educators (Faulkner and Ward, 1983; Macleod-Clark et al, 1985). It is also important that nurses have the ability to recognise opportunities for health education. Kendall has examined the opportunities nurses have in relation to smoking education (Kendall, 1986).

Smoking continues to be the largest cause of preventable disease in the UK. One in 4 of all smokers will die from a smoking related disease such as lung cancer, heart disease or chronic destructive lung disease (Doll and Peto 1981). Current figures suggest that 33 per cent of men and 30 per cent of women in the UK are smokers (OPCS, 1990). Smoking therefore provides an excellent example of an area where nurses can develop and use their skills effectively in health education. Hopefully, it can be seen that the approach suggested is equally applicable to many other areas of health education such as nutrition and exercise.

Framework for health education

Recent research by the authors (Macleod-Clark *et al*, 1990) has demonstrated that health education by nurses can be effective if it is structured and skillful. The suggested framework is based on the nursing process approach since health education should be individualised like all aspects of nursing care. The long-term aim in this case is that the client stops smoking.

Assessment   This involves assessing the smoker in terms of:
- Motivation to give up;
- Health beliefs and worries about smoking;
- Level of knowledge about smoking and health;
- Factors influencing smoking behaviour, eg family circumstances;
- Factual information, eg number smoked per day.

Using interpersonal skills effectively in the assessment stage is more likely to lead to an eventual successful outcome. The skills necessary for effective assessment will be discussed and illustrated with extracts from real conversations between nurses and their clients which have been recorded by the authors in the course of their research.

Questioning skills   Any kind of nursing assessment requires questioning in order to gather information and to build up a complete picture of the client in terms of health and social needs. There are many ways of questioning people but two which can be most usefully employed in assessment are *open* questions and *closed* questions. Open questions usually commence with how, what, where, when, who or why. They allow the respondent to answer in their own words without limitations.

Example 1
N: How keen are you to give up?
C: Well, I know I should give up and I
know I would like to. Its just — I
think it would be difficult.

Open question

In Example 1 the nurse has asked an open question in order to establish the client's level of motivation. It is important to do this in the early stages as an unmotivated client is unlikely to respond positively to any health education intervention. If the client is not motivated then the intervention should focus more on increasing motivation than changing behaviour.

Open questions are also used to find out about the client's belief system. Efforts at health education will be unsuccessful if the nurse and the client have different beliefs and values about health. If the nurse can establish what the client's beliefs are she can work within that client's frame of reference. It cannot be assumed, for example, that everybody is worried about getting lung cancer — many are not.

In Example 2 the nurse is now aware that the client is worried about breathlessness and heart disease. She could now expand on these areas

Example 2

N: What worries you about continuing
     to smoke?
C: Only that, you know, you can't
     breathe properly.
N: Mmm
C: . . . and some people get, you know,
     something wrong with their heart.

but keep the focus of her intervention on what is relevant to the client. It is equally important to establish the worries people may have about giving up smoking.

Example 3

N: What concerns you about giving up
     smoking?
C: I would really worry about putting on
     weight, there's no way I would want
     to do that.
N: Yes, a lot of women are very worried
     about that.

By asking an open question the nurse has established the client's fear of weight gain (Example 3). Obviously, this kind of information about the client is essential before any sort of plan can be formulated. This client will not feel committed to giving up smoking if she is not also given some guidance and support regarding diet and weight maintenance.

Open questions can also be used to gather factual information which will be central to the planning stage, eg "How long have you been smoking?", "How many do you smoke a day?".

Closed questions

Closed questions limit the type of response that can be given — usually to "yes" or "no". In a nursing assessment they are most useful for gathering facts quickly but should not be used to the exclusion of open questions since they do not provide the depth of information required to make a satisfactory assessment.

Example 4

N: Have you ever tried to stop smoking
     before?
C: No.

In Example 4 a simple fact has been established which may have some influence on the outcome of the intervention. For example, it is known that ex-smokers have often made several attempts to stop before they are finally successful so it would be reasonable not to expect that this client will be successful first time.

Listening and encouraging skills   Some of the most powerful skills apparently require very little effort from the nurse. However, it is more difficult than at first appears to both develop these skills and recognise their potential in assessment. Listening means more than just hearing, it means being able to interpret and make use of what is being said. In every day conversation we tend to interupt and talk over each other instead of listening. Traditionally in nursing the nurse has been very much in control of the patient which usually means she has done most of the talking. When helping people to make decisions about their lifestyle and health they should be encouraged to do the majority of the talking so that the assessment made is accurate and client-centered. Encouraging people to talk more usually only requires the nurse to give her full attention and to say things like "uh-uh" or "go on".

Example 5
N: What sort of ways have you thought about giving up smoking?
C: I've tried several times, um, and I've always stopped for about a week.
N: Mmm
C: But I get this really empty feeling inside my stomach.
N: Mmm
C: I get really moody.
N: Uh-uh
C: And I've been thinking recently, that instead of just thinking about it, I thought I'm going to set a date.
N: Mmm
C: Its best not to think about it.

As in Example 5, open questioning and encouragement often go together. By listening to this client the nurse can focus her intervention on the information she has learned.

Responding to cues   Cues are hints that the client may give as to real worries not openly expressed. A skillful listener will pick up these cues and encourage the client to talk more about them. Frequently, they may be areas of concern which the client wished to discuss but was unable to — perhaps through fear, anxiety or embarrassment.

In Example 6, the nurse picks up on the client's nervousness by echoing back what the client is telling her. This technique also encourages the

Example 6
C: Um, I've been trying to cut down since I was pregnant.
N: Mmm
C: But I haven't thought about stopping altogether because it calms my nerves.
N: Mmm
C: I've been very nervous during this pregnancy.
N: You're nervous?

client to say more about the underlying cause of the nervousness so that the nurse can focus her smoking education around this, ie explore other ways of coping with anxiety.

Cues will frequently be non-verbal and it is just as important to observe and interpret these signs of anxiety and restlessness such as clock-watching or tearing up a paper handkerchief. An inattentive or worried client will not be able to respond fully to the intervention.

Giving information   During the assessment it may become apparent that there are some areas in which the client needs or requests information. Information given appropriately can enhance the client's understanding of the problem. Information given will refer back to the clients beliefs and worries and should be contained within the client's frame of reference.

Example 7
C: I think with lung cancer, I mean if your lungs pack up you have more or less had it haven't you?
N: Mmm. Yes.
C: I think that's the one that really worries me.
N: Mmm. Women are increasingly getting lung cancer because more women are smoking now. At one time, women used to think it didn't affect them and that more men die. In fact, the statistics are going up for women so it is a definite health risk.

The information given in Example 7 is appropriate because it responds to the client's worry and is given at the client's own level, avoiding jargon. Compare this with the following extract:

N: I'll just explain to you that when you smoke, carbon monoxide attaches itself to the red corpuscles that are in the blood. Blood goes to every tissue in the body so carbon monoxide, which is poison, is being sent everywhere. So what it tends to do to your hands and feet is make them tingle. Do you ever feel tingling?
C: No.
N: You don't?
C: No, never.
N: Well, this is one of the sort of circulatory problems which taken to its end is gangrene, fingers falling off and things like that.

The nurse has saturated this client with unsolicited and inappropriate information. She has used technical terms which may mean nothing to the client and has resorted to terror tactics to gain her client's attention. It is not necessary to tell every client everything you know about smoking.

Where information is given it is often useful to back it up with written material so that the client has a chance to absorb the information quietly

It is often useful to back up information with written material such as this HEA leaflet.

later on. There are many leaflets and booklets freely available on smoking and other subjects from health education units.

In summary, the initial assessment involves the skills of questioning, listening, encouraging, responding to cues and giving appropriate information. The aim of the assessment is to build up a picture of the client, enabling the nurse to focus her intervention within the client's frame of reference.

Planning

When formulating a plan the overall aim should be kept in sight, ie cessation of smoking. However, before a total behaviour change is achieved there may be other short term goals to be met. Such short term goals should be realistic and mutually agreed between the client and the nurse. Frequently, the client may be pleased to accept the nurse's guidance as she will have practical suggestions and access to methods of cessation (see Kendall, 1986) previously unavailable or unknown to the client. However, a plan conceived and imposed by the nurse alone is unlikely to be successful. Some short term goals which may be useful to consider are:

- Create no-smoking areas in the home/car;
- Keep a smoking diary for one week, ie write down how many cigarettes are smoked, when and why;
- Reduce smoking by half within one week;
- Find out where the nearest smokers clinic is.

The overall plan and the short term goals should be based on the needs and beliefs established during the assessment. For example, if a client smokes as a way of relieving stress then the plan should be based on alternative methods of coping with stress. Asking questions such as "How do you think you could go about giving up?" may be useful in giving some initial direction to the plan and in helping the client to feel that she is participating in the lifestyle changes she is making.

Clients often feel that a behaviour such as smoking is outside their control and that the risks of smoking are on a par with the risks of nuclear war for example. Clients should be helped to see that they can control their own behaviour and setting realistic goals often helps to put the behaviour into perspective.

Implementation

Once the client and the nurse have established the "giving up" plan in which there are agreed goals and objectives it is up to the client to implement it. Many smokers will say "It is only me that can do it". This is true, but the client can be helped by offering support. This could be done in the form of leaving a telephone number on which the nurse could be contacted (eg on the ward or health centre) or could be more formalised with future meetings being planned. If it is inappropriate for the nurse herself to offer support (ward-based nurses may find this difficult) then support could be sought from within the family or friendship network. For example, partners may find it helpful to give up together. Some clients might be attracted to group support and in this case a stop smoking group may be appropriate. Whatever form the support takes it must suit both the client and the nurse.

Evaluation

Whenever possible, following an intervention the nurse should arrange to see the client again at least once. This could take place in the home, in the antenatal clinic, outpatients clinic or wherever is most appropriate to the nurse's field of work. This follow-up has a dual purpose. It gives the client something to work towards and allows priorities to be reorganised and goals reset.

If, by the time of the agreed follow-up, there has been no demonstrable change in behaviour, the nurse should not regard her intervention as a complete failure. Many ex-smokers make several attempts before finally giving up and a change in motivation is as successful as a change in behaviour. It may be that the continued interest and support of the nurse will give the smoker the required impetus to give up eventually.

However, a reassessment of the previous intervention will give guidance for tackling problems and setting new short-term goals. If the original plan was unsuccessful it may be necessary to make adjustments or formulate a new one. If the client is successful in giving up smoking then she should be encouraged to continue and where possible continued support offered if required.

In summary, this framework requires the nurse to assess her client, make a plan of action with the client, support and encourage the client in its implementation and evaluate the intervention.

It may at first appear that the framework is complicated and time consuming. However, in their research the authors have found that with practice, it is possible to assess and plan in five to 10 minutes. The framework aims to be flexible and adaptable to various work settings. For example, if ward based nurses find the idea of giving continued support unrealistic due to high turnover of patients then they could either give the client their ward telephone number or refer her/him to one of their community colleagues. Health visitors and district nurses will have more prolonged contact with their clients and may decide to spread the assessment and planning over two visits and they will be more able to offer support over a period of time.

The framework is not rigid and if nurses of all disciplines could adapt it and use it in their every day practise there is potential for a considerable impact on attaining the WHO target of health for all by the year 2000 (WHO, 1985).

References
Cumberlege, J. et al (1986) Neighbourhood nursing – a focus for care. Report of the Community Nursing Review. HMSO. London.
Doll, R. and Peto, R. (1981) The Causes of Cancer. Oxford University Press.
Faulkner, A and Ward L (1983) Nurses as health educators in relation to smoking, *Nursing Times*, Occasional Paper 8, **79**, 15, 47-48.
Judge, H. et al (1985) Commission on nurse education. RCN, London.
Kendall, S. (1986) Helping people to stop smoking. *The Professional Nurse*, **1**, 5, 120-123.
Macleod-Clark, J. Elliot, K. Haverty, S. and Kendall, S. (1985) Helping people to stop smoking – the nurse's role. Phase 1. Health Education Council, London.
Macleod-Clark, J. Haverty, S. and Kendall, S. (1990) Helping people to stop smoking – a study of the nurse's role. *Journal of Advanced Nursing*, **16**, 357-363.
OPCS (1990) General household survey. HMSO, London.
Royal College of Nursing (1990) Strategy for nursing. RCN, London.
United Kingdom Central Council for Nurses, Midwives and Health Visitors. (1986) Project 2000, UKCC.
World Health Organisation (1985) Targets for health for all. WHO, Geneva.

5

Introducing nurses to the counselling process

Patrick McEvoy, RMN, SRN, DipN, RCNT, RNT, BA
Senior Tutor, Department of Postbasic Education, Eastern Area College of Nursing, Southside, Belfast

"Counselling is a personal relationship in which the counsellor uses his own experiences of himself to help his client to enlarge his self-understanding and so make better decisions" (Sutherland, 1973).

"Counselling is a relationship in which one person endeavours to help another to understand and solve the difficulties of adjustment to society" (Heasman, 1969).

"Counselling gives a person the opportunity to discover, explore and clarify ways of living more resourcefully and towards greater well-being" (British Association of Counselling, 1979).

Counselling is a complex process which is difficult to define, never mind teach, as the definitions above indicate. For this reason some people will say such teaching should be left to the professional counsellor, as student nurses may become confused with a concept which is open to so many interpretations.

In the context of nursing, however, I would suggest a simple definition of the concept: "Counselling is an enabling interaction between two people which seeks to support the weaker person as a responsible human being". Within this definition it is difficult to visualise a situation whereby a nurse would care for patients' daily needs and yet avoid involvement in counselling – a nurse cannot provide care without counselling. She does not really have a choice. Patients will inevitably bring their problems to her and she will be expected to counsel as part of her role. In this respect she must frequently respond to the unexpected, whereas full time counsellors work in much more structured situations. The nurse's choice, then, is between counselling in a competent and informed manner or in a haphazard thoughtless fashion. All nurses should therefore be properly introduced to the counselling process at an early stage in their training. Counselling competence, however, cannot be achieved through a one-off experience at the beginning of a nurse's education. Rather, it must weave into her professional fabric throughout her professional life supported by a sound programme of continuing education.

Presenting the skills

Counselling skills need to be presented in such a way that nurses will immediately grasp their relevance to nursing. Initially their interest must be aroused by drawing attention to the problems they will be confronted with in the clinical setting and offering to help find some of the answers. It is useful to give them first hand accounts of counselling situations which develop in the hospital wards. The following points can be emphasised:

- Nurses spend more time with patients than any other health professionals.
- The social distance is least between the patient and the nurse. Therefore it is likely that the patient will feel that he can confide in the nurse more than in anyone else.
- Virtually all ill people have problems which may be amenable to counselling.
- All nurses counsel patients. In many instances counselling is integral to the provision of care; for example, even helping a patient to feel at home in hospital may involve counselling.

Having established that counselling is intrinsically linked with the provision of care, nurses should be placed in small groups and encouraged to discuss their own ideas of counselling. To correct misconceptions, the facilitator must circulate from group to group and make certain all individuals are aware of a simple definition like the one previously mentioned: "Counselling is an enabling interaction between two people which seeks to support the weaker person as a responsible human being". Counselling must never be confused with simply giving advice.

Offering help

Counselling involves one person offering to help another. No-one can help another without at least having begun to understand that person, and one cannot begin to understand others until one understands oneself, so nurses must be aware that effective counselling is unlikely to occur without self-knowledge. It is most unwise for anyone involved in counselling to ignore her own feelings, needs and problems.

The process of self-disclosure can be stimulated by asking each nurse to pair off with someone she does not know intimately and engage in a mutual exchange of personal information. When the pairs have been together for about 10 minutes the tutor should ask couples to become foursomes and repeat the exercise. At this stage the tutor might present each group with some light and amusing topic to discuss such as 'what would you do if a kissogram girl/boy called for you?' Such topics reduce self-consciousness and encourage spontaneity; and it is remarkable how they frequently develop into serious discussion around ethical matters like sexism and sexual behaviour in general. Having broken the ice during these preliminary exercises, nurses can move more confidently into discussion of their own self-awareness in relation to counselling.

Self-awareness includes self-image – how you see yourself; and self-esteem – how you think others see you. Some young people come into nursing with poor self-esteem, and it is essential that this is detected before they move into situations where they will attempt to counsel others. They must be encouraged to be more self-revealing than self-concealing. The facilitator must always be available to listen to nurses talking about their problems, and be willing to help them develop on their own terms. A nurse lacking in self-esteem will very soon get out of her depth in the mental health field. Not all patients will be honest and cooperative. Some will exhibit conscious or unconscious desires to manipulate and frustrate those who offer to help them. Such patients can be adept at getting their own way through covert manipulation. Student nurses are particularly vulnerable. Not wishing to be labelled like "that other insensitive nurse who didn't understand", the inexperienced nurse may be too eager to be helpful. She must know there will always be someone to whom she can turn for support; someone who will enable her to ask herself questions like, "Am I being taken beyond my responsibilities as a nurse?", and "What does this patient really want?"

Attitude of the counsellor

Unhealthy attitudes on the part of nurses can also inhibit counselling. Research has clearly indicated that counselling is only successful when the counsellor displays warmth, sensitivity and understanding, and is willing to meet patients with an open attitude. Relationship is infinitely more important than technique. Successful counsellors radiate sincerity and are able to confront in a constructive manner. Of course, not all nurses will possess these qualities, but they must be made aware of the desirability of developing their personalities along these lines if they are to help patients cope with their problems.

As the facilitator discusses these matters with nurses, she should pay particularly attention to individuals who express reservations about these ideas, for their defence mechanisms may be rejecting some aspects of counselling, for example self-disclosure, on emotional grounds. On the other hand, it may be that the concepts have not been sufficiently explained. Since counselling is based on ideas borrowed from other disciplines such as philosophy, psychiatry and theology, different meanings may become attached to words, with consequent confusion.

Counselling concepts are difficult to comprehend in the abstract and for ethical reasons cannot be freely tested with patients, so nurses must be placed in simulated situations which will enable them to get the feel of the skills involved. Three or four of the basic components of counselling should be isolated, and structured opportunities created for the students to practise them. This is usually the prerogative of the facilitator. I would propose the following skills to begin with; attending, listening, leading and demonstrating empathy. More difficult skills such as summarising, reflecting and confronting may be introduced as the nurse gains experience.

Attending This is the giving of undivided attention to the patient who seeks help through:
- eye contact – looking (without staring) in such a way as to communicate concern and understanding;
- a posture which is relaxed and focused towards the patient;
- gestures and facial expressions which are natural, but not excessive or distracting.

Listening "If one gives answer before he hears, it is his folly and shame", (Proverbs 18:13). My favourite definition of listening is "not thinking about what you are going to say until the other person has stopped talking". Many people fail to listen because they are already concentrating on what they wish to say in response. Waiting through periods of silence as the patient summons up courage to delve into painful memories, or pauses to collect his thoughts can be tedious and tiresome, yet nothing destroys counselling as much as excessive talking by the counsellor. A nurse who talks a lot to patients may give good advice, but this is seldom heard and even less likely to be acted on. Listening is one of the most effective ways of caring.

Nurses must be made aware that if they find themselves talking a lot to patients, this may be an expression of their own insecurities. They may feel unable to handle situations which they don't fully understand or find too emotional or threatening. If so, they should be advised to withdraw and seek help from more experienced people. Listening is essentially a sensitive monitoring of the other person's words to try to understand his perceived problems and underlying emotions.

Leading Despite the emphasis on listening as the core of counselling, the patient must obviously be asked some questions, but how? Questions should be simply phrased and asked one at a time, avoiding those which can be answered by a simple yes or no. Questions involving the use of the word 'why' are also undesirable since they may appear too judgmental. Open-ended questions such as; "You said a few minutes ago that you have been having difficulties at work. Tell me a bit more about this?" are far preferable. The judicious use of questions can gently lead the patient into productive channels of exploration. The competent counsellor will ask the patient those questions which he should be asking of himself. Subtle questioning can also help the patient inject a sense of order and perspective into his life situation.

Demonstrating empathy This is the ability to demonstrate to a person that you can view the situation from his point of view. It is vital that nurses can clearly distinguish between empathy and sympathy. Empathy is to understand the feelings of another person; sympathy is being affected yourself by the same feelings experienced by the other person, and is a hidden danger for the inexperienced nurse. Empathy embraces the ability of the counsellor to remain impartial and not allow her own feelings to intrude into the counselling situation. It is an elusive quality which cannot always be conjured up because it seems the right way to feel. It is related to experience. The closer the nurse's own life experience to that of the patient the more likely she is to understand how the patient feels. On the other hand, sympathy can easily replace empathy if the nurse becomes over-involved with an individual's problems.

The success of any attempt to teach counselling is closely related to the graded presentation of the relevant skills together with a plan to teach them in an interesting and purposeful manner. I have always found simple, direct person-to-person methods most effective. Using a battery of media, including closed circuit TV, tapes and films can be distracting and confusing for students and facilitator alike. Role play supported by group discussion is obviously the medium of choice.

To facilitate this approach, an easy relationship between facilitator and nurse is essential. There must be a considerable degree of mutual trust and acceptance. Initially the role model must be willing to demonstrate the skills herself. Lack of finesse need not be a drawback. A highly skilled model may actually increase performance anxiety in nurses, whereas a model who copes in spite of shortcomings will encourage nurses to launch out themselves.

Having demonstrated the selected skill, the facilitator may place the nurses in groups of five to practise the skill. They can take on the following roles; patient, nurse, patient observer, nurse observer, and group coordinator. Each must move through each of the roles, and sufficient time must be set aside after each piece of role play for discussion of the performances. This feedback is most important; it is at this point that self-insights can be sharpened and good techniques reinforced. However, unless such discussions are carefully controlled they can harm individuals. Undue criticism or embarrassment will discourage sensitive nurses.

The group facilitator must guide such discussions so that they inform, build up confidence and promote openness and peer support. Nurses can learn to support each other, and this is invaluable in the clinical situation. The nurse must be made aware that she is not expected to solve a patient's problems; only help him accept responsibility for solving his own problems. Finally, she should be taught the value of referral. Frequently she will be best able to help a patient by referring him to someone whose training, experience or availability will be of special assistance; for example, a ward sister, social worker, or hospital chaplain. Referral must never be interpreted as incompetence, and it should be done in such a way that the patient does not feel dismissed. Nurses need the maturity to accept and respond openly to the needs of students and those with less experience than themselves who are still struggling to develop a coherent self-image. Secure in your own self-image, you should remain open to continual learning. Your personal view of the world is one among many; and your ethical standards, whatever their intrinsic merit, may not be shared by a new generation of nurses. Moralising has no place in counselling or in the teaching of counselling. Nurses will become competent counsellors through developing self-awareness, and related experiences of helping patients to cope with their problems. You, as an experienced professional will be their sounding board and companion along the way.

References
Burton, G. (1979) Interpersonal Relations. Tavistock publications, London.
Collins, G. (1985) Christian Counselling. Hazell Watson and Viney Ltd, Aylesbury.
Heasman, K. (1969) Introduction to Pastoral Counselling. Constable, London.
Hurding, R.F. (1980) Restoring the Image. Paternoster Press, Exeter.
Minshill, D. (1982) Counselling in psychiatric nursing. *Nursing Times*, 7 July.
Rogers, C. (1961), On Becoming a Person. Constable, London.
Salaman, G. (1983) Counselling organisations: trust or conspiracy? *Nursing Times*, 19 January.
Spy, T. and Stone, J. (1982) So you think you know about counselling? *Nursing Times*, 21 May.
Stewart, W. (1979) Health Service Counselling. Pitman Medical Publishing Co., London.
Tournier, P. (1957) The Meaning of Persons. SCM Press Ltd., London.
Tschudin, V. (1982) Counselling Skills for Nurses. Balliere Tindall, London.
Wallis, J.H. (1973) Personal Counselling. Allen and Unwin, London.

6

Counselling: basic principles in nursing

Philip Burnard, PhD, MSc, RGN, RMN, DipN, CertEd, RNT
Director of Postgraduate Nursing Studies, University of Wales College of Medicine, Cardiff

During the past five years the idea that nurses in all specialties should develop appropriate skills in communicating with and helping their patients has received much attention. Often, however, basic counselling skills are taught without supporting theoretical rationale. This chapter sets out some basic principles based on those found in humanistic psychology theory and in the literature on client-centred therapy, with the aim of offering a 'theoretical scaffolding' on which to build good practice. The principles are presented dogmatically for the sake of clarity but, like all principles, they are open to debate, clarification and development. A further reading list is offered to be used as a guide to tracing the ideas back to source.

The terms 'counsellor' and 'client' are used through the chapter. 'Counsellor' means any grade of nurse acting as counsellor. 'Client' means anyone with whom the nurse is interacting in a counselling capacity. Thus a client may be a patient, a colleague or a friend. Table 1 shows the basic principles of counselling.

> 1. The client knows best what is best for them.
> 2. Interpretation by the counsellor is likely to be inaccurate and is best avoided.
> 3. Advice is rarely helpful.
> 4. The client occupies a different 'personal world' from that of the counsellor and vice versa.
> 5. Listening is the basis of the counselling relationship.
> 6. Counselling 'techniques' should not be overused; however:
> 7. Counselling can be *learned*.

Table 1. Basic principles in counselling.

The client knows what is best for them   We all perceive the world differently having had different personal histories which colour our views. Throughout our lives we develop a variety of coping strategies and problem solving abilities which we use when beset by personal problems. Central to client-centred counselling is the idea that, given the space and time, we are the best arbiters of what is and is not right for us. We can listen to others, and hear their ideas but in the end we as individuals have to decide upon our own course of action.

Belief in the essential ability of all people to make worthwhile decisions for themselves arises from the philosophical tradition of existentialism. Existentialism argues, among other things, that we are born free and that we 'create' ourselves as we go through life. For the existentialist, nothing is predetermined, there is no blueprint for how any given person's life will turn out. Responsibility and choice lie squarely with the individual.

No one is free in all respects. We are born into a particular society, culture, family and body. On the other hand, our *psychological* make up is much more fluid and arguably not predetermined. We are free to think and feel. One of the *aims* of counselling is to enable the client to realise this freedom to think and feel.

Once a person has to some extent, recognised this freedom, he begins to realise that he can change his life. Again, in humanistic or client-centred counselling, this is a central issue: that people can change. They do not have to be weighed down by their past or by their conditioning (as psychoanalytical and behavioural theory would argue): they are more or less free to choose their own future. And no one can choose that future for them. Hence the overriding principle that the client knows what is best for them.

Interpretation by the counsellor is likely to be inaccurate and is best avoided To interpret, in this sense, is to offer the client an explanation of his thinking, acting or feeling. Interpretations are useful in that they can help to clarify and offer a theoretical framework on which the client may make future decisions. However, they are best left to the client to make.

As we have seen, we all live in different perceptual worlds. Because of this, another person's interpretation of *my* thinking, acting or feeling will be based on that person's experience — not mine. That interpretation is, therefore, more pertinent to the person offering it than it is to me, coloured as it is bound to be by the perceptions of the other person. Such colouring is usually more of a hindrance to me than a help.

It is tempting for others to lace their interpretations of a person's action with 'oughts' or 'shoulds'. Thus an interpretation can quickly degenerate into moralistic advice which may lead to the client feeling guilty or rejecting the advice because it does not fit into his own belief or value system.

Advice is rarely helpful Any attempt to help to 'put people's lives right' is fraught with pitfalls. Advice is rarely directly asked for and rarely appropriate. If it is taken, the client tends to assume that 'that's the course of action I would have taken anyway' or, he becomes dependent on the counsellor. The counsellor who offers a lot of advice is asking for the client to become dependent. Eventually, of course, some of the advice turns out to be wrong and the spell is broken: the counsellor is seen to be 'only human' and no longer the necessary life-line perceived by the client in the past. Disenchantment quickly follows and the client/counsellor relationship tends to degenerate rapidly. It is better then, not to become an advice-giver in the first place.

There are exceptions to this principle where advice giving is appropriate; about wound care or medication for example. In the sphere of personal problems, however, advice-giving is rarely appropriate.

Different 'personal worlds' of client and counsellor Because of varied experiences, different physiologies and shifting belief and value systems, we perceive the world through different 'frames of reference'. We act according to our particular belief about how the world is. What happens next, however, is dependent upon how the world *really* is. If there is a considerable gap between our 'personal theory of the world' and 'how the world really is' we may be disappointed or shocked by the outcome of our actions.

It is important that the counsellor realises that her own belief system may not be shared by the client and that her picture of the world is not necessarily more accurate.

A useful starting point is for the counsellor to explore her own belief and value system before she starts. She may be surprised at the contradictions and inconsistencies that abound in that 'personal world'! She is then in a better position to appreciate the difference between her belief system and her client's.

The counsellor's task is to attempt to enter and share the personal world of the client. This is often described as developing empathy or the ability to non-judgementally understand the particular view of the world that a person has at a particular time. That view usually changes as counselling progresses, after which the client may no longer feel the need for the counsellor. When this happens, the counsellor must develop her own strategies for coping with the separation that usually follows.

Counselling is a two-way process. While the client's personal world usually changes, so may the counsellor's. It can, then, be an opportunity for growth for the counsellor as well as the client.

Listening is the basis of the counselling relationship To really listen to another person is the most caring act of all, and takes skill and practice. Often, when we claim to be listening we are busy rehearsing our next verbal response, losing attention and failing to hear the other person. Listening involves giving ourselves up completely to the other person in order to fully understand.

We cannot listen properly if we are constantly judging or categorising what we hear. We must learn to set aside our own beliefs and values and to 'suspend judgement'. It is a process of offering free attention; of accepting, totally, the other person's story, accepting that their version of how the world is may be as valid as our own. Listening can be developed through practice and may be enhanced through meditation. Various experiential exercises have been developed to enable people to learn properly. They need to be used carefully with plenty of time allocated for them.

We need to listen to the metaphors, the descriptions, the value judgements and the words that people use, as they are all indicators of their personal world. Noting facial expressions, body movements, eye contact or lack of it, are all aspects of the listening process.

Many of us have been confronted by the neophyte counsellor whose determined eye-contact and stilted questioning make us feel distinctly uncomfortable! The aim is to gradually incorporate techniques into the personal repertoire. It is important that learner nurses do not adopt, wholesale, a collection of techniques that they have been taught in the school of nursing.

Counselling 'techniques' should not be overused   If we arm ourselves with a whole battery of counselling techniques, perhaps learned through workshops and courses, we are likely to run into problems. The counsellor who uses too many techniques may be perceived by the client as artificial, cold and even uncaring. It is possible to pay so much attention to techniques that they impede listening and communicating.

Some techniques, such as the conscious use of questions, reflections, summary, probing and so forth are very valuable. What one must hope for, is that through practice, such techniques become natural to the counsellor. The process takes considerable time and must be rooted in a conscious effort to appear natural and spontaneous to others.

Counselling can be learned   Counselling is not something that comes naturally to some and not to others. We can all develop listening skills and our ability to communicate clearly with other people, which is the basis of counselling. The skills can only be learned through personal experience and lots of practice, which may be gained in experiential learning workshops for development of counselling skills.

The list of principles outlined here is not claimed to be exhaustive. It attempts to identify *some* of the important principles involved and to explain them. The next stage is to develop counselling theory and skill further through reading and counselling skills courses. The bibliography identifies some sources of further ideas regarding the theory of counselling. These are not the *only* books on counselling but they are up-to-date, readable and currently available in bookshops.

Counselling skills courses are run by a variety of university extra-mural departments; by specialist counselling organisations and, increasingly, as part of the continuing education programmes organised with schools of nursing.

Bibliography
Bond, M. (1986) Stress and Self Awareness: A Guide for Nurses. Heinemann, London.
    A practical book which explores methods of coping with emotions and personal problems.
Burnard, P. (1985) Learning Human Skill: A Guide for Nurses. Heinemann, London.
    An introductory text on self-awareness and experiential learning. Contains a series of exercises on counselling skills training.
Burnard, P.(1989) Counselling Skills for Health Professionals. Chapman and Hall, London.
    A guide to many aspects of counselling theory and skills.
Claxton, G. (1984) Live and Learn: An Introduction to the Psychology of Growth and Change in Everyday Life. Harper and Row, London.
    A stimulating and eclectic approach to the question of how people learn and change. A very readable book.
Nelson-Jones, R. (1981) The Theory and Practice of Counselling Psychology. Holt, Rinehart Winston, London.
    A very comprehensive account of most aspects of counselling.
Rogers, C.R. (1980) A Way of Being. Houghton Mifflin, New York.
    A sensitive book by the late Carl Rogers founder of 'client-centred' counselling, which explores the nature of empathy and the therapeutic relationship.

7

The path towards a common goal: structuring the counselling process

Alun Jones, RMN, RGN, Dip. Psych., MA, CPN Cert.
Clinical Nurse Specialist, Liaison Consultation Psychiatry, Countess of Chester Hospital

Therapeutic communication is an aspect of patient care which is of concern to all nurses. With the development of clinical nurse specialism nurse/patient interactions are becoming increasingly sophisticated, and specialist nurses have helped increase awareness of the effectiveness of facilitative communication in providing the psychological component of care.

Many nurses, however, are beginning to develop their role beyond the deployment of effective communication in the clinical setting. The alignment to specific theoretical communication frameworks such as individual, family group and marital therapies has brought about a new breed of nurse, the nurse counsellor. These are increasingly becoming identified as 'experts' in areas of communication previously considered the province of psychologists and medical practitioners.

When determining whether to enter a counselling relationship with a client, the nurse is accountable to both the organisation and professional body. However, it is also the nurse's responsibility to provide the setting for a safe and effective working alliance with the client. This means setting limits, defining parameters and negotiating boundaries for a highly personal but always professional relationship. This chapter examines this important, but often neglected, aspect of the counselling relationship.

Structuring the counselling process

Structure in counselling has been defined as a "joint understanding between the counsellor and the client regarding the characteristics, conditions, procedures and parameters of counselling" (Day and Spartico, 1980). Structuring refers to the interactional process by which structure is reached - the means by which the counsellor and client together define the guidelines governing the counselling process. This involves activities such as informing, proposing, suggesting, recommending, negotiating, stipulating, contracting and compromising. Day and Spartico argue that although structure is fundamental to the therapeutic relationship, it is often neglected in the counselling process.

Support for this view exists throughout counselling and psychotherapy literature; Green *et al* (1989), for example, believe that structure and limits are indispensable markers in any therapeutic or counselling situation - whether implicit or overtly stated, they are necessary for effective outcomes and achieving therapeutic goals.

Structure within any counselling relationship cannot be avoided, and will either evolve or be developed (Day and Spartico, 1980). It is important that client and counsellor have a similar view of the structure of the relationship if counselling is to progress as smoothly as possible. Day and Sparico call for an explicit structure within a counselling relationship, and offer guidelines which constitute the basis of a framework. These are:

- the structure should be developed rather than allowed to evolve;
- the client and counsellors' perception should be similar;
- structure should support counselling goals rather than impede them.

Egan (1986) supports the notion that structure is a basic tenet of the helping situation. He believes the 'helping' process should be owned by the helper and client alike, and there should be a basic understanding of the major goals and procedures used in the process, so that both people own the same thing. Egan proposes the negotiation of a contract which would provide the structure required to achieve therapeutic outcomes. The two following case outlines illustrate the effectiveness of structuring in counselling relationships.

Structuring in practice
Counselling to overcome low self-esteem   Sally, a 34-year-old married woman, came into counselling due to persistent depression and a 'failure' in her marital relationship. It soon became apparent that Sally's self-esteem depended on affirmation and approbation from others in her life - a sort of 'living for others'. Sally was very astute at recognising other people's needs, and fell into the theme of 'being for others' in order to illicit favourable behaviour to gratify her own needs. 'Living for others', however, left Sally feeling angry, resentful and ultimately compounded her feelings of despair and low self-esteem.

This pattern soon established itself in the counselling sessions, and the therapy became a vehicle for Sally to search out the counsellor's own needs. She would speak of the counsellor as 'attractive and intelligent', 'warm and kind', and played the part of the unfortunate client to make him look after her. Sally would give long monologues about her relationships and sexual activities which made it difficult for him to respond appropriately, and allowed her to avoid confronting her emotional distress. Initially, the counsellor failed to recognise this behaviour for what it was, believing the sessions to be facilitative and therapeutic. He had, in fact, become seduced by Sally's manner in much the same way as had happened in her previous relationships.

If allowed to continue, this scenario would eventually have led despair, disillusionment and further unhappiness in Sally's life. This, however, was quickly recognised in the counsellor supervision group, and the use of structure in the session was discussed at length and implemented. Explicit structure in the relationship was of immense importance to the outcome of therapy, and for Sally the experience of participating in an openly structured relationship enabled her to observe herself in a healthy relationship which she had had a role in constructing.

The lack of initial structure within the session had allowed Sally to replay unaccounted her conflictual relationship theme in therapy. The recognition of the need for 'explicit limits' in the counselling process proved an important lesson for the counsellor, who was relatively inexperienced; while he had previously acknowledged the need for structure in relation to the practical and consumer issues of the counselling relationship, such as length, time and place of sessions, method of recording sessions and an outline of the method of therapy, he had not yet realised the importance of explicitly stating the 'process issues' (Stewart *et al*, 1978). This entails a definition of counselling, client and counsellor roles and expectations, as well as identification of goals. These 'process issues' were attended to in subsequent sessions, allowing the therapeutic process to focus on Sally's emotional distress. Supervision had given the counsellor invaluable insight - in the absence of adequate structuring, Sally's distorted sense of reality would only have been confirmed, eventually rendering the working alliance untenable.

Counselling in hospital   Brian, a 50-year-old teacher, had suffered previous chest infections and had been admitted to the medical ward for the second time with respiratory distress. He was not responding to treatment, appeared edgy, anxious and withdrawn, his sleep and appetite were poor, and he also had difficulty breathing. However, he found difficulty in sharing his fears and anxieties with the nursing staff.

Stewart *et al* (1978) state that "if a person seems unsure, hesitant or insecure the counsellor should provide structure immediately. On the other hand, a client may readily begin sharing a concern and thus the provision of a structure at this time would be an intrusion upon the person's desire to share that concern. If this is true the counsellor can provide structure at a later date in the initial interview". This provides a useful basis from which to begin to effectively structure the counselling process taking place in the high stress setting of the general hospital.

While for some patients, fear and anxiety will impede effective communication, others will experience a desire to share their concern openly, but may later experience guilt, anger and shame at their action. Formal structure can establish a facilitative framework which can prove therapeutic and, importantly, provide an element of protection for the counsellor and client. Brian's obvious anxiety and hesitance when introduced to the counsellor suggested that early structuring of the session would reduce the amount and intensity of anxiety to reasonable working levels amd reduce the likelihood of con-fusion and conflict at the important initial moments of the relationship.

It is possible to structure a relationship even within the restricted confines of a hospital bedside: the counsellor sat so as to allow both parties to look away, thus avoiding direct eye contact. He introduced himself to Brian stating who he was and what time he was available for the interview (practical issues). The counsellor also encouraged discussion on the confidential nature of the relationship and Brian's right to decline the intervention (consumer issues). Finally, he encouraged dialogue on the nature of their relationship, and discussed and defined possible therapeutic outcomes (process issues).

This early structuring of the relationship provided Brian with an optimum safe coalition in which to explore feelings which were already at "the edge of awareness" (Rogers, 1961). This allowed him to reformulate his problem, converting feelings of distress, fear and confusion into clearer sequences of thought (Ryle, 1975).

Benefits of structure

Both brief and long-term counselling situations can be greatly enhanced through the introduction of structure. It is important, however, to avoid allowing structure to evolve, as it should be developed in a skilled and conscious manner. For many nurses, developing counselling skills aligned to an identified theoretical framework may be relatively alien to their culture, but avoidance of an explicit structure can also be due to personal factors, such as fear of self-assertion and subsequent fantasised rejection.

We need to develop this important aspect of overall counselling skills. Understanding the benefits of structure to the counselling situation can allow nurse counsellors to feel able to negotiate structure, without necessarily perceiving its introduction as threatening either themselves or the client. The two interventions described above illustrate the importance of structure to good therapeutic outcomes. In both cases, the clients' positive experience in therapy was greatly enhanced by the process.

It is important to feel comfortable with the application of theory to practice, even though structure should be introduced with caution. Pietrofesa *et al* (1978) indicate that too much or too rigid a structure can be constraining for both client and counsellor, while Benjamin (1974) and Winnicot (1971) assert that ill-timed and lengthy structuring or an overly orderly counsellor can result in confusion or resistance or interrupt the continuity of the therapeutic process.

In Sally's case, although the process issues of structures were introduced appropriately, earlier attention to these factors may have reduced the likelihood of 'acting out' behaviours or resentment which could have impeded effective counselling. In Brian's situation early attention to these issues facilitated the use of the therapeutic relationship in a safe context. It is important to be aware of the need to perhaps hold back to begin with and introduce structure later in the initial interview.

In all cases, however, it is necessary to recognise the dynamic and collaborative nature of structuring: it should be a joint understanding and it is of the utmost importance that client and counsellor together define the guidelines which are to govern the counselling process in each individual case.

References
Benjamin, A. (1974) The Helping Interview (2nd Ed.). Bosta Houghton Miffin, .

Day, R.W. and Spartico, R.T. (1980) Structuring the counselling process. American Association for Counselling and Development. *Personal and Guidance Journal*, **59**, 246-49. In: Dryden, W. (Ed) Key Issues for Counselling in Action. Sage Publications, London.

Egan, G. (1976) The Skilled Helper (3rd Ed). A Systematic Approach to Effective Helping. Brooks/Cole, California, USA.

Green, S. A., Golberg, R. L., Goldstein, D. M., Leibenluft, E. (1988) Limit Setting in Clinical Practice. American Psychiatric Press, Washington, USA.

Pietrofesa, J.J., Hoffman, A., Splete, H.H., Tinto, D.D. (1978) Counselling Theory Research and Practice. Rand and Nally, Chicago, USA.

Rogers, C. R. (1951) Client Centred Therapy: Its Current Implications and Theory. Constable, London.

Ryle, A. (1979) The focus on grief interpretive psychotherapy dilemmas traps and snags as target problems. *British Journal of Psychiatry*, **134**, 46-50.

Stewart, N.R., Winbarn, B.B., Johnson, R.G., Burks, H.N.Jr. Engelkes, J.R. (1978) Systematic Counselling. Prentice Hall, London.

Winnicot, D.W. (1971) Playing and Reality. Tavistock, London.

Applying
Communication Skills

8

Tablets to take away: why some elderly people fail to comply with their medication

Sally Quilligan, RGN, DipN
Currently studying BEd (Hons) at South Bank Polytechnic

In 1981, Bliss revealed that drug related problems accounted for 10 per cent of all hospital admissions in elderly people. While some of these could be explained by the age-related changes in physiological and metabolic processes and by polypharmacy, some were also a consequence of patients failing to take their medications correctly (Bliss, 1981). My own experiences as a medical ward sister appeared to support this finding and stimulated me to investigate the problem at a local level. In doing so I was surprised to see that, although nursing studies about discharge planning and self-medication briefly mention the problem of non-compliance with medication, there have to date been few detailed nursing papers (Entwistle, 1989).

Increased life expectancy

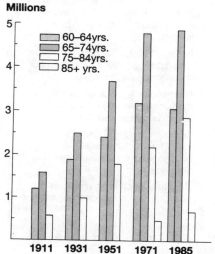

Figure 1. Population trends above 60 years, adapted from Social Trends (1987).

In 1980, Williamson reported that one quarter of all elderly patients admitted to hospital suffer from four or more chronic conditions, and that 80 per cent of all elderly patients take some prescribed medication. Statistics (Figure 1) clearly demonstrate that elderly people have an increase in life expectancy, and although this demographic trend may be attributed to many causes, a major factor is medication.

There is, however, strong evidence to suggest that elderly people frequently fail to comply with their medication regime – the Royal College of Physicians (1984) emphasised this in their report demonstrating that 75 per cent make errors in their compliance to prescriptions, of which 25 per cent are potentially serious. An extensive literature search seems to demonstrate that compliance with long-term medication is about 50 per cent. Non-compliance with a drug regime may disrupt or reverse the possible benefit of the preventive, curative or palliative effect the drug provides. It may involve the patient in further investigative procedures, cause discomfort and physical suffering. Illness

1. The medication to take home is checked by a trained nurse, but invariably given to the patient by a student nurse.

2. The medication is handed to the patient at their bedside less than an hour before discharge.

3. Little attempt is made to check the patient's knowledge about the medication.

4. With the occasional exception of patients on Warfarin and steroids, no explanation of likely side-effects is given.

5. Patients' ability to open containers, dispense their medication, or read the labels is not checked.

6. No mention is made about the danger of hoarding previously prescribed medication.

7. Occasionally, family members are told when to administer the drug, but there are no planned teaching sessions.

8. No explanation is given of how to obtain a new prescription unless the patient asks.

9. No reference is made in the care plan to this aspect of discharge preparation.

Table 1. Outcome of observations.

and possible readmission to hospital may upset daily routines, disrupt social relationships with family and friends and possibly induce deep anxiety for the elderly person. With dwindling resources and the current NHS crisis, the additional cost generated must also be considered.

This appears to suggest that failure of elderly people to take their medicines correctly after discharge from hospital does have far-reaching consequences. It is surely in the healthcare professional's and society's interest to ensure elderly people are able to administer their drugs safely and correctly.

Fully aware of the importance of correct medication administration among elderly people after discharge from hospital, I decided to review current practice within my own clinical area, a four ward medical unit. This proved a salutary experience as shown by the outcome (Table 1), and I would suggest that the results might be mirrored on hundreds of other wards up and down the country.

Factors affecting non-compliance

"Reasons for error and non-compliance are varied and . . . external factors such as poor record keeping by healthcare professionals . . . inadequate labelling, packaging and presentation may all contribute to the problem, as may the patients' knowledge of their medication and the availability or lack of adequate instructions in their safe and appropriate use" (Parish, 1983).

Size, shape and colour of pills   "The white one is my water pill." Past experience has shown me that some patients relate the action of their drug to its colour. The World Health Organisation (1981) recognises this and suggests that where several drugs are prescribed they should be of different shapes and colours. This may however be failing to treat the patient as an individual, assessment might reveal many elderly people who would know exactly which tablets and what dose to take. The shape of the tablet also needs to be easy to handle. Limited movement and painful joints are a feature of the lives of many old people and they may find it difficult to pick up small, round tablets. Even if a suitable form of medication is prescribed, a repeat prescription may, as Warren (1985) notes, be a different brand or generic product, and this variation in the tablets' appearance may be a contributing factor to drug non-compliance.

Containers   "We have established beyond reasonable doubt that it is difficult, if not impossible, for some elderly patients to open childproof containers and remove tablets from bubble packs without shooting them across the floor" (MacGuire, 1987). In 1983 Parish clearly stated that healthcare professionals should be alert to the fact that child resistant containers are a potential source of medication error. This is reinforced by Halworth's (1984) outpatient study of 92 elderly people, in which he found that a quarter of them admitted to having transferred their tablets to an alternative container. Clearly, blister packaging, foil packaging and childproof containers present difficulties, indeed childproof would appear to generally be synonymous with elderly proof.

Davidson (1973) demonstrated that a glass container with a screw top lid was the most convenient for elderly people to use. However, this requires a firm handgrip, and handgrip becomes progressively weaker with age, which may explain Bellamy's (1981) more recent finding that many elderly people could not completely close screw-capped containers. The ability to open a container depends on eyesight as well as manual dexterity, and Coote (1984) proposes that people with poor eyesight should place each prescription in a different shaped bottle. In my experience I have found patients prefer a clear glass palm-sized bottle with screw cap or push-on lid. There are, however, those with particular needs who will find even these difficult. Coote (1984) suggests that for people with severe hand tremors, the use of Dines high impact polystyrene tubs with pull-off lids may be beneficial.

Labelling   "Pharmacists should provide typewritten labels with clear and complete instructions and ensure that the patient can read and understand the label" (*Drug and Therapeutics Bulletin*, 1980).

It is common knowledge that part of the ageing process results in a loss of visual acuity and may result in a loss of ability to read effectively. Although labels are now computer printed, they are often too small and difficult for elderly people with poor eyesight to read. It is, then, somewhat alarming to consider that in Halworth's (1984) outpatient study, 34 per cent stated that if the instructions were not on the label they would not remember how to take their drugs correctly. It is also disturbing to note that Bliss (1981) revealed that 50 per cent of GPs' repeat prescriptions have no instructions other than take as directed.

Instructions themselves can cause problems if ambiguous. 'One tablet three times daily', or 'one tablet at breakfast, lunch or dinner' may, as MacGuire (1987) notes, cause problems – when is dinner, what is lunch? It may then be better to state take one tablet at 08.00 hrs, 12 noon, 18.00 hrs. What is certain is that research has demonstrated associating specific times of day with medication may improve compliance (*Drug and Therapeutics Bulletin*, 1980).

Written instructions   "Written information about the medication each patient is taking, which they could take home, may help to increase their knowledge level and indirectly compliance" (Waters, 1987). In 1970, Skeet argued that written instructions for patients to take home would increase understanding and memory. Although not all elderly patients need additional instructions, those with memory or hearing impairment may find some useful.

The progressive hearing loss associated with ageing results in a progressive loss of ability to hear high frequencies and may significantly affect ability to understand speech. In a community survey of over-70 year-olds, Gilhome (1981) found 60 per cent had some hearing impairment and, of more concern, 25 per cent of these refused to accept any suggestion that they might have a hearing impairment. This must alert nurses to the fact that elderly people may try to hide their hearing loss and that verbal instructions may often need to be written down.

Memory aids   "Intellectual decline is not a universal and inevitable part of growing old" (Redfern, 1985), but 25 per cent of the population over 80 are moderately severely demented (Cormack, 1985) and many others who are not demented experience short-term memory loss. People with memory or orientation problems may experience difficulty and fail to take their medication as directed, and will require to be given extra time when preparing for their discharge. Even after this, some may have such severe problems that they are unable to manage, but others may benefit from learning to use a memory aid.

Memory aids range from the simple device made by the family, such as setting out doses for a day or week in egg cartons, to the more complex commercial product such as the Dosett Box. I could find no recent research to support the type of simple device already discussed, but it may act to encourage the family and or friends to become involved in reminding the patient about adhering to the drug regimen. The use of commercial aids to improve compliance is somewhat debatable. A ward using the Dosett Box system within my clinical area found it complicated, and the *Drug and Therapeutics Bulletin* (1980) notes that they may be difficult to use and awkward to refill.

Patient teaching   "We believe that teaching patients to take their medication correctly should form part of the rehabilitation programme for patients leaving hospital" (Crome *et al*, 1980). The review of current practice indicated that the information given to patients about their medication was hopelessly inadequate, and Wilson Barnett (1985) suggests that the implication of discharging patients home unprepared and without adequate knowledge is that they will fail to cope.

The benefits of using teaching plans as a means of improving knowledge and compliance have been clearly demonstrated (MacDonald, 1987). However, the author found little evidence that nurses recognise their role in relation to teaching about medication, and no reference to formal teaching on medication on any of the care plans.

The literature does appear to identify that there is no framework for patient education. Instruction is sometimes given in the form of informal chats in response to questioning, or as Price (1984) notes, as a menu or list of facts to be taught after a specific operation or procedure. This type of patient education is self-limiting and a framework is required which all nurses, including students, can use with ease. The familiar format of the nursing process as utilised by Wilson Barnett (1985) provides a basis for such patient teaching.

The way forward

This review of the literature has shown that many of the factors that influence medication compliance have been recognised for as long as a decade. It is suggested that in many clinical areas the importance of this information is being ignored and that nurses need now to consider the significance of their role in this important aspect of care.

References

Bellamy, K. *et al* (1981) Letter: Granny-proof bottles. *Journal of the Royal College of General Practitioners*, **31**, 2, 124.

Bliss, M.R. (1981) Prescribing for the elderly. *British Medical Journal*, **283**, 203–06.

Coote, J. (1984) Helping the elderly with their medicines. *The Pharmaceutical Journal*, November 17, 608–09.

Cormack, D. (Ed) (1985) Geriatric Nursing – A Conceptual Approach. Blackwell Scientific Publications, Oxford.

Crome, P. *et al* (1980) Drug compliance in elderly hospital in-patients. *The Practitioner*, **224**, 782.

Davidson, J. (1973) Presentation and packaging of drugs for the elderly. *Journal of Hospital Pharmacy*, 31, 180–84.

Drug and Therapeutics Bulletin (1980) Helping elderly patients to manage their medicines. *DTB*, **18**, 23, 89–91.

Entwistle, B. (1989) A problem of compliance. *Nursing Standard*, **20**, 3, 33–35.

Gilhome-Herbst, K.R. and Humprey, C.M. (1981) Prevalence of hearing impairment in the elderly living at home. *Journal of the Royal College of Practitioners*, **31**, 155–60.

Halworth, B.R. and Goldberg, L.A. (1984) Geriatric patients' understanding of labelling of medicines. *British Journal of Pharmaceutical Practice*, **6**, 6–14.

MacDonald, E.T. *et al* (1977) Improving drug compliance after hospital discharge. *British Medical Journal*, **2**, 618–21.

MacGuire, J. *et al* (1987) Two pink and one blue. *Nursing Times*, **83**, 2, 32-33.

Parish, P. *et al* (1983) The elderly and their use of medicine. Kings Fund Project Paper, No. 40, Kings Fund, London.

Price, B. (1984) From hospital to home. A framework for patient education. *Nursing Times*, **80**, 8 Aug, 28–30.

The Royal College of Physicians (1984) Medications for the Elderly. Report of the Royal College of Physicians. *Journal of the Royal College of Physicians*, **18**, 7–17.

Skeet, M. (1970) Home from Hospital. Macmillan, London.

Waters, K. (1987) Discharge planning: an exploratory study of the process of discharge planning on geriatric wards. *Journal of Advanced Nursing*, **12**, 71–83.

Williamson, J. (1978) Principles of drug action and usage. In: Isaacs, B. (Ed) Recent Advances in Geriatric Medicine. Churchill Livingstone, Edinburgh.

Wilson-Barnett, J. (1985) Principles of patient teaching. *Nursing Times*, **81**, 13, 28–29.

World Health Organisation (1981) Health Care in the Elderly. Report of the Technical Group on use of medicaments by the Elderly. *Drugs*, **22**, 279–94.

9

When should you take your tablets? Teaching elderly people about their medication

Sally Quilligan, RGN, DipN
Currently studying BEd (Hons) at South Bank Polytechnic

If 10 per cent of hospital admissions of elderly people can be linked to drug-related problems (Bliss, 1981), this must in part reflect that the present level of patient teaching about medication is inadequate. As Wilson Barnett (1985) has suggested, the implication of discharging a patient home without adequate knowledge is that they will fail to cope.

In 1977 MacDonald found that a predischarge counselling session of 15 minutes improved compliance by as much as 50 per cent, and there is much recent evidence to demonstrate that teaching is beneficial and may improve knowledge and compliance (Johnston, 1986). There is, however, little documented data to show that nurses recognise their role, in relation to teaching about medication. Within my own clinical area, while patient teaching was viewed as important, it was often omitted when the ward was busy. In addition, there was no reference to formal teaching about medication on any of the care plans. This accords with Water's (1987) experience in the North of England.

Lack of framework
What the literature does appear to identify is that there is no framework for patient education. Instruction is sometimes given in the form of informal chats in response to questioning, or as Price (1984) notes, as a menu or list of facts to be taught after a specific operation or procedure. This type of patient education is self-limiting – we need a framework which all nurses, including students, can use easily. The familiar format of the nursing process (Wilson Barnett, 1985) provides such a basis.

Who should perform the teaching? This appears to be another point for debate. Many writers suggest pharmacists should counsel patients (Sweeney, 1989; Johnston, 1986), whereas others suggest that because nurses spend most time with patients, it should be primarily their role (Royal College of Physicians, 1984). I would argue that it is the teaching *per se*, rather than who does the teaching, that matters.

Teaching patients to take their medication correctly should, as Crome (1980) suggests, form part of the rehabilitation programme, and should begin with the first nursing assessment following admission. The nurse must assess what precipitated this admission and ask the next of kin to bring in all the tablets patients have at home. It may also be necessary to ascertain how willing the family are to become involved in a teaching plan. As patients' conditions improve, the drug round can be used to assess their knowledge about both their disease and why they have to take their medication. Drug rounds thus become part of the learning process, and where appropriate, this could eventually be in the form of carefully supervised self-medication. Patients would then have a chance to familiarise themselves with their medication and discuss any needs or worries, while the nurses would have the opportunity to assess patients' knowledge, evaluate previous teaching and also identify those patients who may fail to take their medication due to physical or mental impairment and thus alert the community services. Following the drug rounds, nurses and patients could establish new goals – further individualised teaching sessions, involving patients' families wherever possible, can then be planned around patients' needs.

The drug round could thus provide continuous assessment and evaluation, and nurses would, as Redfern (1985) suggests, prepare patients for discharge throughout their hospital stay. Progress and teaching sessions given could then be formally documented within patients' care plans.

Suggested framework

The following framework is one way of ensuring elderly patients are given enough support in learning about their medication. It takes the steps of the nursing process as its structure.

Patient assessment

1. Does the patient understand his or her disease, and why their tablets must be taken?
2. Does the patient want to learn? Is he or she able to learn?
3. Can family be involved in the process?

Planning teaching   Use realistic, clear, *joint* goals on agreed topics and if possible arrange discussions when family can be present. Set dates and times for the sessions to ensure they are not missed.

Implement   Limit teaching to three topics in each session. Discuss the patient's worries and check previous knowledge. Remind the patient of the topic and goal, and limit the session to 15 minutes maximum.

Evaluate   On-going assessment of medication and the teaching programme is required (see Table 1).

By using this simple framework the patient's individual needs may be accounted for. Below is a checklist of areas that, ideally, most patients

1. Patient must be able to explain to the nurse at the end of session what has been discussed.
2. The patient's knowledge, needs and worries should be reassessed when he or she receives drugs on drug round, thus demonstrating change in knowledge.
3. A follow-up questionnaire should be conducted on discharge, to gain feedback on whether the teaching helped.
4. The nurse should assess the experience and recognise any lack of knowledge.

Table 1. Evaluation.

should be aware of.

Many intrapersonal factors such as motivation may influence compliance with medication following discharge and over this the nurse has no control. With a little planning the nurse can provide the elderly person with a real choice. With a sound knowledge base and user friendly medication they can now decide whether or not to comply rather than being in many cases simply unable to comply.

References
American Society of Hospital Pharmacists (1984) Guidelines on pharmacist conducted patient counselling. *American Journal of Hospital Pharmacy*, **41**, 331.
Bliss, M.R. (1981) Prescribing for the elderly. *British Medical Journal*, **283**, 203–06.
Crome, P. *et al* (1980) Drug compliance in elderly hospital in-patients. *The Practitioner*, **224**, 782.
Gooch, J. (1985) Medication to take home. *Professional Nurse*, **1**, 1, 15–16.
Johnston, M. *et al* (1986) Facilitating comprehension of discharge medication in elderly patients. *Age and Ageing*, **15**, 304–06.
MacDonald, E.T. *et al* (1977) Improving drug compliance after hospital discharge. *British Medical Journal*, **2**, 618–21.
Price, B. (1984) From hospital to home: a framework for patient education. *Nursing Times*, **80**, 32, 28–30.
Redfern, S. (1985) Nursing Elderly People. Churchill Livingstone, Edinburgh.
The Royal College of Physicians (1984) Medications for the Elderly. Report of the Royal College of Physicians. *Journal of the Royal College of Physicians*, **18**, 1, 7–17.
Sweeney, S. *et al* (1989) the impact of the clinical pharmacist on compliance in a geriatric population. *The Pharmaceutical Journal*, Feb 18, R4–R6.
Warren, J. *et al* (1985) Drug compliance in the elderly after discharge from hospital. *The Pharmaceutical Journal*, April 13, 472–73.
Waters, K. (1987) Discharge planning: an exploratory study of the process of discahrge planning on geriatric wards. *Journal of Advanced Nursing*, **12**, 1, 71–83.
Wilson-Barnett, J. (1985) Principles of patient teaching. *Nursing Times*, **81**, 8, 28–29.

10

Mums and dads need care too: supporting parents of babies in neonatal units

Alison J. Stewart, RGN, RM, RHV, MSc
Research Midwife, Bristol Maternity Hospital

Becoming a parent can be a time of crisis, with severe emotional upset and tension, while pregnancy is a transition period from independence to being responsible for the nurture of a helpless being. LeMasters (1979) found that 83 per cent of parents rated the arrival of their first child as a crisis event. The main problems cited were 'unpreparedness' for the realities of caring for a baby, such as tiredness, coping with feeds and a crying baby, all of which tend to be minimised by the romantic media image of perfect parenthood, with the cooing and chubby baby. For women the period of upset and confusion is heightened by the physical strain of labour and the changes which occur in the puerperium. Caplan (1965) has argued that life crises occur when a state of disequilibrium occurs and that for parents this is normally a short-term state as role readjustment occurs.

The arrival of the anticipated normal, healthy baby can be a positive event and do much to ease the adjustment of roles and ideas, but parents whose baby requires admission to a neonatal unit (NNU) do not have the comfort of cuddling their baby whenever they wish, helping them to perceive themselves as parents. For these parents the predominant feelings may be negative and long-lasting: aggression, anxiety, frustration, shock, fear, confusion, guilt and failure at the need for admission and the separation from their baby (McGovern, 1984; Alderson, 1983). Each parent is an individual and will bring a different set of beliefs, fears and needs with them. One of the main difficulties for parents is finding out what their role is in a NNU. How fulfilled they feel and how developed that role is depends on the staff.

As a visitor?
Twenty years ago, parental entry to NNUs was severely restricted and subject to staff dictates, in an attempt to avoid cross-infection. Parents were cast in the role of visitors, with the connotation of being invited and grudgingly allowed in, rather than having a right to come and go at will. The situation has now radically altered, due to staff awareness and the

efforts of pressure groups such as National Association for the Welfare of Children in Hospital (NAWCH), from the mid 1980s most units have had 'open' visiting – 24 hours per day (Thornes, 1985). Encouragement and explanation can familiarise parents and help them to feel less like intruders, as can facilities to make them more comfortable, such as kitchen, toilets and television, and the availability of information leaflets.

Parents as carers

Increasingly we are seeing families as 'healthcare agencies' responsible for the provision and maintenance of the health of its members. As Price (1987) notes, this can involve various functions: protecting and nurturing; lay care partners assisting professionals; pressure groups on behalf of the patient.

Normally, after the child is born, parents assume the responsibility for meeting his or her needs, such as feeding, changing and cuddling. Babies admitted to NNUs are separated from their parents, whose role as parents and providers is demeaned or totally negated, making them feel useless. They may see their child as belonging to medical/nursing staff and be too awed, frightened or overwhelmed by the surroundings to suggest that they become involved in providing care. Staff in NNUs need to take the initiative to suggest various ways in which parents can care for their baby (Table 1) to enhance their self-esteem as parents, which may be severely damaged by the birth of a baby who is not 'perfect'. Caring

- Cuddling the baby – providing comfort and contact.
- Feeding the baby – tube/breast/bottle.
- Choosing or providing milk, eg humilacting breast milk or deciding on a particular brand.
- Nappy changing/cord care.
- Cleaning the baby's mouth with moist cotton wool buds if not on oral feeds.
- Removing phototherapy goggles during nappy care.
- Stroking/massaging the baby's head.
- Putting toys, photos or pictures in the incubator/cot.
- Bringing the baby's own clothes and dressing him/her.
- Assisting nursing staff, handing items as needed, steadying tubes/probes when changing the baby's position or sheets.
- Maintaining a weight/progress chart and photographic record of changes.

Table 1. Suggestions for parental involvement in care.

activities also offer opportunities to meet and bond with the baby – separation has been cited as a cause of failure to bond, and early contact can have a long-term beneficial effect (Klaus and Kennell, 1976).

Physical care
The extent to which parents will become involved in the physical care of a baby will depend on parental inclination, unit policy and staff encouragement. For example, some units are happy for parents to perform tube-feeds once they have been safely supervised. However, even within a unit there may be variations between staff in how much they encourage parents to do. Thornes (1985) pointed out that "an inconsistent approach from staff does not encourage confidence. Cases have been reported of mothers who carried out a procedure successfully one day but were prevented from doing the same tasks by a different staff member the following day." A specified unit policy and documented approach of what aspects of care parents can be involved in can reduce this confusion. Care should also be taken to ensure that parents arrive when care is needed; coinciding with the time for observations, feeds and nappy changes: this may be a particular problem once the mother is discharged home, and will require liaison to avoid her making wasted journeys when feed times change.

Feeding the baby, whether by tube, bottle or breast, is often seen as the ultimate expression of care and love. Whatever the method, parents need to be taught how best to do it and given handy hints about baby behaviour, such as dealing with winding and hiccups. Mothers expressing milk for babies who are not currently enterally feeding need considerable support and praise, since it takes considerable effort and determination to continue.

It is equally important for staff on the unit to teach parents how to change nappies and wash their baby's face, since these skills are not instinctive. Any parent, regardless of how many previous children they may have had, tends to welcome a few reminders – and anyone is daunted at the idea of trying to juggle sticky tapes of a nappy inside an incubator. If parents are to feel confident carers they need sufficient support to achieve an appropriate level of competence.

Emotional care
It is vital that parents realise they provide comfort and security for their baby. They need to be taught how to cuddle a baby attached to probes, ECG monitors and drip, and can actively contribute to the baby's emotional development by providing sensory input and stimulation. For example, photos of parents/siblings can be stuck to the incubator or cot at the level of the baby's head so that as he or she turns from side to side the photos are there. Tapes of soft music or parents' voices reading a story might be played in the incubator or nearby, while pieces of sheepskin for the baby to lie on can provide tactile stimulation and

warmth, and small toys and mobiles can personalise the area surrounding the baby, making it feel more like home. At the end of the day parents need to feel they are providing the loving touch.

If they are not allowed or encouraged to develop their caring role, the danger exists that parents may have difficulty in assuming or resuming it when the baby gets better and is ready to go home. Some parents find it difficult to believe their baby is judged 'well' and that they are now competent to look after him or her, which may cause ambivalent feelings about taking the baby home (Salitros, 1986). Involving parents in care throughout their baby's stay in hospital can alleviate some of the panic experienced on discharge (Hawthorne, 1984).

Planning for discharge and equipping parents with information and skills to cope at home should be an integral part of neonatal care. However, discharge preparation can be woefully inadequate, and frequently parents are not asked what they wish to know. Marshall (1987) discovered that:

- Skills such as bathing were taught by junior, inexperienced staff with little room for parents to practise themselves.
- Social and psychological preparation appeared to be the most neglected area, such as what to expect in terms of future behaviour and problems.
- Discharge was based on the medical model – that the baby was better, and not on a holistic one of when family and baby were ready.

A consistent, well-planned and documented approach appears necessary for successful discharge, and it may be useful to conduct a survey of parents to find out what they want to know. Many units also have various facilities to aid the transition to home (Table 2).

- Mother and baby rooms in NNUs, where parents 'room in' for several nights prior to discharge and give 24 hour care to the baby while medical/nursing advice and treatment is still on hand.
- Transitional Care Units (TCU) where parents can care for babies in a more homelike setting, with staff available when necessary to perform and advise on care.
- Specialist support (eg, Family Care Team midwives or health visitors) in the community who may visit daily or weekly over a period of weeks or months as necessary. They liaise with the unit, meet the parents prior to discharge and appreciate the needs of these particular babies and families when setting down at home.

Table 2. Facilities to help parents adjust to being carers.

Learning about their baby

As intensive care becomes more complex, the battery of clicking, flashing, whirring and bleeping equipment may be a source of horrified fascination and fear. Seeing a member of the family amidst all this technology can cause emotional crisis (Daley, 1984). The two main expressed wishes of families tend to be:

- that they are informed truthfully of the patient's condition;
- to know the best care is being offered (this may involve nurses in explaining the need for and value of equipment).

This places a considerable onus on staff to provide sufficient explanation and information – and to repeat it, as most parents in a shocked state cannot readily assimilate it initially. In addition to learning what is happening to their baby, parents also need time to come to 'know' their baby. They need to see the child as an individual and to be able to interpret/perceive his or her reactions and needs.

Parents as guardians or advocates

An important aspect of being a parent is to protect children from potentially harmful events. Their capacity on the unit is to represent the best interests of their child and to reflect the needs and wishes of the child if he or she could express them. This means parents should be involved in treatment decisions: frequently they are seen as being too over-wrought to be able to participate intelligently in decisions. Taylor (1986) points out that "Being emotionally troubled does not make parents unintelligent, nor prevent them from using the intelligence they have". The danger is that staff may develop strategies to give information in short bursts and then become engrossed in care of, and procedures with, the baby, thus terminating spontaneous conversation and discussion. This is frequently a consequence of work pressures and may be one of the disadvantages of busy regional units taking all the 'difficult' cases as opposed to the steadier work pace of provincial units.

Parents as part of a family

In an intensive care situation it is easy to focus attention on the critically ill patient and fail to see the family holistically, with an established network of relationships. The involvement of siblings in NNU can reduce the conflicting demands on parents and minimise the sense of alienation or resentment siblings may feel towards the baby as the focus of attention. Involvement can include nappy changes, cuddling the baby and keeping a weight chart.

The clinical, overcrowded environment of NNU is not conducive to lengthy visits from children at any age – the provision of toys, a play area and even a playworker can help make visiting a success.

If they are to effectively care for their baby, all parents need help, which often comes from family, friends and professionals. Numerous reasons may cause parents to need and/or seek counselling, support and just a chance to chat. McHaffie (1987) found in a group of mothers on NNU with a low birthweight baby that all apparently needed "someone who can be quiet and still, who will listen attentively without interfering, who will be comfortable simply to be with rather than preoccupied by doing things". She argues that this is part of the nurse's or midwife's role. However, with current staffing levels there is little time to stop and listen for hours, nor may nurses feel competent to deal with some of the emotions encountered. Sources of help are listed in Table 3.

- Family/social worker – attached to the unit with counselling skills – acts as liaison between parents and staff: his or her job is to have time for the parents.
- Linkworkers/interpreters can be invaluable when communicating with other cultures – to ensure adequate explanation and ascertain any particular religious/cultural requests.
- Chaplains/religious workers may be contacted by nurses and parents to come and visit on the unit and offer comfort – possibly suggest a christening for a very sick baby.
- Psychotherapist referral if one is attached to the unit. Vas Dias (1987) cites the use of techniques to help families come to terms with their baby or his or her death.
- Parent/staff support groups – at an informal level, introductions by staff of mothers to each other, and at a more formal level with organised meetings.
- Contact addresses of people who are willing to 'adopt' parents who may have transferred many miles from home to the facilities available in a regional unit.

Table 3. Sources of help for parents.

One method of particular value to help parents share and express their feelings has been the use of parent or parent-staff support groups. These can be useful sources of comfort and feedback. Otherwise "parents may feel it is inappropriate to criticise one aspect of the care while being so grateful for the clinical care their baby is receiving" (Thornes, 1985).

Parents as members of the unit?

As staff, we need to adopt a positive partnership with parents and make sure we recognise the contribution that they alone can make to their child's wellbeing. Everyone's aim is for the babies on NNUs to recover and to be discharged into the care of confident and competent parents – we are just the facilitators in this process.

References

Alderson, P. (1983) *Special Care for Babies in Hospital*. NAWCH, London.
Caplan, G. (1964) *Principles of Preventive Psychiatry*. Tavistock Publications, London.
Daley, M. (1984) Families in critical care. *Heart and Lung*, **13**, 3, 231–37.
Hawthorne, J. (1984) Support for parents of babies in special care baby units. *Midwives Chronicle*, **97**, 1157, 170–74.
Klaus, M.H. and Kennell, J.H. (1976) *Maternal Infant Bonding*. C.V. Mosby, St. Louis.
LeMasters, E.E. (1979) *Parenthood as a Crisis*. Family Service Association of America, New York.
Marshall, J. (1987) A review of the discharge preparation and initial community support given to families of neonates after surgical intensive care. *Intensive Care Nursing*, **2**, 101–06.

McGovern, M. (1984) Separation of the baby from the parents. *Nursing Times*, **80**, 4, 28-30.
McHaffie, H. (1987) Isolated but not alone. *Nursing Times*, **83**, 28, 73–74.
Price, B. (1987) Happy families. *Nursing Times*, **83**, 47, 45–47.
Salitros, P. (1986) Transitional infant care: a bridge to home for high risk infants. *Neonatal Network*, Feb. 35–41.
Taylor, P. (1986) Promoting parental care of high risk babies. *Aust. Nurses Journal*, **15**, 8, 31–33.
Thornes, R. (1985) Parent participation. *Nursing Mirror*, **160**, 12, 20–22.
Vas Dias, S. (1987) Psychotherapy in SCBU. *Nursing Times*, **83**, 23, 50–52.

Bibliography
Two books which are very readable sources of information aimed at both staff and parents:
Alderson, P. (1983) *Special Care for Babies in Hospital*. NAWCH, London.
Redshaw, M. *et al* (1985) *Born Too Early*. Oxford University Press, Oxford.

11

Preparing children for hospital

Christine Eiser, BSc, PhD,
*Senior Research Fellow, Department of Psychology, Washington Singer Laboratories,
University of Exeter*

Lesley Hanson, BA, RSCN, HVCert,
School Nursing Sister, Exeter Health Authority

Hospital admission can be a frightening experience for children, particularly those who experience traumatic injury or sudden onset of chronic disease. To prepare them for the possibility of admission, it has been advocated that school-based education programmes be implemented (Elkins and Roberts, 1983; Peterson and Ridley-Johnson, 1983). This approach may also benefit children who are generally anxious about more routine visits to a doctor or dentist (Roberts et al, 1981).

One common approach to school-based intervention is the organised hospital tour. McGarvey (1983) reports that a programme for preschoolers, in which they were encouraged to "see, feel and experience" what happens in hospitals, was well received by children, teachers and parents. Three children who were subsequently hospitalised as emergency admissions were reported to adjust well.

An alternative technique involves setting up a 'play hospital' in school, and encouraging children to participate in both structured or free play situations (Brett, 1983). Elkins and Roberts (1984) set up a play hospital and used hospital volunteers dressed up as medical personnel to explain the equipment and procedures. The 25 children who took part in this activity subsequently reported fewer medical fears and were more knowledgeable about medical events than a control group of children.

Setting up a play hospital

This chapter is concerned with our own experiences in setting up a play hospital in primary schools, and describing the children's responses. The purpose of the study was twofold: to increase children's hospital related knowledge, and reduce anxiety and fear. Since some of the children were quite young, we did not feel verbally based assessments, such as interviews or questionnaires, were appropriate as the main techniques for evaluation. Instead, we focused on qualitative changes in the nature of children's play. Groups of three children were videotaped playing with the equipment on two separate occasions, four weeks apart. During the intervening period, children were given the opportunity to handle and play with the equipment under the guidance of a school nurse and mother helpers. We hoped that, as a result of experience with the equipment and a range of educational activities, we would be able to identify changes in play, reflecting improved knowledge and attitudes towards hospitals and medical personnel.

Method

Subjects   The children all attended a small first school (catering for five- to eight-year-olds) in a rural Devon town. There is little local industry, and unemployment is relatively high. The school, like most others in the district, caters for children predominantly from working and lower middle-class homes. None of the children suffered from any chronic condition, or had personal experience of hospital other than as an outpatient. Subjects were drawn from the reception class (five to 5½ years) and the third and fourth year (seven to eight years). They were collected from the classroom in groups of three (normally same-sex triads), selected by the teacher. Selection was random, rather than in terms of friendship patterns or ability levels. In all, 14 triads of five-year-olds and eight triads of eight-year-olds took part in the study.

Apparatus   A miniature hospital was set up in an empty classroom in the school. It was divided into four areas.
- The **reception** area consisted of a table and two chairs opposite each other. On the table was a telephone, notepad and pencil. There was also a display rack containing a selection of health education leaflets.
- The **hospital ward** consisted of two beds made with blankets, and a baby's cot, complete with doll. There was a food table on one of the beds, and a 'drip' hanging at the side. On a small table nearby were several pairs of rubber gloves, cotton facemasks and head covers (of the type used in surgery). On a series of open shelves was an array of medical equipment, including a stethoscope, syringe, tweezers, respiratory mask and nursing bowls.
- In the **X-ray** area was a hard table covered with a sheet. Above the table was a pretend light that could be swung through a semicircle, and two X-rays were hung on the wall.
- In the **surgery** areas, another hard table was covered by a sheet. There was also another green sheet on top, with a hole through which the 'surgery' could be performed. On nearby shelves were a number of surgical overalls, hats, masks, gloves and overshoes. In addition, there was a set of surgical equipment.
  We also had a selection of dressing-up clothes: nursing uniforms of several grades (dark blue for sister, light blue for staff nurse, green for students); a doctor's white coat, and various 'patient' outfits – pyjamas, nighties and dressing-gowns.

Procedure

The 'hospital' was set up in a spare classroom. Children were brought into the hospital in groups of three, and invited to play with the equipment for 10 minutes. Over the following month, a number of activities were organised. The children were brought back to the hospital on several occasions, by the school nurse and mother helpers. On these occasions, some of the equipment was pointed out, and ward and surgical procedures explained. Other activities included a visit to the children's ward at the local hospital, and visits to the school from an ambulance and crew, health visitor and a guide dog and owner. Each class also undertook a health-related group project.

At the second filming, children were again brought to the 'hospital' in groups of three (as before) and told that this was their last opportunity to play with the equipment before it was moved to another school. Again, their play was videotaped during the 10-minute session.

Results

Area of activity   During the first play session, most groups of children focused all their activities on the ward area, with only two groups using the surgery and one using X-ray equipment. During the second session, all groups organised their play throughout all areas of the hospital. Games were more sequenced – patients were 'admitted' to the ward, and subsequently moved to X-ray and surgery, before being discharged.

Use of equipment   Children used a range of equipment at both sessions, although at first the stethoscope, syringe, bandages and masks were used considerably more than other pieces of equipment. During the second session, there was much greater use of all the equipment, with less emphasis on the stethoscope and syringe. There were also differences in how the children used the equipment. During the first session, play was often quite rough. Children were quite aggressive in the way they gave injections, for example. On the second occasion, all children were considerably more gentle, and apparently more aware of the impact of treatment on the patient. 'Patients' were therefore likely to be warned that an injection might hurt.

'Healthcare staff' behaviour   There were substantial changes in the activities, particularly of nursing staff. During the first play session, nurses' activities involved care-taking, making beds, offering food and drink, or giving medicines. On the second, nurses spent a lot of time at the desk writing, or making phone calls. The role of the nurse seemed to have shifted from caretaker, to administrator!

Hospital atmosphere   On both occasions, children created an atmosphere of tension and emergency on the ward. Play invariably involved treating the very sick or dying, and speed and urgency characterised the interactions and conversations of staff.

Additional evaluations   All the children greatly enjoyed their time in the play hospital, and were keen to participate. Eleven children were interviewed in depth about their reactions to the project, and asked to describe what they had learned. All appeared to have benefitted substantially, both in terms of special information acquired, and in the development of non-fearful attitudes to hospital.

Does the play hospital work?

The ultimate justification for school-based preparation for hospitalisation may well be that children are less anxious and fearful about admission. There are, however, many practical difficulties involved in such an evaluation, particularly in that there may be a long interval between the intervention and admission, and that other mediating factors might then determine the child's behaviour. Such arguments have been put forward, and along with financial cuts, resulted in a reduction in these activities (Azarnoff, 1982). Certainly, the changes we identified were short-term, and we cannot speculate on the long-term value of our intervention.

Even within the short-term, however, we feel we can point to some increase in children's hospital-related knowledge. At the second session, children's play reflected greater awareness of a range of medical equipment, as well as knowledge of activities typical of admission, X-ray and surgery, and ward procedures.

There were also changes in hospital-related attitudes. The children seemed to have gained empathy with the patient's role; nurses were careful to warn patients of impending pain. In this respect, children seemed to have acquired very realistic appraisals of what happens in hospital. They were not only more aware of different equipment and techniques, but also aware of the potentially painful nature of medical treatment.

Perhaps more unfortunate was the change in children's perceptions of the nurse's role. During the first play session, 'nurses' cared for patients and tried to make them comfortable. On the second 'nurses' were preoccupied with administrative tasks, and had little, if any, time left for patient care. There also appeared to be greater awareness of a hierarchy among staff, with junior nurses being subordinate to more senior staff. To some extent, this kind of play may be closer to reality than that shown prior to the intervention, nevertheless, it seems somewhat regrettable.

Given the potential stress associated with hospitalisation (Peterson and Ridley-Johnson, 1980), it is important to develop a range of preparatory techniques for children. The school-based educational programme appears to have considerable merit, not least because it can be made available to all children before the need arises. It is not altogether clear at what level the programmes are successful; whether by increasing hospital related knowledge, reducing anxiety or helping the child develop skills to cope with hospital procedures. The success of the latter, described as 'stress-inoculation' procedures (Zastowny et al, 1986) in reducing stress in other situations (public-speaking [Cradock et al, 1978], and dental treatment [Klingman et al, 1984]), attests to the potential value of this approach in preparing children for hospitalisation.

At a practical level, the success of the play hospital is probably as dependent on the energy and enthusiasm of staff and children as on the particular contents. The overriding feeling of those who took part, however, both adults and children, was that the experience was worthwhile, and everyone learned a lot.

References

Azarnoff, P. (1982) Hospital tours for school children ended. *Pediatric Mental Health*, **1, 2**.

Brett, A. (1983) Preparing children for hospitalisation – a classroom teaching approach. *Journal of School Health*, 53, 561-63.

Cradock, C., Cotler, S., Jason, L.A. (1978) Primary prevention: Immunisation of children for speech anxiety. *Cognitive Therapy and Research*, **2**, 389-396.

Elkins, R. and Roberts, M. (1983) Psychological preparation for pediatric hospitalisation. *Clinical Psychology Review*, **3**, 275-295.

Elkins, P. and Roberts, M. (1984) A preliminary evaluation of hospital preparation for nonpatient children: Primary prevention in a 'Let's pretend hospital'. *Children's Health Care*, **13**, 31-36.

Klingman, A., Melamed, B.G., Cuthbert, M.I., Hermecz, D.A. (1984) Effects of participant modelling on information acquisition and skill utilisation. *Journal of Consulting and Clinical Psychology*, **52**, 414-422.

McGarvey, M.E. (1983) Preschool hospital tours. *Children's Health Care*, **11**, 122-124.

Peterson, L. and Ridley-Johnson, R. (1980) Pediatric hospital response to survey a prehospital preparation for children. *Journal of Pediatric Psychology*, **5**, 1-7.

Peterson, L. and Ridley-Johnson, R. (1983) Prevention of disorders in children. In Walker, C.E. and Roberts, M.C. (Eds.) Handbook of Clinical Child Psychology. Wiley-Interscience, New York.

Roberts, M.C., Wurtele, S.K., Boone, R.R., Ginther, L.J. Elkins, P.D. (1981). Reduction of medical fears by use of modelling: A preventive application in a general population of children. *Journal of Pediatric Psychology*, **6**, 293-300.

Zastowny, T.R., Kirschenbaum, D.S., Meng. A.L. (1986) Coping skills training for children: Effects on distress before, during and after hospitalisation for surgery. *Health Psychology*, **5**, 231-247.

Acknowledgements

This work was funded by the Nuffield Foundation. We would like to thank Miss Joan Cudmore and the staff and children of Cowleymoor First School, Devon and Philip Gurr for technical assistance. James Lang assisted with some of the children's interviews.

12

Communication can help ostomists accept their stoma

Ian Donaldson, RGN DIPN

The author was studying for a BEd (Nursing) at the Polytechnic of the South Bank, London, at the time this chapter was written.

Throughout this chapter, for reasons of conciseness, the female gender has been used to describe nurses of either gender and the male to describe patients of either gender.

Ward based nurses can play an important part in helping ostomists to adapt to their new situation, enabling them to reintegrate into society. Many wards do not have access to the services of a full time stoma therapist, and so general nurses need to be able to care for and assist ostomists. A recent study showed that many nurses feel unprepared for the complexities of stoma care (Monnington, 1987), so ostomists on their wards are likely to have little preparation for their future life.

In most cases, the formation of a stoma is life improving (eg, ulcerative colitis) or life saving (eg, perforated diverticulum). Some surgeons regard stoma formation for cancer as life saving, but this disregards the patient's expectation of the diagnosis of cancer, which to most people means unpleasant death (Broardwell and Jackson, 1982).

Devlin (1985) refers to ostomists as "people who have traded death for disablement", and this hints at the profound effect this type of surgery has on the individual. Society values health as desirable but its picture of health is of someone who has total control over bodily functions and is odour free. The formation of a stoma removes the patient's ability to control elimination and presents the possibility of leakage or release of flatus in any situation, a similar picture to an incontinent person. Fear of rejection by family and friends due to stigma is particularly acute, so new ostomists have to face many problems and anxieties before they feel able to return to their previous social situation (Kelly, 1985).

Preoperative care
It is useful to consider preoperative care under the two broad headings of physical and psychological. As with general surgery, physical preparation is usually carried out effectively, but it is important that issues such as siting the stoma are dealt with. An incorrectly sited stoma can cause much distress and may reduce the ostomist's ability to cope with the stoma in the future. The type of clothing the patient wears, skin creases and his ability to reach and see the site must be considered. Some

ethnic groups have been reported to accept their stoma better if it is sited above the umbilicus, as the discharge is then associated with clean food contained in the stomach rather than bowel contents (Whitethread, 1981). It is also important to take into consideration the ostomist's cultural/ spiritual background for other reasons. For example, the concept of cleanliness is very important to Muslims; faeces are considered unclean and so a stoma will present a Muslim with difficult problems. The requirement that he is 'clean' before prayer will mean frequent appliance changes, similarly his right hand should be kept clean and should not handle faeces. This obviously will present great difficulties to any Muslim trying to change his appliance one handed. Difficulties like this can greatly inhibit acceptance of a stoma, and it is important that the nurse is aware of these as potential problems and is prepared to support the patient.

Many studies have indicated that preoperative information giving and visits reduce anxiety, which is not only beneficial for the patient, but also for the nurse. Anxiety has been recognised as a barrier to learning, so it is of great advantage to have a less anxious patient postoperatively. Sadly, this area of patient care is all too often neglected. It is important for the nurse to assess what the patient is aware of and be prepared to put right any misconceptions he may have. Both nurses and doctors are much to blame for giving inadequate information. How often have we heard or used the phrase "don't worry its only a little bag on your tummy". Are these the reassuring words we should be using? Ridgeway and Matthews (1983) describe a method called cognitive coping, in which the patient is encouraged to identify fears and anxieties about the operation and its after effects to the nurse and to highlight the areas in which he is most concerned. The nurse and the patient then deal with these fears, either by presenting them in a positive light or dealing with any misconceptions. This positive reappraisal involves an altered perception of the threatening situation; the nurse provides the patient with accurate information that he can understand, and which he can use to cope with the impending situation. For example, a patient with colitis who is about to have a permament ileostomy may be helped to reflect on the fact that afterwards he will not have to repeatedly come back to hospital due to remissions, and his health will improve. A patient who has just been told he needs a colostomy due to a perforated diverticulum will be greatly relieved to hear this type of surgery is life saving and the stoma is usually only temporary. It has to be accepted however that patients are often sceptical of information and need to see the evidence. Associations such as the Ileostomy Association can provide visitors, who are ostomists themselves, and can show the patient that normal life afterwards is possible. Care must be taken, however, to ensure the 'visitor' is experienced and a suitable role model. Most ostomists' postoperative problems can be placed in two groups; physical and psychosocial, and both are of importance when planning appropriate care.

Physical care

It is useful to note that the patient's ability to change his appliance is usually, (though not always) the criteria used for discharge, so it is an important nursing aim to assist the patient to be responsible for his own self-care actions (Orem, 1985). Inherent in this statement is that the nurse is an educator. Orem breaks down self-care deficits (inability to care for oneself) into three areas: knowledge, skill, and motivation. It is useful for the nurse to consider these areas when planning care. To give self-care, the ostomist needs the necessary knowledge and skills to care for the stoma on a daily basis, and will need to develop skills related to changing his appliance (when and how to change), and knowledge as to how to obtain, store and dispose of the appliances. He will also need to learn about diet, skin care, how to deal with problems such as leaks, skin excoriation, odour and flatus and when to seek medical advice.

The nurse should be constantly aware that she is teaching the patient, so he can return to his home and normal activities. Many patients will return to houses without inside toilets; similarly, one who wishes to return to work as a travelling salesman will need to be able to deal with his stoma in a variety of settings. Awareness of what the patient is intending to return to is obviously important.

When planning the patient's care with him, it is important that realistic goals are negotiated and set. The patient is likely to become despondent if he is told "don't worry we'll have you managing this next week" and next week arrives and he has not been able yet to master emptying his appliance. However, if realistic short term goals are set (eg, will be able to apply clip to drainable appliance), when they are met the patient will feel a sense of achievement. Using short term goals as building blocks allows the patient to progress at his speed and can also be used to show him that he *is* making progress.

The right environment

When teaching the patient the nurse must ensure that the right learning environment is created. It is absolutely no use to try and teach someone who is in pain or tired. Showing the patient equipment and using diagrams can be useful, and it is vital that the nurse avoids using jargon. If the patient does not understand he may not ask and so will not learn. An important aspect of teaching is to assess what the patient has actually learnt. All too often it seems nurses believe that if they have told the patient what to do then he will do it. The patient's level of comprehension must be assessed – it is not enough just to give information and expect the patient to act on it, and recall of information does not necessarily mean that the patient comprehends it. Comprehension is vital if the patient is to apply this knowledge to solving new problems he may encounter.

Psychosocial care

As already mentioned, stoma formation has an immense impact on the

patient's psychological and sociological wellbeing. Most patients suffer from low self-esteem postoperatively, usually due to altered body image. The patient's level of self-esteem is a result of evaluation of his self concept, of which his body image is a part. Body image is 'how we see ourselves', and includes not only our physical appearance but also our beliefs, goals and other people's opinions of us. According to Meisenhelder (1985) the perceived respect, love and approval of people close to us (significant others) have a considerable effect on our self-esteem. She suggests three groups of people who can raise the patient's self-esteem:
- other patients in a similar situation;
- family and friends (significant others);
- nursing and other medical staff.

As patients do not stay in hospital for any great length of time, they don't often get the opportunity to meet others in a similar situation. However, self help groups can be beneficial to the patient as they allow him to meet others in a similar situation to him with whom he can talk and discuss problems. A fellow ostomist is unlikely to give him a negative appraisal or avoid him, and this will therefore create an atmosphere conducive to raising his self-esteem. He may also be able to obtain practical advice that will be useful in future.

In the postoperative period the patient will be testing his family and friends to find their response to his stoma. Their acceptance of the stoma is a major help towards the patient's sucessful adaption to the stoma (Broardwell and Jackson, 1982). He will use their responses as predictors of future interactions with other people, so a negative appraisal (actual or perceived) from the patient's significant others will only confirm his fears that he has become a social outcast. The nurse can help by preparing and supporting family and friends so they can help raise the patient's self-esteem and increase the likelihood of his acceptance of the stoma.

According to Porrit (1984) the nurse can raise the patient's self-esteem by effectively communicating a sense of worth and value for the patient, showing that he is truly valued as a human being. This can be achieved through touch and reflective listening, an approach she calls 'unconditional positive regard' through which the nurse can help the patient explore his feelings and fears without judgement.

Ostomists fear rejection by others and worry about how they will relate to them. If this fear becomes all consuming, the ostomist may retreat from social contact. Studies have shown (Devlin, 1971; MacDonald and Anderson, 1984) that many ostomists retreat from social life. Nurses can help them cope with any insecurities they may face due to their attempt to reintegrate back into society. Price (1986) suggests a framework for this (Table 1) which gives patients three possible approaches to use. Preparation of these responses can give them confidence when meeting people who know they have been in hospital. By using simple interventions like those discussed in this chapter, nurses can assist ostomists greatly in accepting their stomas.

	POSSIBLE APPROACH USED		
Relevant person.	OPEN FRANK.	MODIFIED FRANK.	RESTRICTED.
Spouse.	✓		
Children.		✓	
Close colleagues	✓		
Other colleagues.			✓
Close relative.		✓	
Distant relatives.			✓

Table 1. A framework for reintegration. **Open frank:** explanation showing of new image, equipment and aids. Recognition and comment made upon aetiology and prognosis as understood. Frank expression of how new image makes you feel. **Modified frank:** Explanation of current physical shape/image but not showing actual part of body that is changed. Indicate how you feel in general terms. No comment on aetiology or implications for the future. **Restricted:** Indication that operation has taken place but no direct reference to new image.

References
Broardwell, D. and Jackson, B. (1982) Principles of Ostomy Care. C.V. Mosby, London.
Devlin, B. (1985) Second opinion. *Health and Social Services Journal*, **95,** 4931, 82.
Devlin, B. et al (1971) Aftermath of surgery for anorectal cancer. *British Medical Journal*, **3,** 413-418.
Kelly, M. (1985) Loss and grief reactions as a response to surgery. *Journal of Advanced Nursing*, **10,** 517-525.
Meisenhelder, J. (1985) Self-Esteem: A closer look at clinical interventions. *International Journal of Nursing Studies.* **22,** 2, 127-135.
Monnington, M. (1987) Teaching and counselling support for new stoma patients – a survey of the views of patients and trained nurses. Unpublished MSc thesis. Kings College, London.
Macdonald, L. and Anderson, H. (1984) Stigma in patients with rectal cancer: A community study. *Journal of Epidemology and Community Health*, **38,** 284-290.
Orem, D. (1985) Nursing: Concepts of Practice. Mcgraw Hill, New York.
Porrit, L. (1984) Communication: Choices for Nurses. Churchill Livingstone, London.
Price, B. (1986) Keeping up appearances. *Nursing Times*, **82,** 40, 58-61.
Ridgeway, V. and Matthews, A. (1982) Psychological preparation for surgery: A comparison of methods. *British Journal of Psychology*, **21,** 271-280.
Whitethread, M. (1981) Ostomists; A world of difference. *Journal of Community Nursing*, **5,** 2, 4-10.

13

Ensuring dignity and self esteem for patients and clients

Christine Morgan, RNMS, RGN

The author was Ward Sister, Bennetts End Hospital for the Mentally Handicapped, Hemel Hempstead, at the time that this chapter was written.

When I started training as a general nurse after working as a Registered Mental Handicap Nurse, several things struck me about the differences and similarities between the two care settings. I saw how vulnerable people become once they change from day clothes into pyjamas, and the impact of this on their self esteem, and I was also struck by the lengths to which designers had gone in the planning of general hospitals to ensure patient privacy was preserved, in total contrast to my experiences in institutions for mentally handicapped people. I knew that the dignity of mentally handicapped people is threatened by the attitudes of both the public and many care staff, and realised that these also prevail in general care and can affect patients similarly. These threats should be minimised for all patients, and nurses can have a major role in this. It is an essential aspect of nursing which I feel is frequently neglected.

Christine Morgan.

The dignity and self esteem of patients and clients must be uppermost in the mind of every nurse who assesses and plans care for their individual needs. Dignity and self esteem are closely linked (Figure 1): people can only behave with dignity if they have a reasonably good opinion of themselves, and their self-esteem depends, in part, on their freedom from conditions and situations which reduce their dignity.

Dignity: the state or quality of being worthy of honour or respect; sense of self-importance.

Self esteem: a good opinion of oneself.

When individuals from any social class or group are dependent on others to meet their living needs, a number of things threaten their dignity and self esteem. They also become very vulnerable once they change out of their day wear and into pyjamas. I wonder how many nurses are aware of this? Illness and physical weakness also increase this vulnerability. The impact of dependence and vulnerability on a person's dignity and self esteem is clearly much more profound for a long stay client.

Mentally handicapped people

The factors which threaten a person's dignity and self esteem may be even greater in both number and effect if that person is mentally handicapped. The nature of their handicaps (which may be multiple, and may include physical handicaps) may make it difficult for them to articulate their feelings and responses to the situation they are in, and may mean that they also have a particularly high degree of dependency on their carers, and for an indefinitely long period.

The attitudes of their carers and of society may reinforce their dependency, and actually limit their real capacity for independence. Someone who is treated as a child may have little motivation to behave and view themselves in any other way, even though they may be capable of more adult thought and action. The design of the buildings in which many mentally handicapped people live may also threaten their dignity and self esteem — the contrast between the design and facilities of a general hospital and those of many institutions for mentally handicapped people is very striking.

How can dignity and self esteem be preserved? With the development of systematic planning of individual patient care, nurses have become more aware of the need to consider the patient as a whole person, not only having an illness or handicap but also thoughts, feelings and opinions. Having and demonstrating respect for an individual reinforces his or her self esteem, and nurses play an important role in maintaining this by assessing an individual's needs and also his capabilities. The nurse can easily find out what the patient can do for himself and encourage him to do as much as his condition will allow.

'Personal' procedures

In the past, prior to an abdominal operation, patients were *given* a pubic shave; now nurses have started to question whether the person is capable of performing this for themselves, and if so, why they shouldn't be allowed to do so. The nurse could simply check to make sure that it is done thoroughly. This reduces embarrassment and a sense of helplessness on the part of the patient and also perhaps, that of a young and inexperienced junior nurse. Ensuring dignity and self esteem requires that the patient or client must have some say and control over what happens to him while he is in hospital, because 'self' esteem and 'self' worth are only achievable while he is actively involved, actively participating in his own care. Relatives or close friends could also be involved more in the care of patients, perhaps with washing and dressing.

Privacy

Being forced to undergo certain procedures, or to eliminate or vomit without privacy is an intensely degrading situation for most people. Provision for privacy is generally much better in most general hospitals than in most institutions for mentally handicapped people. In many general hospitals designers and planners have gone to great lengths to ensure that patients' privacy is preserved. Wards are cubicalised; there are usually sufficient bathrooms and showers, even bidets in some wards; also numerous toilets; some patients have single rooms, and there are screens around beds to give added privacy. There may be treatment rooms on all wards, where patients can have dressings changed and removed privately.

In most hospitals for mentally handicapped people, facilities are much poorer. Toilets are not cubicalised and often have no doors; bathroom doors don't have locks; some have no doors at all; there may be a large number of clients having to share the one bathroom and there is often no place for clients to dress and undress in private. These problems are very much structural and not readily changed by the nurse. But this lack of provision for privacy should not lead anyone to assume that it is therefore not important to their clients, and more strenuous efforts are required to ensure some privacy despite the lack of available resources.

Elimination   Many patients become constipated, partly as a result of their inactivity but also due to their acute embarrassment at having to perform a very private activity in a 'public' place. The nurse should consider allowing the patient to go to the toilet once he is mobile enough, possibly helping him there and back, and should also put a mobile screen in front of the toilet or bathroom entrance to give it the sense of privacy, if it lacks a door.

Effective communication   If the details of procedures are explained to the patient beforehand, he will be much better prepared for what is to come, and the fact that the nurse respects his need for this information supports his self esteem. It is important, for example, before passing a nasogastric tube, to explain what one is going to do, why, and what the patient will experience, and also to discuss how he can help in the procedure. Underpinning all nursing action is the need for effective communication. Not only is it important to explain procedures, but the way we communicate is vitally important. Hanley and Hodge (1984), used the term "controlling language" to describe a type of speech which reinforces the parent-child relationship between nurse and patient. This communication style is often seen in settings where patients are most vulnerable, such as in Mental Handicap and Elderly Care settings.

It is also important to examine the inappropriate use of first names of patients, and the thoughtless use of endearing terms such as "deary" and "lovey" which only serve to lower self esteem.

Feeding   Many mentally handicapped clients have multiple handicaps — some are physically disabled and blind. What can be worse than being fed without knowing from which direction the spoon is coming; what is on the spoon, and being unable to say they don't like what is being given? It is essential to communicate with the client, tell him what is being given, encourage him to hold the spoon, so he is aware of it and knows it is not just going to arrive at his mouth apparently from nowhere.

This communication demonstrates the nurse's respect for the patient, contributes to raising his opinion of himself and also gives him some control over what happens to him.

Living space and style of dress   Recent research (Blunden, 1985) has shown that simply allowing patients to display their own belongings, giving them their own living space, and involving them in decision-making on changes in their environment, brings about a marked improvement in their apparent dignity and consequently their attitude towards care.

In mental handicap hospitals, simple and inexpensive measures can be taken, such as arranging existing furniture in such a way as to allow the client some control over an area he can recognise as his own living space. Encouraging him to have his own belongings, to display pictures, and if possible to have his own front door key; arranging the decor of living areas and also his style of dress in ways appropriate to his age will all contribute to the individual's dignity and self esteem.

Ensuring dignity and self esteem

Many features of illness, handicap and of the various settings for care and essential clinical procedures potentially threaten an individual's dignity and self esteem.

Much of the freedom, and many of the everyday experiences which we take for granted, have to be compromised and modified if we are ill, or become handicapped in some way. The dependence we must then place on others deprives us of some of the control we normally expect to have over our own lives.

Perhaps the most important question we as nurses should ask ourselves about our patients and clients is: 'would I accept this situation for myself, a friend or relative?' If the answer is 'no' then we must take steps to improve the care we give, and the environment in which our patients and clients live. Most of all, we need, at all times, to respect them as individual people.

NB Throughout this chapter the male gender has been used to refer to all patients and clients, but is intended to include both male and female patients and clients.

References

Blunden, R. (1985) A New Style of Life: a study of the impact of moving into an ordinary house on the lives of mentally handicapped people. Mental Handicap Applied Research Unit, Wales.

Hanks, P. (Editor) (1979). Collins Dictionary of the English Language. William Collins Sons and Co Ltd, Glasgow.

Hanley, I. and Hodge, J. (1984) Psychological Approaches to Care of the Elderly. Croom Helm, London.

Bibliography

Blows, H. and Alcoe, J. (1985) Lifestyles for people with mental handicap. E.S.C.A.T.A.
A staff training exercise based on the principle of normalisation.

Blunden, R. (1980) Individual plans for mentally handicapped people. Mental Handicap Applied Research Unit, Wales.
A guide to implementing individual programme plans for mentally handicapped people.

Chilman and Thomas (1981) Understanding Nursing Care, Second Edition. Churchill Livingstone, Edinburgh.
A textbook designed to help learners and qualified nurses to develop a sympathetic and perceptive approach to care.

Elliott, J. and Bayes. K. (1972) Room for Improvement: a better environment for the mentally handicapped. King Edward's Hospital Fund for London.
This discusses the ways in which simple, cost effective measures and attention to design can create a more homely and therapeutic environment for mentally handicapped people in both in and out of hospital.

English National Board, (1985) Caring for people with Mental Handicap. ENB, London.
This package for learners is based on the 1982 syllabus for the RNMS course.

14

Educating patients at home

Pauline Bagnall, SRN
Angela Heslop, DipN(Lond) RCNT SRN
Research Fellows, Department of Medicine, Charing Cross and Westminster Medical School, London

Teaching involves application of good communication skills, and the outcome can have dramatic and positive effects on the quality of life and wellbeing of patients, particularly those whose illness or disability is long-term. This chapter outlines a study which was undertaken to assess the value of educating patients with chronic respiratory disease about their condition.

Recommendation

Chronic respiratory disease is an important cause of disability, a fact recently recognised in a report from the Royal College of Physicians (1981). It recommended that a Respiratory Health Worker (RHW) should be appointed on a trial basis to visit and care for people suffering from chronic lung disease at home.

A controlled trial, to evaluate the effect of RHWs, was undertaken in 1984 (Cockcroft et al, 1986). Seventy-five patients were randomised to one of two groups: 42 patients to the intervention group (visited by the RHW) and 33 patients to the control group.

The aims of the study were to improve the patients' quality of life and to reduce their hospital admissions. Two nurses, (the authors) with experience of looking after people with chest disease were employed to fill the Respiratory Health Worker post. In addition one had experience of working in the community. People were visited approximately monthly, intervention being mainly preventive, supportive and educative.

Methods

The Royal College of Physicians' Report suggested that one role of the RHW might be 'promoting respiratory health education and practices' (Royal College of Physicians, 1981). In our study both the intervention and the control group completed questionnaires at the beginning and end of the study year. There were specific questions about knowledge of condition and medicines, as well as questions about smoking habits and activities of daily living. Our brief was to be educators and we knew that the patient's education was to be a measured outcome of the research.

We concentrated on the individuality of the patient, using Roper's model (Roper et al, 1983) incorporating a problem solving approach. On the first visit we assessed the patient in terms of daily living activities and knowledge of chest disease and medicines. For example, was it known what the illness was called, how it affected the patient and what the names and actions of the medicines were? From this first assessment problems would be identified and goals set. On each subsequent visit we would evaluate the patient's progress and redefine goals as appropriate.

Education programme

Most patients in the study had not been expected to learn about their disease or medicines before. Many had left school at an early age and so to learn was a new experience. They had other health problems besides chest disease such as poor eyesight, impaired hearing and other illnesses. They had also lost loved ones and a sense of worth. When deciding how to structure the teaching programme all these factors had to be taken into account.

We worked with each individual in his/her home; tailoring the teaching to his/her needs. However a basic format did emerge. From the initial assessment on the first visit areas of knowledge which were lacking would be identified. It was first established that medicines were being taken as prescribed. If this was not so it was corrected and explanations were given about the appropriate use of medicines. Another priority was to establish if the patient knew how to recognise deterioration in lung disease (usually secondary to infection) and in this event what action to take. Gradually over the course of the year each patient's knowledge of his illness and management increased as he was able to assimilate information about anatomy and physiology of the heart and lungs and names and actions of his medicines.

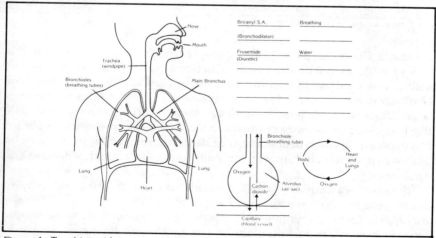

Figure 1. Teaching aid.

A teaching aid (Figure 1) was designed and given to each patient to keep. It was used to present facts visually with colours. The information was given in simple terms with both anatomical and colloquial names used. For example, the lungs were often described as being analogous to sponges with blue blood going in and red blood coming out; the bronchi were often referred to as breathing tubes. Where possible Health Education Council pamphlets about diet and smoking supplemented the teaching. The aim was to increase the patient's understanding of his disease and of how to cope with particular problems.

Date	Problem	Goal LT-long term, ST-short term.	Care Plan	Date	Evaluation
1st visit	Mr L is unable to recognise deterioration in his lung disease.	LT Mr L will tell me at the end of the year the significance of discoloured sputum and the action to be taken. ST Mr L will tell me next visit what colour sputum should be, what green/yellow sputum may indicate and what he will do if this occurs.	Explain to Mr L the importance of green/yellow sputum and that a chest infection may be present. Tell him to call his GP should this occur.	2nd visit	Mr L told me his sputum should be white and that green/yellow sputum indicates a chest infection is present when he will call his GP.
2nd visit	Mr L does not check the colour of his sputum every day.	ST Mr L is to tell me that antibiotics will be prescribed by the GP for a chest infection, that the full course should be taken and if he is not better he is to contact his GP again. He is to check the colour of his sputum daily.	Explain to Mr L why it is important to check his sputum every day. Explain about antibiotics.	3rd visit	Mr L told me antibiotics will be prescribed for a chest infection and it is important to finish the whole course. He also said he will contact his GP again if he is no better and that he checks his sputum daily.
3rd visit	Mr L does not have a reserve supply of antibiotics at home.	ST Mr L is to ask his GP for a reserve supply of antibiotics to keep at home. He is to start a course if his sputum changes colour, complete the course and contact the GP if he is no better. He is to tell me next visit how many times a day he takes the antibiotics and for how long.	Explain about the role of reserve antibiotics.	4th visit	Mr L told me he did get a reserve supply of antibiotics from his GP and had commenced a course 3 days ago because his sputum became green. He is taking 1 tablet 3 x a day for 7 days. He will get another reserve supply when this course is completed.

Table 2. Part of the education programme for Mr L.

Table 2 illustrates part of one patient's teaching programme. Mr L is a 59 year old man with chronic obstructive airways disease. On the first visit it was established that he continued to smoke, did not know how to detect deterioration in his lung disease and did not know the names or actions of his medicines. From this example it can be seen that gradually the knowledge base was built up so that Mr L became responsible for this aspect of his own health and confident in caring for himself. A similar plan was used to help him stop smoking and learn about his disease and medicines.

Education was not only confined to these areas. Some patients were overweight in which case advice about diet and the use of weight charts was given. Other patients were underweight and required some simple cooking lessons. Improving mobility was another major area of our work. Some patients enjoyed programmes to increase their activity. For example, one lady wanted to walk to the library to change her books. We started a training programme in which she started walking around her flat more often; this was gradually extended to walking outside to the rubbish shute every day and eventually she reached her stated goal which was the library. It was important to acknowledge the progress made with encouragement and congratulation.

Patients' response

Most patients wanted to learn more about their disease and medicines. We structured our work on individual patient care so that they were taught as much or as little as they wanted to know. Some found it difficult to retain information, in which case the priority was to make certain that medicines were being taken correctly and that the patient could act appropriately on signs of deterioration. Others wanted to have more detailed knowledge about how the heart and lungs interact and the way in which their medicines acted. An important point to remember was that on some visits education was not of primary importance to the person concerned. In one instance a lady's budgerigar — her 'companion' — had died the previous day. It would have been inappropriate to talk about her medicines when she wanted to talk about her grief. Some of the patients 'prepared' for our visits. One man said he always looked at his list of medicines before a visit because he knew he would be asked about them. Other patients had their medicines on the table ready. Nearly all said that they had valued the time to learn, the individual teaching they received and the opportunity to ask questions. Most importantly, they valued the knowledge which enabled them to look after themselves.

Effectiveness of the programme

The questionnaire replies about knowledge of condition and medicines were evaluated by two physicians not involved in the study. Knowledge was scored as being either poor, adequate or good and an assessment was made of whether knowledge had improved, remained the same or become worse over the course of the year. There was no significant difference between the groups in their knowledge of their condition or medicines at the beginning of the study. At the end of the study significantly more people in the RHW group than in the control group had improved their knowledge of their condition (combined X^2 5.62,

Changes during the study		RHW Group	Control Group
Physician 1			
Number with knowledge:	Worse	3	2
	The same	15	15
	Better	14	6
Physician 2			
Number with knowledge:	Worse	3	0
	The same	15	19
	Better	14	4

Table 3: Knowledge of condition as assessed by two independent physicians, based on questionnaire answers.

p<0.05)(Table 3) and a similar trend was seen for knowledge of medicines.

The teaching programme was goal directed. Of the education goals set, more than 75 per cent were considered by the RHWs to have been achieved by the patients concerned.

Personal experience of the project

Before I (Pauline Bagnall) joined the research project my teaching experience was limited to a teaching exercise I did during the Cardiothoracic Nursing Course ENB 249 and a few short sessions I gave to nurses on the ward. I had not been involved with teaching patients. I spent much time discussing with my colleague how we would approach the teaching aspect of our new role. We were aware that our patients would be elderly and that education might be a new experience for them. I was also aware that this was 'research' and that my work was being monitored and measured. I therefore wanted my patients to learn.

Initially I was shocked at how little knowledge these people had and therefore tried to give them too much information all at once. Gradually I learned to give only as much information as the patient wanted or needed. I also learned to give the information in order of priority — making sure the patient was safe.

Several insights came to me as a result of my participation in this work. I realised that all my patients were chronically ill at home and they had all learned to cope and adapt to their problems in a variety of ways. I had previously only nursed people in hospital where it is difficult to visualise how someone manages at home in a tiny house rather than in a big new hospital. Another insight arose because I was visiting patients in their homes where they not I were in control. I also had no hospital routine or uniform to support me. I had only my personality and expertise to offer. For the first time I felt truly accountable for what I was doing. I was visiting a patient in his home independently and over the course of a year I had a responsibility to help him to cope with his disability. I learned to value my role as a nurse and at the same time to respect each patient as an individual person.

Education needs

It has been recognised that patients need to have information, and guidance to understand this information in order to care for themselves (Redman, 1981). It is also known that understanding their disease and medicines improves patient compliance (Weibert and Dee, 1980). There has been an increasing interest in patient education since the early 1970s and most writers support the idea that nurses should teach patients (Cohen, 1981). Yet, in 1985 Wilson-Barnett published a paper saying that despite all the evidence ''when nurses are questioned they accept that patients' information needs are not met'' (Wilson-Barnett, 1985).

There seem to be many reasons for this lack of teaching. Wilson-Barnett goes on to say that ''teaching does not occur because nurses are inadequately qualified" (Wilson-Barnett, 1985). Learning to teach is not a defined subject in the curriculum for nurse registration. Nurses on average spend only 10 per cent of their time communicating with patients (Macleod Clark, 1983) yet the few studies that have addressed the function of nurses as health educators have all concluded that such patient/client teaching as is done, is done by nurses (Gleit and Graham, 1984).

An important aspect of the research was our role as educators. The results confirm that our patients did learn more about their disease and medicines and how to cope with their disability. The reasons for this success are many. The teaching programme took place in the patient's home which seemed to produce a more conducive atmosphere both for teaching and learning than the busy, noisy hospital. Whenever possible the family also learned and therefore supported the patient. The information was given in small measures and repeated if necessary. This opportunity for repetition and recall helped the patient to fully understand before moving on. Continuity of the visits and the development of a relationship sustained for six-to-nine months was important in the learning process. The patient learned to trust us and felt able to talk about problems he may not have mentioned before.

All the patients were attending the Department of Medicine of a large teaching hospital and had suffered from chronic lung disease for many years. They had all been in hospital several times, yet their knowledge at the beginning of the study was very poor. There is clearly a need to introduce teaching programmes in hospital before discharge, to be continued by community nurses at home. It is the experience of other authors (Wilson-Barnett, 1983; Nuffield Working Party, 1980) and our own experience in this study that patients do want to know more and nurses may be the appropriate people to teach them. We believe it will be beneficial for nurses to know that their work has enabled patients to become more confident and able to take care of themselves.

References
Bagnall, P. and Sigsworth, J. (1988) Living with lung problems. *Professional Nurse*, **3**, 12, 514-7.
Cockcroft, A., Bagnall, P., Heslop, A. et al (1986) Controlled trial of a respiratory health worker visiting patients with chronic respiratory disability. Submitted to the *British Medical Journal*. **294**, 225-7.
Cohen, S.A. (1981) Patient Education: a review of the literature. *Journal of Advanced Nursing*, **6**, 1, 11-18.
Gleit, C.J., Graham, B.A. (1984) Reading materials used in the preparation of nurses for the teaching role. *Patient Education and Counselling*, **6**, 1, 25-28.
Macleod-Clark J. (1983) Nurse patient communication – an analysis of conversations from surgical wards. In: Wilson-Barnett, J., (Ed), Nursing Research: Ten studies in Patient Care, Wiley, Chichester.
Nuffield Working Party (1980) Talking with Patients: A Teaching Approach, Nuffield, Provincial Hospitals Trust.
Redman, B.K. (1981) Issues and Concepts in Patient Education, Appleton-Century-Crofts, New York.
Roper, N., Logan, W., Tierney, A.J. (1983). Using a model for nursing, Churchill-Livingstone, Edinburgh.

Royal College of Physicians (1981) Disabling Chest Disease: Prevention and care. *Journal of the Royal College of Physicians of London*, **15**, 2, 69-87.

Weibert, R.T., Dee, D.A. (1980) Improving Patient Medication Compliance 1, Medical Economics Company, New Jersey.

Wilson-Barnett, J., Osborne, J. (1983) Studies evaluating patient teaching: implications for practice. *International Journal of Nursing Studies*, **20**, 1, 33-44.

Wilson-Barnett, J. (1985) Principles of patient teaching. *Nursing Times*, **81**, 8, 28-29.

Acknowledgements

We are grateful to Dr A. Cockcroft and Professor A. Guz, Department of Medicine, Charing Cross and Westminster Medical School, for their advice and support.

15

The Denford meeting: airing staff concerns

Janice Sigsworth, RGN
Formerly Senior Staff Nurse, The Charing Cross Hospital, London, now Ward Sister at University College Hospital, London

There are many factors in health care which can cause stress – the business of caring for ill people in itself can be stressful without the other problems of staffing, pay and communication and 'problem patients' which can crop up. A medical ward in the Charing Cross Hospital, London attempted to alleviate some of the factors causing stress among ward staff by holding a monthly meeting in which problems could be aired and difficulties with patients discussed.

The ward specialises in the care of breathless patients, and is staffed by two job sharing ward sisters, between eight and 12 registered nurses and eight to 12 student nurses. It is run on a primary nursing system, in which registered nurses care for a group of four to seven patients from admission through to discharge, working with other members of the multidisciplinary team.

The Denford meeting
The monthly meeting is known as the Denford meeting, named after Doctor John Denford, by whom it is chaired. Dr Denford is Director of the Cassel Hospital and a psychotherapist in patient community therapy. The meeting is chaired using a method described by Balint (1964). Research seminars had been organised at the Tavistock Clinic to study psychological implications in general medicine.

These seminars attempted to create a free, give and take atmosphere in which everyone could bring up their problems in the hope of gaining insight into them from the experience of others. The material for discussion at the Tavistock clinic was invariably provided by recent experiences with patients. It was essential for the group leader to refrain from making his own comments and criticisms until everyone had had ample time and space to express their thoughts.

As group leader in our meetings, Doctor Denford's role is to make his contributions ones which open up possibilities for the ward staff to discover for themselves some 'right' way of dealing with patient problems, rather than prescribing the right way to them.

The meeting takes place once a month, usually early on a Monday evening, and is held in the ward sitting room, unless patients are watching television, in which case it is held in the sister's office or an empty seminar room. The date of the meeting is publicised several days beforehand. The topic for discussion is decided by the doctors and nurses on the ward and, as suggested by Balint, is based on problems which arise when caring for patients. This is also publicised before the meeting, which usually lasts for an hour, with light refreshments provided by a nominated ward member – not always a nurse!

The meeting opens with brief, informal greetings as described by Balint. There is no reading from prepared reports or manuscripts – group members are asked to report freely on their experiences with the patients. Use of clinical notes is not encouraged but may be used as an aide-memoire. The aim is for group members to include as full an account as possible of their emotional responses to the problem, or even their emotional involvement in the patients' problems.

Such a frank account of the emotional aspects of the nurse/doctor-patient relationship can be obtained only if the atmosphere of the discussion is relaxed enough to enable group members to speak freely. Menzies (1960) states "The core of the anxiety situation for the nurse lies in her relationship with the patient. The closer and more concentrated this relationship the more likely the nurse is to experience the impact of anxiety, therefore the Denford meeting provides an excellent opportunity and environment to discuss and express these feelings." While a solution to the problem is often not found, staff are generally more aware of their own feelings and more clear about the needs of the patient.

Why is the meeting necessary?

As early as 1970 Menzies' attention was repeatedly drawn to the high level of tension and anxiety among nurses. The work situation arouses strong and mixed feelings in the nurse: pity, compassion, love, guilt, hatred and resentment towards the patients who arouse these strong feelings. Menzies examined the techniques employed by the nursing profession to contain and modify anxiety and hypothesised that nurses' struggle against anxiety can lead them to develop socially structured defense mechanisms such as restricted contact with patients through task allocation.

Kelly (1986) concluded in her study that patients who exhibit deviant behaviour are regarded as unpopular, which this supports Stockwell's theory (1984) that when nonconforming behaviour persists, patients come to be regarded as unpopular. Kelly recommended regular ward meetings to discuss difficulties with patients, and the purpose of the Denford meeting is to explore these feelings. Prior to the meetings, the patient who is causing problems has often been formally referred to the psychiatrist because they have been depressed or because members of the nursing or medical staff are concerned about the aspect of their behaviour.

Case study

George, aged 56, had been admitted to the ward six months previously for weight control, and was readmitted for the same reason. Two days following his readmission he suffered a right cerebral vascular accident. Prior to admission George was socially isolated. He had two female friends who appeared very overpowering, and he appeared to dislike them. He presented a number of problems to the nursing staff.

- He was sexually suggestive to the point of rudeness.
- He would not take his medicines when asked.
- He continually demanded food, telling several different nurses at different times that someone had taken his tray before he had finished.
- Initially he was very ill requiring physical nursing care, and was reluctant to become independent when he was over the acute stage.

During the Denford meeting at which George was the subject of discussion, it became obvious that he angered some staff with the disruptions he caused. Some felt sorry for him and wanted to help, but found this difficult because closeness was restricted by his sexual suggestions. Other nurses said he frustrated them or that they gave him one chance to take his medicines or to get out of bed – if he could not be bothered then neither could they and they would just leave him.

It became apparent that George demanded and got extra attention by all this destructive behaviour. For example, when giving George his medications, which would normally take two or three minutes, he would first refuse to take them, then say he would take them, then drop them on the floor which would require readministration and thus the saga continued. Coupled with this mounting anger and frustration, George appeared to give female members of the team more problems. He would have moments in which he would talk about his past life as a seaman and the places he had visited. This made many nurses feel guilty about their difficulties with him, because he showed that he could be a caring, intelligent person. A plan was formulated to overcome the problems George presented.

1. A day plan was drawn up, negiotated with George. This provided a united front so that if George demanded attention at an inappropriate time we could refer to the plan.
2. The problem posed by George's expression of his sexuality would be approached by two methods to meet the needs of the nurses:
   a. to confront him, telling him how difficult it was to be with him because of his comments;
   b. Some nurses felt they could not do this so they said they would ignore him when he made the comments but go to him at other times.

At the end of the meeting everyone felt optimistic about the plans to help staff cope with George and relieved that it was understandable to dislike George. As the reasons for his behaviour had become clear, however, the negative feelings towards him had subsided.

The Denford meetings give both nurses and doctors the chance to appreciate the difficulties and tensions in each other's work. The discussions allow people to share the troubles that difficult patients can cause, and give staff the chance to present a united front once plans are formulated. They are a useful and enjoyable way of reducing stress and, alleviating problems within patients that cause them to behave in a difficult manner.

References
Balint, M. (1964) The Doctor, His Patient and the Illness. Pitman, London.
Kelly, S. (1986) Nurses' perception of the Unpopular Patient. (Unpublished).
Menzies, I.E.P. (1970) Social Systems as a Defence Against Anxiety. Tavistock, London.
Stockwell, F. (1984) The Unpopular Patient. RCN, London.

16

A means to a long-term goal: helping colleagues become rational career planners

Kevin Teasdale, MA, Cert Ed, RMN
Director of In-service Training, Pilgrim Hospital, Boston

Good quality career counselling is hard to find. Too many people allow their career direction to follow a random pattern, hoping that all will turn out for the best in the end. Even though at the beginning of their careers many nurses may feel compelled to accept the first opportunities that come along, it pays to remember that career options decline as we grow older and that choices made in the past may restrict the freedom to choose in the future. It is an important part of the role of experienced nurses to offer career counselling to more junior staff, to help them to mature not only as nurses but also as rational career planners. To offer this help, it is essential to have a clear model of counselling in mind, and to understand that the process involves much more than simply helping nurses gather information about job vacancies.

• Self-awareness
• Opportunity awareness
• Decision-making
• Handling transition

Table 1. Four key elements of rational career planning.

Rational career planning

Rational career planning involves knowing both oneself and the job market, matching the two, and handling the stress which always comes with change (Teasdale, 1991). All four elements are linked, and a counsellor should help colleagues ('clients') through a cyclical process of exploration and feedback around them. It is important this is a continuing process: as individuals we may move *towards* maturity in rational career planning, but can never fully attain it, since our values, beliefs, abilities and circumstances will change over time, as will the job market. In the past, it was assumed all that was required was opportunity awareness - career counsellors would provide information on jobs which nurses could then act on. This approach is much in need of an update.

John Malkin, Senior Lecturer in Vocational Guidance at Nottingham Polytechnic, has developed a model of career counselling which is a valuable introduction to anyone new to this specialist area. Since many nurses may already be familiar with Egan's model based on exploration, understanding and action (Egan, 1982), this chapter integrates it with Malkin's ideas in order to explain the basics clearly. The integrated model (Table 2) is presented from the counsellor's viewpoint.

Essential preconditions
Pay attention to rights
Develop an equal and adult relationship

Exploration
Agree an explicit contract
Help the client to review his or her career

Understanding
Present a diagnosis
Check out the diagnosis with the client
Proceed only when diagnosis is mutually agreed

Action
Agree the areas the client will work on
Help client to make an action plan

Table 2. The integrated model.

Clients' rights

Whether career counselling occurs at a single interview or as a longer-term counselling contract, certain essential preconditions are necessary for the process to be both safe and helpful. These can be addressed by being open about the rights of both client and counsellor. As a counsellor, you should consider where you stand on the ideas described below, tailoring them to your own views as you think fit.

Confidentiality   This concept needs attention since it often creates profound dilemmas. What if the client tells the counsellor he or she has broken the law or is a drug user? There are limits to confidentiality - it is not an absolute - and the client should be told what these are at the start.

Respect   Try to establish an adult relationship based on mutual respect, while being aware of the potential complications of a relationship in which the counsellor has a position of power in the hierarchy of the organisation. For example, a ward sister might have a vested interest in getting a talented young staff nurse to work in her area, but would be abusing her power position if she used her skills to direct the staff nurse in this way. The ward sister should therefore either let someone else offer counselling, or put her cards on the table right at the start and allow the staff nurse to decide whether or not to discuss career plans with her.

Competence in the counsellor   Competence in this context is often misinterpreted to mean being an expert on the job market or on the availability of postbasic courses, whereas the collection of information is generally best left to the client. A counsellor needs to be competent in the counselling process, of which attention to rights is the cornerstone.

Autonomy   This means clients are capable of making decisions for themselves, and that their right to do so is upheld by the counsellor at all times. Notice that clients' expectations can get in the way of this: they may press you to tell them what they should do, perhaps as a way of avoiding responsibility for the outcome.

Environmental factors   Clients have a right to the things which make counselling interviews possible such as time, punctuality and privacy.

Having an outcome   Counselling is more than listening, and involves helping someone to move in a goal-directed way towards a plan of action. Counselling is not a ritual to be gone through: it leads somewhere, and clients have a right to leave if they are not satisfied with either the process or the direction in which it leads.

Counsellors' rights

Respect   Involves clients appearing at the agreed time, being honest and not just going through the motions of a counselling interview.

To confront clients if they are not being honest   This may mean ending the consultation, but a counsellor should first give the client a chance to explore why he or she is not being honest. It may be because the client is *sent* for the interview (this can occur in tutor/student situations), so check out the client's assumptions about the process first.

Environmental ground rules   Counsellors have a right to be angry if clients are not punctual etc.

To use a counselling model   Within limits, this means the counsellor can direct the sequence of events of the counselling process in line with the model adopted, but the model and sequence must be open and negotiable from the start. A counsellor has a right to explain the process and the client to challenge it at any stage.

To offer a referral   Knowing the limits of your competence, being able to say, "I don't know", and a right not to take on a client.

The integrated model

The counsellor tries to help clients explore factors which are influencing their approach to career development. The counsellor spells out his or her view of the essential preconditions for useful career counselling and clients are encouraged to respond.

Establish a relationship   Develop a mutual dialogue and set the client at ease, taking time for this. Aim for a positive relationship which works at a pace and in a style with which the client is comfortable.

Identify the client's expectations   Ask questions such as: "How can I be helpful to you?" and "Can you begin by telling me what you expect from me?" Very often nurses will expect definite things such as information about a particular course or a specialist career path.

Respond to clients' expectations   Set out the limits of what you are able or prepared to do. Are you willing simply to give information or are you prepared to offer a wider discussion? Explain your agenda as a counsellor in terms of the rights listed above. For example, you might say: "I see my role as helping you to help yourself. I would really like to help you to check out how you are planning and organising your career at present. If you are doing it okay, that's fine, but if not, we will address any problem ahead, and only then take on the specific information issues which you raised. Is that something you are prepared to accept from me, or would you prefer not to go into that depth at the moment?"

Make a contract   If the client wishes to proceed, explain the integrated counselling model and agree how you will operate within it. Spell out your mutual rights in this process, and check agreement. For example, you will help your clients explore the extent to which they are acting as rational career planners by inviting them to talk about their career to date and their values and ambitions for the future. When you feel this has been completed in sufficient depth, explain your diagnosis - stating which areas of career planning you believe they would benefit from working on. Invite them then to discuss this diagnosis with you, and when you are agreed, help them to make their action plan. Check clients actually understand and are willing to accept this process, particularly the formulation and presentation of a diagnosis, and proceed only when you have reached mutual understanding and agreement on this.

Review past and present

Invite clients to explore with you their track record as rational career planners. Clients will explain their career path in their own way, but the counsellor needs to help them review it using the four elements of the rational model.

• **Self-awareness**   Invite exploration along the lines of: "What are you looking for in your proposed career move? Which of your needs do you hope it will satisfy?" "Describe your career to date...start off with when you left school, and at each transition, describe what led up to the move, what you were hoping for from it, and what the outcome was." "What would you say you have learned about yourself so far? What are you particularly good at doing? What are your weaknesses?"

- **Opportunity awareness**   Aim to review how broad a grasp clients have of the range of opportunities open to them. Ask questions such as: "You are thinking of applying for this particular job, were there any alternatives you considered?" "You are thinking of becoming (say) an infection control nurse, what do you know about what an infection control nurse does? What qualifications and experience do panels look for when selecting infection control nurses?"

- **Decision-making**   In terms of matching self to opportunities, aim to assess the level of sophistication in the way the person makes decisions. For example, ask: "Are you someone who plans things out, or do your career moves just happen?" "How much do *you* feel in control of your decisions, and how influential are other people?" "What is your plan of action for moving your career in the direction you want it to go?"

- **Handling transition**   Any change in career path is likely to result in stress, either for the individual or his or her immediate family and friends. It is helpful to encourage clients to explore their previous experience of handling similar transitions. For example: "How do you feel about change, is it something you welcome or fear?" "Thinking about when you first took up your present job, what was the most stressful thing about it?" "How did you handle that stress?" "Do you envisage any problems with your planned move?"

Understanding

Making a diagnosis is an intellectual skill, and demands real concentration. A counsellor must listen carefully to what clients are saying, amassing clues about their strengths and weaknesses as rational career planners. Is a client in charge of his or her own career direction? Is there a pattern of growing self-awareness in career planning? Does the person's career track record show if his or her job expectations were met by their outcomes or not? Is the person aware of the full range of opportunities available? Does the client's assessment of his or her strengths and weaknesses tally with career evidence? Is the client thinking short- or long-term? Can he or she cope with the pressures of change? What are the client's favoured coping styles?

As a counsellor, your knowledge of the particular work area does not have to be high. You are trying to form a judgement on your clients' capacity to take rational action concerning their careers, and to present it to them in an honest yet supportive way. To make such a judgement demands intellectual honesty, especially when trying to help a friend.

Explaining a diagnosis is challenging, demanding both honesty and caring. If the contract was carefully discussed and agreed at the start, the diagnosis is more likely to be given fair consideration by the client. For example the counsellor might say "I think you might benefit from being clearer about what you want from your career, not only now, but over the next five to 10 years. From what you have told, you seem to have made some spontaneous career decisions in the past, which have not always worked out as you wanted. Also you seem to have set your sights too high for what you were able to cope with at the time. How do you feel about what I am saying so far?"

Many counsellors who were trained in a non-directive style of counselling will initially find this approach quite alien. Notice however that the counsellor is *not* saying "I don't think this is the right job for you", but is addressing the planning **process,** not its content. Provided the contract was understood and the interview process made open, the client continues to retain control throughout.

Finally, the counsellor must aim to establish mutual agreement. Diagnosis must, again, be mutually agreed, with the counsellor working within limits the client can accept. If the client accepts only part of the diagnosis, it may still be possible to work usefully on the area of agreement. Only in extreme cases of wide disagreement should the counsellor consider offering a referral. If the groundwork was done and the counsellor made the whole process open to the client, a reasonable level of mutual agreement will generally be possible.

Action

Begin by agreeing a plan of action This involves problem-solving in the areas identified for further work. Try to help clients to summarise for themselves which aspects of the rational model they feel they need to work on in greater depth. Self-awareness issues will lend themselves to further analysis of values and wants. Opportunity awareness means seeking information in a systematic way. Matching the two will usually involve detailed consideration of alternatives, and explicit explanation of the reasons for accepting or rejecting them. Transition issues are directly related to the field of stress management. The actual techniques employed at the problem-solving stage will depend on the preferences of the client and the outlook of the counsellor. The bibliography gives some references and contacts which may be helpful at this stage.

References
Egan, G. (1982) The Skilled Helper. Brooks/ Cole, California.
Teasdale, K. (1991) A structured way to fulfil ambition. How to make rational career plans. *Professional Nurse*, **6**, 11, 644-48.

Bibliography
Priestley, P. *et al* (1978) Social Skills and Personal Problem Solving. Tavistock, London.
    A valuable source book on problem- solving.
Teasdale, K. (1991) A structured way to fulfil ambition. How to make rational career plans. *Professional Nurse*, **6**, 11, 644-48.
    Self-help ideas which can be adapted to the counsellor-client context.

Useful address
ENB Resource and Career Services, Woodseats House, 764 Chesterfield Road, Sheffield S8 OSE. Tel: 0742 551064.
This is a confidential information and careers advisory service available to nurses.

Health Education

17

A preventable tragedy: the nurse's role in preventing coronary heart disease

Patricia A. Black, BA (Hons), RGN, PG Dip HV
Health Visitor, Croydon Community Health Trust

Coronary heart disease occurs when there is insufficient blood supply to the myocardium (the muscular wall of the heart). The myocardium needs a large supply, as it functions continuously, and must adjust its output to meet the requirements of the body tissues. Terms used in connection with CHD (the precursive condition) include angina pectoris, myocardial infarction and atherosclerosis.

Angina pectoris Insufficient oxygen is supplied to meet the myocardium's total energy requirement. Sufferers experience a choking, severe pain in the chest, generated by the heart muscle fibres. Attacks are often caused by physical exertion or emotional stress.

Myocardial infarction (coronary thrombosis/occlusion – MI) A coronary artery becomes blocked, causing that area of the myocardium to become necrotic due to lack of oxygen.

What is CHD?
CHD is a 'deficit' disease – it is said to occur when the blood supply to the heart is reduced by blockage of the coronary vessels. Two conditions contribute to this – atherosclerosis and arteriosclerosis.

Atherosclerosis Fatty substances, composed of lipids and cholesterol, are laid down in the lining of the arteries. The 'silting' process usually builds up gradually, but it interferes with the nourishment of the intima cells, causing their death and leading to scarring and calcification. The process also reduces the lumen, while the scarring and calcification roughen the arterial walls.

Reduced lumen and roughened walls lead to reduced blood supply because the blood flow is slower, and there is a tendency for clots to form in the artery. If a clot or a piece of fatty tissue breaks away, it will travel through the arterial system until it becomes too large for the carrying vessel and occludes it. If the vessel is a coronary artery, a coronary thrombosis (MI) results. Factors contributing to atherosclerosis include smoking, hypertension and hyperlipidaemia.

Arteriosclerosis   This is a gradual loss of elasticity in the arterial walls, due to calcification and thickening. It tends to be accompanied by high blood pressure (due to the extra effort needed to pump blood through a narrower space) and seems to precede the internal organ degeneration which is part of the ageing process. Diabetes seems to accelerate ageing degeneration of the vascular system.

The cost of CHD

Approximately 180,000 people die from CHD each year in the UK, and the cost of treatment is over 50 million and accounts for over 200,000 bed days each year (Health Education, 1987). If CHD could be prevented, lives would be saved, there would be a substantial saving and beds would be freed to shorten hospital waiting lists.

Can anything be done to prevent CHD? A recent World Health Organisation report (1986) concluded that diet is the most critical factor in determining the level of CHD in a society, reinforcing the report by the Committee on Medical Aspects of Health (COMA, 1984). This report is particularly important in the UK, as it was government commissioned, and as such will form the basis of any future policy changes. The chief recommendations are shown in Table 1. It may be helpful to briefly examine and update these recommendations.

> ★ Reduce fat intake to not more than 35 per cent of the daily calorie requirement, with 15 per cent or less supplied by saturated fats.
> ★ Salt intake not to be increased, and if possible, decreased.
> ★ Sugar intake should not be increased – and it was noted that reduced sugar intake would benefit other conditions, such as dental caries.
> ★ Increase intake of fibre-rich carbohydrates to provide the energy requirement previously met by fats. This intake should be increased by around 50 per cent, which would mean an average daily intake of 30g.

Table   1.   The   COMA   Report's   main recommendations.

Fat and cholesterol are broken down in the body to produce lipids, which do not readily dissolve, and are carried around the bloodstream as complex particles known as lipoproteins. When first absorbed by the gut, digested fats and cholesterol are formed into a chylomicron – the largest lipoprotein particle. These are too large to convey their energy into the cells, so they are further broken down into free monoglycerides and free fatty acids to provide energy. This makes the lipoprotein smaller and heavier – high density lipoprotein (HDL), and these have been shown to remove cholesterol from the arterial wall, so they may be said to be cardioprotective (Miller, 1977).

The HDLs travel in the bloodstream until they reach the liver, where their cholesterol content, along with any endogenously produced cholesterol, are shaped into very low density lipoprotein (VLDLs). The VLDLs in turn circulate in the blood, and lipoprotein lipase transforms them into HDLs and low density lipoproteins (LDLs). LDLs provide energy for cell membrane metabolism, but any surplus appears to contribute to atherosclerosis (Heller, 1986).

Saturated fats

Levels of LDLs and plasma cholesterol have been shown to be increased by consumption of saturated fats (WHO, 1986), although there is currently some doubt about the validity of this. However, eating less saturated fats, and replacing those eaten with polyunsaturated and monounsaturated fats may reduce the level of plasma cholesterol and LDLs. Until evidence to the contrary is conclusive, it is as well to assume this is true – a reduction in fat consumption is unlikely to harm healthy people in the UK. (Not all elevated levels of plasma cholesterol are due to excessive fat intake – other causes include diabetes, nephrotic syndrome and hypothyroidism.)

Recent research has indicated the consumption of oily fish, such as herring, tuna and mackerel or fish oil appears to significantly reduce incidence of mortality in those who have recently recovered from MI (Burr, 1989), and indeed the incidence of CHD among races whose diet is high in oily fish, such as the Eskimos, is almost negligible.

Salt reduction is recommended because excessive salt tends to raise the blood pressure. Since there is so much 'hidden' salt in most readily available prepared foods in the UK, it is unusual for normal, healthy people to suffer from a lack of sodium. However, it can happen, particularly if people exercise in direct sunlight on a hot day, and symptoms include cramps, nausea, weakness and vomiting.

It has also been suggested that the salt to potassium ratio may be more important than the amount of sodium consumed. If this is the case, increasing intake of fruit, vegetables and wholegrains would have the same effect as cutting down on salt, but conclusive evidence is awaited.

Sugar does not provide any real nutrients, although it does provide calories. This means excess sugar consumption can lead to weight gain, or even malnutrition, as the appetite may be satisfied before the body has had sufficient nutrients. While moderate obesity is not in itself a risk factor in development of CHD, it is usually accompanied by altered glucose tolerance and hypertension (Shaper, 1985), which does increase the risk. One of the most accurate ways of assessing whether an individual has a 'weight problem' is by using the body mass index. This is calculated as $\frac{\text{Weight}}{\text{Height}^2}$ (in kg/m^2) (Table 1). A body mass of 20-25 is acceptable, 30 is obese and 40 grossly obese.

Increased fibre-rich carbohydrate intake is recommended not only to replace fats in energy production, but because the soluble type of fibre found in oats and oat bran, for example, appears to help lower blood cholesterol by inhibiting atheroma formation. Although fibre also helps prevent constipation, if taken in excess (eg, three bowls of raw bran per day) it can inhibit the absorption of essential minerals such as zinc and magnesium. This is unlikely to harm people taking fibre from a range of sources, as the amount of fruit, vegetables and pulses they would have to eat would mean they were also taking in large amounts of these minerals.

Other factors affecting risk of CHD include intake of caffeine – which increases the blood pressure, and alcohol, which can lead to obesity. Southgate (1990) has also suggested that the frequency of eating may affect the metabolism of glucose, cholesterol and lipid. Research suggests that the traditional three meals a day may not be as easily metabolised as a large number of smaller meals or snacks, and may contribute to surplus LDLs in the blood.

Patient education

Since diet appears to be the most critical factor in influencing the rate of CHD in the population, healthcare by encouraging people to adopt healthy eating habits nurses may significantly affect this. Patients or clients will, however, have individual perceptions about their situations, and will also have certain expectations about the advice nurses may give – it is quite possible that they may dismiss it as irrelevant to them if the threat of CHD is not real to them.

Several subjective factors determine whether people act on information they receive, based on whether they have been satisfied by past contact with healthcare professionals, how likely they believe they are to experience CHD, how severe they believe CHD to be, and whether they feel it is worthwhile to change their lifestyle (eg, will they get CHD no matter what they do?) (Becker, 1974). Diet is a way of life and should be enjoyable, so a positive approach should be taken at all times, so it is essential to develop an empathetic communication with clients, trying to 'enter' their lifestyle. Each client will need an individual approach, but the underlying strategy should include short-, medium- and long-term goals (realistically, a small change that is maintained is better than a radical one that is not). A method of evaluating the change should also be devised, and this may require several follow-up visits for clients to receive support and encouragement. It may be helpful to stress that one lapse does not make it pointless to continue with a healthy lifestyle programme, and that it is the cumulative effect that is important, not each individual meal.

A positive message

If too much stress is placed on what should not be done, and what must be given up, clients are more likely to reject the advice entirely – they are not ill yet and probably want to continue with their current way of life. This is known as 'dispositional attribution' – the more severe a threat, the more people continue to feel they enjoy the behaviour eliciting the threat, and while they may alter their behaviour for a while, the change is unlikely to be maintained. A positive approach – suggesting a different behaviour would be beneficial is usually more successful. Positive change is adopted without undue fear, so it is more likely to become permanent, and people are more likely to have a positive attitude towards the recommended behaviour (Aronson, 1963).

Teaching can follow a basic strategy: begin from existing knowledge; ensure information is presented in a logical manner, using relevant materials; involve the client in identifying and planning changes and aim for an achievable goal (Ewles and Simnett, 1985).

References
Aronson, E. and Carlsmith, J.M. (1963) The effect of the severity of the threat on the devaluation of forbidden behaviour. *Journal of Abnormal and Social Psychology*, **66**, 548–88.
Burr ,M.L. *et al* (1989) the effects of changes in fat, fish and fibre intake on death and myocardial reinfarction trial (DART). *The Lancet*, **8666**, 757–60.
Becker, M. (1974) The Health belief model and sick role behaviour. *Health Education Monograph*, **2**, 409–19.
DHSS/Health Education Council (1987) Look after your heart: campaign strategy. DHSS/HEC, London.
Ewles, L. and Sinnett, I. (1985) Promoting Health: a Practical Guide to Health Education. John Wiley, Chichester.
HEC (1987) Broken Hearts. HEC, London. Miller, N.E. *et al* (1977) High density lipoprotein and coronary heart disease: a prospective case-control study. *The Lancet*, **i**, 965–68.
Shaper, A.J. *et al* (1985) Risk factors for ischaemic heart disease: the prospective phase of he British Regional Heart Study. *Journal of Epidemiology and Community Health*, **39**, 179–209.
Southgate, D.A.T. (1990) Nibblers, gorgers, snackers and grazers. *British Medical Journal*, **300**, 6718, 136—37.
WHO (1986) Community prevention and control of cardiovascular disease. Technical report series 732, WHO, Geneva.

Handout: reduce your risk of heart disease

Heart disease happens when the blood supply to the heart muscle is limited because the arteries become too narrow. If enough blood can't get to the heart, part of it won't work properly, and may even die. Arteries narrow because fatty substances stick to the inside walls and food can't pass through properly – this is a bit like a pipe furring up in your water system at home (see diagram).

About 180,000 people in the UK die each year from heart disease, but there is a lot you can do to stop yourself becoming one of them.

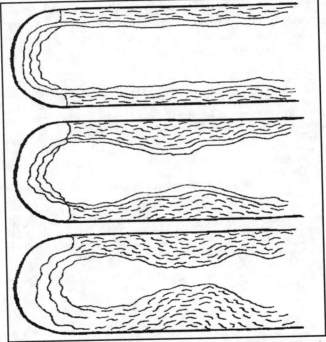

Fatty substances in the blood can clog up the arteries, making it more difficult for blood to pass through them.

What you can do

Regular exercise will not only benefit your heart, but it will also help keep your weight steady. You can walk briskly to the shops or to work, swim or go to an exercise class once a week or more, but you should try to do at least three sessions of 15–20 minutes a week.

• Another way you can help yourself is to try to avoid stressful situations. This is not always easy, but for example if taking the kids to the supermarket is a nightmare, why not try to arrange for a friend to look after them while you shop. Then you can look after hers in return. Stress at work can be difficult to avoid, but make sure you have a break in the middle of the day, and walk around to clear your head.

• If you smoke, you could try to cut down, and eventually stop altogether. Smoking narrows your arteries, stopping blood getting to your heart, as well as causing other serious illnesses.

Diet

When it comes to heart disease, the old saying 'you are what you eat' seems very true. By changing to a healthier diet, you can do a lot to reduce your risk of getting heart disease.

Fat   There are three types of fat – saturated, polyunsaturated and monounsaturated. Saturated fat helps make the substance that clogs your arteries, so if you cut down on this, you will help your arteries stay clear. 'Hard' fats, like butter, block margarine and lard are usually saturated. Try replacing them with polyunsturated fats or low fat spreads.

• The fat on meat is saturated, so look out for lean cuts when you shop, and cut off any fat you can see (although there will still be fat in the meat). Stewing meat can be precooked and left to cool, so the fat can be skimmed off easily. As long as you take care to cook and store it properly, it will be just as enjoyable. When you cook things like stews and casseroles, you can use less meat, and replace it with beans and pulses, or more vegetables.

• Processed meats like sausages, meat pies, pates, most minced meat, tinned meats and fatty cuts like shoulder of lamb contain high levels of fat. Try to avoid these, or cut down on the amount you eat. Some sausages are now lower in fat, which is better for you, but they do still contain some fat. Also remember that fat is often hidden in foods like biscuits and cakes, and this is usually saturated.

• Fish and poultry have less fat than red meat – try using these instead (remove the skin from poultry before you cook it though, as that is fatty). Oily fish such as mackerel, herring and tuna are very good for your heart, as they seem to reduce the amount of fatty substance in the blood, so try to eat more meals with these fish in.

• When you are cooking, avoid frying wherever you can, and steam, bake, poach and grill food instead. When you do fry, use cooking oil instead of butter, lard or dipping, and look on the label to check it is polyunsaturated or monounsaturated.

● Skimmed and semiskimmed milk is now widely available, and if you change to one of these, you won't notice the difference before long. There are also plenty of low fat cheeses available now, and these can be used just like ordinary cheese.

Sugar Sugar provides 'empty' energy, which means it doesn't give you any nourishment, just calories. There are plenty of ways to cut down on sugar now – buy diet fizzy drinks and put sweeteners in tea and coffee, and when you buy tinned fruit, get the sort in fruit juice rather than syrup.

● Alcohol is also high in calories, but without any nourishment – try to limit the amount you drink. You can make it go further by adding mixers or drinking soft drinks or alcohol free drinks in between.

Salt This is linked with high blood pressure and may lead to strokes. It is hidden in most ready prepared food, especially tinned and packaged brands, so before you add more salt yourself, taste your food and see if it really needs more. Salt substitutes are now available, containing less sodium, so you could try using these instead – although you should check with your doctor before you try these if you suffer from renal impairment or diabetes.

Fibre This is good for you – it helps you feel full up and prevents constipation. Some fibres can actively help prevent fatty substances from clogging your arteries, like those found in oats, beans, pulses, fruit and vegetables.

This handout is just a little information to help you get the best in terms of health. If you want more information, ask your nurse, who will be glad to help. The most important thing to remember is that life is to be enjoyed, and you are more likely to do that if you are healthy. If you start to make the sort of changes given here, you are giving yourself a better chance of staying healthy.

18

Motivation can prolong life expectancy: a health education programme to help people give up smoking

Janice Clarke, RGN, DipN, BSc (Hons), PGCEA
Nurse Teacher, Southampton University College of Nursing and Midwifery

Smoking significantly increases the risk of developing coronary heart disease (CHD). Although people may wish to give up smoking, it is not always possible to do so independently. This chapter describes how a health education programme was devised to help people stop smoking, and which is formulated jointly by both patients and nurses.

Aims

Health education aims to change an unhealthy aspect of a person's life. It can be interpreted as being "concerned with learning to live in the healthiest way possible" (Redman, 1980). Implicit in this statement is the assumption that there is a desire to live healthily, and that health educator and client agree as to what is meant by 'health', which is a concept in its own right and can incur many interpretations.

Green (1979) defines health education as "any combination of learning opportunities designed to facilitate voluntary adaptions of behaviour (in individuals, groups, or communities) conducive to health". This implies that health education has an individual and social function, consists of any learning opportunities, be they formal or informal, and aims to promote a voluntary change in behaviour. Central to this approach is that individuals' needs must be listened to before the health plan can begin, and that coercion is not acceptable. Nurses need to develop specific skills to implement effective health education (Macleod-Clark, 1990), and must be taught to maximise their effectiveness.

Health education plan

The healthcare plan described in this chapter can be taught in a hospital ward for people admitted with signs of CHD. In a hospital situation there are many constraints (such as the time available for teaching and learning and the availability of human and financial resources), but where possible, most individualised plans, such as this, should be performed on a one-to-one basis.

Time required for the programme can be restricted to half an hour in the afternoon for two to three days, and the plan was formulated with such a time constraint in mind to achieve the aims and objectives set by patient and nurse. People who have CHD tire easily so such a time span would also accommodate their physical limitations. The plan could be implemented at the bedside by giving resources such as booklets and other material. If, however, the patient's condition means he or she cannot leave the ward initially but self-help organisations and relatives need to be contacted, portable telephones can be brought to the bedside.

The framework for the plan adopted a problem-solving approach as described by the nursing process (Kratz, 1979). Any health education plan should involve the individual when setting aims and objectives, and identifying the stages, to allow for clarification and effective communication between patient and nurse. Such an approach allows the power to lie with the individual, correlating with Orem's (1985) perspective of self-care and the acknowledgement that people must ultimately live on their own without a health educator.

> The plan consists of four parts:
> - client assessment to identify needs (including motivation, previous knowledge, health education needs and lifestyle);
> - health education plan (aims and objectives);
> - implementation of plan (method and content);
> - evaluation (summative and formative).

Table 1. Health education plan.

The assessment stage is considered to be the precursor to the remainder of the plan, when needs are identified, which then facilitate the aims, objectives, methods and content to be devised. This chapter will identify pertinent client factors and, through the assessment process, analyse why certain aims, objectives, methods and content were devised (Tables 1, 2, 3 and 4).

There are several factors which need to be assessed:

- extent of existing knowledge of CHD and known effects of smoking;

- ability to learn;

- motivation to learn/personality;

- learning style most appropriate to the individual;

- influence of primary socialisation on health matters.

Extent of knowledge base
The first objective allows people to identify why they smoke, enabling

them to question the influences on their lifestyle, strengthening their resolve to stop and prepare for a different lifestyle. A baseline of knowledge can be obtained by questioning and asking them to express in their own words their understanding of their disease, so that any gaps in the clients' understanding of the causes and effects of CHD can be clearly identified.

Those who seem willing to discuss their understanding of CHD and its links with smoking are showing they accept smoking is a causative factor. Nurses can then point out that smoking is undesirable and threatens to cut short their lifespan. Clients who are contemptuous of or deny the evidence for any correlation of smoking to heart disease present a greater clinical and educational challenge.

Assessment
1. Extent of knowledge base in relation to CHD and the known effects of smoking
2. Ability to learn
3. Motivation to learn/personality
4. Learning style most appropriate to the individual
5. Influence of primary socialisation

Aim
Client will gain knowledge of the pathological effects of cigarette smoking in relation to CHD and subsequently stop the practice to improve health and life chances

Client
1. Identify and understand the reasons why he or she smokes
2. Be aware of research findings on the effects of smoking in relation to CHD
3. Appreciate the need to stop smoking to avoid complications of coronary artery disease
4. Identify strengths and weaknesses in self to achieve stated goal of stopping smoking
5. Set a goal to stop smoking completely from a fixed date
6. Identify members of family and/or friends (significant others) who will be supportive and use them as additional resources of support
7. Contact an organisation who helps stop smoking and inform them of the decision

---

Table 2. Health education plan ideally devised between patient and nurse.

The plan acknowledges that people must understand the effects of smoking on their health to be successful. Use of the most up-to-date research about smoking is vital to show its effect on CHD. It is then assumed clients will make their own informed decision as to the health benefits to be gained from actively stopping smoking (Nutbeam, 1987). If nurses just related the dangers of smoking, the element of personal control and decision-making would be denied.

Assessment of the knowledge base facilitates planning and goal setting for client and nurse, and allows the content and method of the plan to be developed. By listing the reasons for smoking, a personal and public confrontation is achieved. Clients are asked to write down their identified reasons for smoking and then try to explain them to both themselves and the nurse. They are also asked to state the date they first started smoking (to make them realise just how long they have been smoking) and how many cigarettes per day are smoked. Such exercises allow them to assess themselves and the effects of smoking on their health. Research can then be presented in the form of articles, prepared booklets, photographs of diseased lungs and hearts, together with mortality figures of heart disease of smokers and non-smokers.

Rahe *et al* (1975) and Gregor (1981) studied people following myocardial infarction and their response to information from prepared booklets, and their results showed higher knowledge scores following issue of the booklets proving them to be useful. Nurses can then evaluate the knowledge gained through question and answer technique. Finally, assessment and identification of clients' knowledge base means more information can be collected as to their ability to learn.

• Formative
• Diary kept by the client. Self-assessment as to the actuality of stopping smoking. Oral questioning to evaluate the knowledge base of information.
• Summative
• Extent of success in terms of the plan structure

Table 3. Evaluating process.

Ability to learn

This can be gauged by talking to the individual: certain subjective and objective observations can be made to gather data about people's ability to learn, to allow the nurse to make an assessment: do they understand easily? Do they ask questions or does their body language express confusion? Can they follow directions, pay attention, see, hear, communicate? Do they understand abstract ideas?

Learning theorists have distinguished three types of learning, cognitive, affective and psychomotor (Coutts and Hardy, 1985). In learning to stop an addictive behaviour, all three domains must show change. Age is another factor to consider: the rate of learning - not necessarily the ability to learn - may have slowed down. It may therefore be necessary to repeat information, making sure it is given in small amounts and is also available in writing. Older people will also have had more experiences and so will learn "in response to their own needs and perceptions, not those of their teachers" (Curzon, 1985). Educational level will also indicate the smoking pattern prior to the disease process. More informed people generally tend to smoke less (Fuchs and Farrell, 1982), although of course, people from all social classes and educational levels do smoke.

Anxiety levels induced by being in hospital will also affect individuals' ability to learn. It is well documented that anxiety levels rise considerably on admission to hospital (Cassem *et al*, 1970), and this can be detrimental to learning. The use of printed material therefore allows people to read when they feel able, and can concentrate. The plan is based on a simplistic approach to help overcome any barriers that hospitalisation and illness can produce.

Motivation to learn

Motivation is a vital ingredient to learning, and can be interpreted as consisting of "internal processes which spur us on to satisfy some need" (Child, 1977). It can also help nurses predict the outcome of a potential change in behaviour. The various theories of patient compliance are useful indicators of assessing individual's possible compliance rate.

Locus of control This model balances a continuum of internal and external motivation. It is also similar to the attribution theory. Seligman (1975) studied the concept of locus of control, whereby some people express internal or external attributions which affect their ability to control their lives, or accept a helpless self-concept called 'learned helplessness'. Control is a dominant feature of human relationships, and any health education plan should incorporate a controlling factor for the client.

People who believe outcomes are dependent, at least partially, on actions they take are internally orientated. They will consider that if smoking is harmful to their health, by stopping the habit they can help themselves. People with an external orientation often do not believe there is a connection between individual action and outcome, and present a greater challenge to the health educator. This attitude can, however, be changed by identifying the external aspect, and giving control and decision-making power. This gives them a realistic experience in which they can be active and take some control of their life and health. Goals would be set by the individual him- or herself to stop smoking on a certain date at a certain time, and agreed in a contractual arrangement with the nurse. This expresses a facilitative approach from the nurse and a controlling role from the client.

Health belief Becker (1975) designed a health belief model to discover why compliance to health education was poor. Four dimensions were identified as useful in assessing how to teach people to stop smoking: perceived susceptibility; perceived seriousness; perceived benefit and perceived barriers.

This model helps people identify their strengths and weaknesses, and how these affect the likely success of the plan (Redman, 1980). Understanding the aspects of this model may therefore help people recognise their own strengths and weaknesses. The model may, for example, show people that their life is at risk from smoking, that they could imminently die or become a 'cardiac cripple', diminishing their quality and quantity of life, and that by stopping smoking they would improve quality and quantity of life, even though they may initially experience withdrawal symptoms. The model can be criticised because it only considers actual behaviour, whereas intention to perform that behaviour is another important variable.

Reasoned action theory Ajzen and Fishbein (1975) developed Becker's model further by considering the relationship between beliefs, intentions and actions. They assumed that behaviour is under voluntary control, and people will intend to perform a behaviour if they evaluate it positively. If a person decides not to smoke and this is his or her intention, then their behaviour should reflect this. The authors also recognised that people are influenced by what others think, so they should identify 'significant others' in the positive sense in the plan.

Ajzen and Fishbein's theory of reasoned action assumes people take action or do not take action based on their beliefs and values learned in life situations or from significant others (Kolton and Piccolo, 1986). Such a theory has influenced this plan, as clients negotiate with the health educator throughout all the stages of setting aims and objectives. The process then allows them to fully understand the aims and plan, and also allows the nurse to see whether or not they believe they will gain any benefit from stopping smoking. People who leave hospital intending to stop smoking have a greater chance of fulfilling that intention than those who do not.

Perception and actuality are not always the same, and belief is an important variable. Similarly, perceived and actual control may differ. Ajzen discovered that people who believe they can achieve a desired aim are more likely to perform the appropriate action to do so. Attitude is another important aspect, so an exploration of attitude is reflected in the plan when people are asked to identify strengths and weaknesses, appreciate the need to stop smoking and identify and understand the reasons why they smoke. Attitudes to the interpretation of research findings on the effects of cigarette smoking on CHD are also relevant. Although this chapter has concentrated mainly on personal motivation, many sociological factors influence people's motivation and ability to give up smoking, such as social class and peer group interaction.

Learning style

Learning style is related to the motivation to learn and the client's personality. People with an 'internal' style will probably want to discover information by themselves, discuss it with their family and friends and health facilitator and then make their own judgements. Those with an 'external' style will probably wish to rely on being given information, and will require positive feedback and praise.

Talking with a patient will show whether he or she prefers to be told factual information or read, work with others or alone, watch videos, require much praise and encouragement to cut down on smoking by one cigarette a day or stop completely immediately. This plan reflects an individual who had an informal learning style, where some variety of method is necessary to keep attention and stimulate him or her into active learning rather than passive information gathering.

Content	Method
List the reasons why you smoke	Question and answer
State the date you started smoking	Written evidence and admission of smoking
State how many cigarettes you smoke. Work out how much they cost per month	Assessment of the reason for smoking
(Nurse gives information that clearly states the known effects of cigarette smoking in relation to CHD)	Articles, booklets, photographs, mortality figures
Appreciate the known benefits of stopping smoking	
Through negotiation, set the date to stop	Client decision-making and commitment
Decide on mode of informing family and friends verbal, face-to-face, telephone, letter, note	Client decision-making. Forming a contract with family
(Nurse gives address of support groups)	Client control to contact support group
Formulate a list of strengths and weaknesses influencing these objectives, identify resources available	

Table 4. Method and content of plan.

Influence of socialisation

Primary socialisation is the intricate process of developing values, norms and beliefs indicative of the social group one matures into. Kirscht (1983) suggests "individuals engage in health related behaviours because the behaviours are actively supported or promoted by the norms and beliefs of specific groups", and smoking can be seen in this light. If the family accepts smoking as a norm, there would be no drive to stop, or suggest it was contrary to health. This presents difficulties if smoking must cease on health grounds. It then becomes desirable for the family to change their beliefs and norms. A supportive approach is desirable, so family involvement should be encouraged to produce a permanent change in the beliefs, norms and thus behaviour.

Attitude to health is another important influence. Strauss and Weeks identified that working-class people have a present day orientation to health (Brearley, 1978) and may not think in terms of preventive health by stopping smoking. Middle-class people were identified by Milio as having a future-orientated attitude to health (Brearley, 1978), and would consider the importance of action to secure a healthy future. Another useful socialisation theory is Bandura's social learning theory (1977) which suggested that people learn behaviours from observing a model. In family or influential grouping, for example, the parents may have set the example to smoke. In health education, this can be used to an advantage if the health educator acts as a role model.

Evaluation

Evaluation can be another educational aspect that can encourage people to stop smoking. It can reinforce the desired behaviour, helping people realise whether the desired behaviour has been obtained (formative evaluation) and assist the health educator to assess the devised teaching plan and approach used (summative evaluation). Oral questioning is useful to evaluate informational aspects of the health plan, while asking clients to keep a diary of their thoughts, feelings and health-related actions can also be a helpful method of evaluation.

Taxonomies have been created to assess the level of knowledge acquired, such as Bloom (1964), Eisner (1969) and Steinaker and Bell (1979), with each adopting a different approach to education and evaluation. According to these authors, evaluation on the part of the client has to be self-assessment. Only the client really knows whether the behaviour has been changed, as people can easily convince others they have stopped smoking, but can only be true to themselves.

Another useful method is the triad evaluation structure outlined by Donabedian (1966), involving examination of the setting in which the education is performed. If resources are adequate, it is assumed education will be of a satisfactory standard. Process examines the actions and skill of the educator whereas outcome considers the patient outcomes, which were written in the plan as measurable objectives.

A health education programme provides an ideal format to help people give up smoking. By assessing and evaluating an individual's attitudes towards smoking, a structured plan can be developed which sets realistic stages and guidelines to help ease the process. Central to the programme's success is that the individual maintains overall control, and that the nurse ensures he or she is and remains well-motivated.

References
Ajzen, I. and Fishbein, N. (1975) Belief, Attitude, Intention and Behaviour: an introduction to theory and research. Addison-Wesley, Massachusetts.
Bandura, A. (1977) Social Learning Theory. Prentice Hall, New Jersey.
Becker, M. and Maiman, L. (1975) Socio-behavioural determinants of compliance with medical care recommendations. *Medical Care*, **1**, 18, 10-24.
Brearley, P. *et al* (1978) The Social Context of Health Care. Robertson and Blackwell, London.
Bloom, B.S. (1964) Taxonomy of Educational Objectives: the classification of educational goals. Cognitive Domain, (Handbook). Longman, London.
Cassem, N.H. *et al* (1970) Reactions of coronary patients to the CCU nurse. *American Journal of Nursing*, **17**, 2, 319.
Child, D. (1977) Psychology and the Teacher (2nd Ed). Holt, Rinehart and Winston, London.

Coutts, L.C. and Hardy, L.K. (1985) Teaching for Health. Churchill Livingstone, London.

Curzon, L.B. (1985) Teaching in Further Education (3rd Ed). Holt, Rinehart and Winston, London.

Donabedian, A. (1966) Evaluating the quality of medical care. *Millbank Memorial Fund Quarterly*, **44**, (part 2), 166-206.

Eisner, E.W. (1969) Instructional and expressive objectives. In: Popham, W.J. *et al* (Eds) Instructional Objectives. Ranc McNally, Chicago.

Farrell, P. and Fuchs, V. (1982) Schooling and health: the cigarette connection. *Journal of Health and Economics*, **1**, 217-30.

Green, L.W. (1979) Health promotion policy and the placement of responsibility for personal healthcare. *Family and Community Health*, **2**, 3, 51-56.

Kirscht, J. (1983) Preventative health behaviour; a review of research and issues. *Health Psychology*, **2**, 277-301.

Kratz, C. (1979) The Nursing Process. Bailliere Tindall, London.

Kolton, K.A. and Piccolo, P. (1988) Patient compliance; a challenge in practice. *Nurse Practitioner*, **13**, 12, 40.

Nutbeam, D. (1987) Controlling a killer. *Nursing Times*, **83**, 15, 24.

Macleod-Clark, J. *et al* (1990) Helping people to stop smoking: a study of the nurse's role. *J. of Adv. Nrs.*, **15**, 3, 357-63.

OPCS (1987) Deaths by Cause. OPCS, London.

Orem, D. (1985) Nursing: Concepts of Practice. McGraw Hill, New York.

Redman, B.K. (1980) The Process of Patient Teaching in Nursing . Mosby-Year Book, St Louis.

Scheffler, I. (1966) Philosophy and Education (2nd Ed). Allyn and Bacon, Boston.

Seligman, M. (1975) Helplessness. Freman, San Francisco.

Shaper, A.G. (1989) Epidemiology. *Practice Nurse*, **12**, 7, 307-10.

Steinaker, N.W. and Bell, R.M. (1979) The Experimental Taxonomy: a new approach to teaching and learning. Academic Press, London.

19

An exhibition to eradicate ignorance: setting up a continence resource centre

Elspeth Gibson, RGN, NDN, PWT
Nurse Teacher, Buckinghamshire College of Nursing and Midwifery

Incontinence is a sensitive subject, and people who have difficulties with continence, and their carers, often find it difficult to talk about the problem, even to trained, sympathetic professionals. One way of easing the problems and breaking the taboos caused by this lack of communication is to set up a continence resource centre (CRC). If it is properly used and publicised, the CRC may also go some way towards eradicating the general public's ignorance about incontinence and make it less distressing for sufferers.

What is a CRC?

How can I promote continence? What does it mean? What products are available? Is this free? On prescription? Can I buy it? Do you supply it? I am doing a project on incontinence, do you have any articles or books on it? What does a 'slipad' look like? Why are there so many different types of catheters and drainage bags? Do you have any leaflets on....? Is there more than one kind of male urinary sheath? What on Earth is a pubic pressure flange? Where can I show some samples of different products to my disabled son so he can decide for himself which are best for him?

All these questions will be familiar to those working in the field of continence promotion. Most of the answers are filed away in the heads of continence advisors, but others take time to look up. A CRC is a display of anything concerned with continence problems, from information, leaflets and booklets to samples of the products available and sources of further help, presented in a clear, accessible way. People can visit it alone or accompanied by the continence advisor to discuss their individual needs. As a permanent exhibition, it allows anyone wishing to use it to easily obtain information with or without help from a professional. This can cut down on embarrassment and waiting time, and make best use of the time of the continence advisor or other professional who is usually asked the routine questions.

Who is it for?

The CRC can be situated on a hospital, health centre or any other appropriate place where it will be seen by those who need it. It is there to inform and help clients, carers, healthcare professionals and anyone else who wishes to know more about the subject. They can find out where to go for help with a specific problem, look at pads to see what is available and decide which type is most suited to their needs, and learn more about the causes of and remedies for continence problems. Hopefully, feeling more informed (and armed with a few technical terms to reduce embarrassment), clients may also feel more able to discuss their problems with professionals, but those who unfortunately are unable to overcome this embarrassment at least have a source of information they can consult in confidence, instead of suffering in silence as so many do.

Ideally the CRC should be situated in a room of its own, where people can wander round without embarrassment. Space in hospitals and health centres, however, is often at a premium, and if this is not possible, and it must be situated in a public area, the use of screens can help make it feel more private.

Layout and design of the CRC

The CRC set up in Chalfont and Gerards Cross Hospital was modelled on the major museums, such as the Natural History Museum and the Science Museum in London, who display their collections with accompanying information. Exhibits in the CRC were thus accompanied by written educational material including client/patient suitability, assessment, availability, sources of further information, leaflets and useful addresses. For example the section on the male urinary sheath included text explaining the 'system' and a range of samples, with information on sizes, types and availability. The CRC aims to emphasise the importance of the individual's own wants and needs, and hopefully helps people find a sensitive and individual answer which suits them in their own environment.

Commercial companies were extremely helpful in supplying both samples of their products and up-to-date information to accompany them. It is vital, however, in setting up a CRC to ensure the information is comprehensive and current, and that any developments are quickly incorporated. This involves keeping a good ongoing relationship with both commercial companies and voluntary and other organisations who work in continence promotion.

The CRC is aimed at clients, carers and professionals, so it is vital that information is presented in an easily accessible form. It should be clearly broken into sections, so relevant information is easy to find, and technical terms should be included, but clearly explained. Table 1 gives a suggestion of how the CRC can be broken into sections.

If only a certain range of pants and pads are available to the health authority, this should be made clear, but as comprehensive a range as possible displayed, together with information on performance, price and availability, so that those who buy these products can choose the one most appropriate to them, having had a chance to look at the options first. Professionals can also easily see what stock they are able to order for their clients, and choose the items which will best enhance their quality of life.

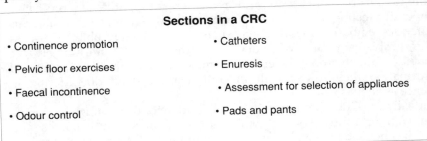

Sections in a CRC

• Continence promotion	• Catheters
• Pelvic floor exercises	• Enuresis
• Faecal incontinence	• Assessment for selection of appliances
• Odour control	• Pads and pants

Table 1. Suggested layout for a CRC.

To ensure the information in the CRC is up-to-date, a current events board can be used to display new developments, books, research results, additions to the FP10 list and new products before they are incorporated into the main body of the exhibition. This means they can be instated quickly, and are less likely to lay around waiting for an appropriate quiet period when the exhibition can be reorganised to fit them in.

Evaluation

It is difficult to formally evaluate a CRC, because it is set up to be used informally. However, a questionnaire can be circulated among professionals and students for their comments, allowing developments to be made where necessary, and clients can be asked if they have found the CRC of benefit during consultations. Another source of comment is the inclusion of a 'visitors' book', in which those using the CRC are invited to make comments and requests. These measures help ensure the CRC is as useful as possible to those who use it, and that information is conveyed at the appropriate level.

By the time the Chalfonts and Gerards Cross CRC had been open a year, it had stimulated the production of five student projects on continence problems, and a visit to the centre had been written into a district nurse's orientation programme for nursing auxiliaries. It made the job of continence advisor easier and far more rewarding, as clients are better informed and their distress and embarrassment is minimised. The time and effort put in to setting up the CRC and to keeping it up-to-date have been repaid many times over both in satisfaction and actual time savings.

20

The dry season: promoting continence in the South West

Diane Lofting, RGN, DN, HV, FETC
Continence Manager, Bath District Health Authority

Some eight years ago, convinced that there was a more effective way of promoting continence and managing incontinence within the Bath District Health Authority, I assisted in the setting up of a working party which included nurses, a urologist, a geriatrician, and a nurse employed by a private company. Its conclusions resulted in the birth of our continence unit, based at St Martin's Hospital in Bath, serving an area crossing two boundaries - Wiltshire and Avon/Somerset - with a total population of over 404,000. Our department was extremely fortunate to be managed in its early days by Janet Blannin, who has done so much to promote continence both nationally and internationally, and to put our own unit firmly on the map. From humble beginnings, it now employs a full-time continence manager, and two part-time continence advisors.

Our team supports the concept that incontinence is common, but that it can be successfully treated, or at least well-managed. We aim to give people suffering from incontinence access to effective and appropriate assessment, followed by relevant treatment and management. The team also aims to ensure recognition of incontinence and continence promotion as a national health issue by providing various courses and study days for different branches of the caring professions, and to educate the community in general to recognise incontinence as a common condition for which treatment can and does work. We hope to increase public awareness of the availability of discreet and sensitive management for incontinence, and to make younger people aware that continence in later life can be promoted by preventive measures.

Education

Incontinence is a problem for both patients and carers. Its effects account for an alarming percentage of nursing time, and obviously its effective management or eventual cure will be hugely beneficial for everyone concerned. We aim to educate both professional carers and the general public alike, in the hope that as many sufferers as possible will be cured, and that the 10 per cent of patients with intractable incontinence may be managed as sensitively and effectively as possible with the minimum of physical and emotional distress.

The ENB 978 course is held twice yearly in conjunction with the

Education Department for qualified nursing staff with a special interest in continence promotion and the management of incontinence who may wish to specialise in this particular field. A four-day introduction to the field is held three times a year for trained staff, and a basic half-day course once a month for new nursing staff in the district. This short course enables the continence team to introduce themselves and to briefly outline the aims of the department and its work. A two-day course for carers of all disciplines working in the social services sector is held four times a year, and we also run a variety of one-off study days, such as a recent workshop on male catheterisation. Our education programme includes night nursing staff, and we have recently introduced a course aimed at staff caring for people with a mental handicap.

Our target has been to provide education for carers of all disciplines, and the subsequent results and attitudes have been extremely encouraging. We aim to teach participants on all our courses to take a holistic approach to the care of their patients, assessing their physical, physiological and social needs; nursing interventions such as bladder retraining, toileting programmes and pelvic floor exercises, which can be put into practice in a caring situation, are covered in some detail. The various factsheets and literature handed out at these courses have recently been published as a simple handbook, 'A Guide to Continence Assessment and Bladder Retraining', which has been well received both within Bath Health Authority and further afield.

The clinics

According to statistics, approximately 14 per cent of the population suffers from incontinence at some point in their lives. About 1 per cent of people with incontinence living in the Bath district currently use our services, which means there could still be a further 20,000 suffering in silence. Our computer carries records of over 4,000 people, of whom 1,800 are currently receiving some form of treatment from us.

During a typical month, we run approximately 12 clinics (including two consultant clinics and two special appliance clinics) in the unit at St Martin's Hospital, for which we use the nursing service provided by the Thackraycare Dispensing Appliance Centre in Bristol. We see about 60 patients in these clinics, and our own statistics show that approximately 85 per cent keep their appointments. Patients can refer themselves to our clinics, but we also receive an ever-increasing number of referrals from GPs, consultant urologists, gynaecologists, and neurologists, as well as from Bristol consultants.

In addition to the clinics here at St Martin's, continence clinics are held regularly at various clinics and health centres throughout the district. Our resource nurses run eleven such clinics, usually on a monthly basis, and will ask the advisors for additional advice should they require it. We have an ever-increasing number of nurses on our register throughout the district, who have completed either the ENB 978 or the four day promotion of continence course, and have expressed willingness to act as resource nurses, helping patients and advising staff involved in the care of people with incontinence and associated problems.

All our patients are assessed either in the clinic by one of our advisors or at home or school by the district nurse, school nurse or health visitor. All completed assessment forms are forwarded to our department for transfer onto our computer and for monitoring by the advisors, who will offer help and advice where necessary before the form is returned to the nurse or health visitor. All continence supplies for the whole district are ordered from our department and despatched from the central supplies unit to 15 health centres and clinics throughout the district for collection by patients. A home delivery service operates within Bath itself for people unable to collect their own supplies, and the possibility of streamlining this service and eventually extending it to cover the whole district is being explored.

Several months ago a monthly walk-in clinic was set up in Boots the Chemist in Bath city centre, and is proving tremendously popular. We are also frequently asked to give talks about our work to organisations such as the WRVS, the Townswomens' Guild and many others, and these talks are always well received. As a result of increased advertising and publicity, more people, many of whom have suffered in silence for years, are aware that help is available and are coming forward.

Budgets

In many respects our department is money-generating. We encourage companies to advertise their products in our unit, for which we make an annual charge. We frequently participate in seminars and exhibitions and help to organise open days, and profits from such ventures are used to pay for advertising the unit in surgeries, chemists and the local press. Disposable pads and pants are the direct budgetary responsibility of the Continence Manager, but male incontinence appliances such as sheaths and legbags are covered by the Drug Tariff and are obtainable on prescription. Dispensing appliance centres are licensed to dispense all the appliances in parts IXa, b and c of the Drug Tariff; part IXb covers incontinence appliances. Financed by dispensing fees, the appliance practice nurse provides a valuable free appliance fitting service to our department, and is bound by the code of practice drawn up by the British Surgical Trades Association to offer a totally independent service and unbiased advice to patients. This nurse also visits people at home as required, and keeps in touch through the Thackraycare Centre, which dispenses prescriptions and organises delivery to the patients. This gives us a specific person, particularly skilled in teaching intermittent self-catheterisation, to whom all children who require this method of continence control are referred. Our unit is extremely fortunate to be able to use this invaluable service.

Looking to the future

Having reduced the problem of incontinence to a minimum here at St Martin's Hospital through effective education, we aim to expand our programme of education to encompass all the other hospitals within the Bath district, as well as the social services and residential homes.

Eight years on, our team has expanded and the number of people we are able to help has increased considerably, as has the numbers of carers attending our courses. Nevertheless there is still a lot to do, such as the introduction of a comprehensive home delivery service and reusable pads. Our computer needs to be updated and linked to the main supplies computer to facilitate more effective stock control and budgeting.

The task has not been easy, but our unit now plays an extremely important role in educating other carers in the effective assessment and management of incontinence. It ensures more sensitive and appropriate care for people with continence problems, while effective management and possible cure reduces the need for aids and appliances. Combined with more effective use of nursing time, this reduces costs and provides an improved service to people in hospital and in the community. Armed with a dedicated and enthusiastic team, true commitment and a sense of humour, such spectacular results will continue to be achieved.

21

A smooth start to a new age: helping women cope with the menopause

Patricia A. Black, BA(Hons), RGN, PGDipHV
Health Visitor, Croydon Community Health Trust

Menopause - the last menstrual bleed - is pinpointed retrospectively; it is said to have occurred following 12 months amenorrhoea. The mean age of appearance is 50 years, which seems unaffected by age at menarche, puberty, heredity or weight - although smoking seems to lower it (Wilson, 1985). It is preceded by the climacteric (perimenopause) - two or three years of fluctuating oestradiol levels resulting from erratic ovarian function, which leads to ovarian oestradiol gradually declining until the ovarian follicles fail to develop and the last menstrual bleed occurs.

Hypothalmic-pituitary hyperactivity may occur 10 or 15 years before the menopause, to compensate for the ovarian follicles' increased resistance to maturing and the subsequent decrease in follicular hormone secretion. It may be determined by raised follicle stimulating hormone (FSH) and later raised luteinising hormone (LH) levels, with a precise indication of entry into the menopausal state being by a plasma FSH level of >15 i.u./litre (Chakravati, 1976).

At first sight it may appear that the menopause and the way women cope with it is not an immense social problem - it is, after all, a natural part of the ageing process. However, 30 per cent of a woman's life may be spent post menopausally, so around 10 million women in the UK are post-menopausal. Any problems with the menopause and its sequelae will therefore have an economic and emotional impact on society.

The menopause can be perceived as a positive time for change and self-development (Neugarten, 1980) or as a negative one, involving concepts of 'partial death' or grieving for the loss of ability to reproduce (Deutsch, 1945; Klaus, 1974). Which way individuals perceive it seems to depend mainly on their knowledge of what to expect, cultural myths surrounding the event, particular symptoms experienced, and the value the woman places on herself. If nurses are to materially contribute to women's positive interpretation of the menopause, they need to be fully aware of the physical and psychological effects that may be experienced, why they occur, the myths surrounding the event and the techniques and treatments that may be used to help.

Physical symptoms

Physical symptoms are short- and/or long-term. The most frequently mentioned short-term symptoms are hot flushes, night sweats, headaches, weight gain and vaginal dryness. Although currently there is no clinically demonstrable cause for hot flushes and night sweats, it is suggested they may be due to the cyclic release of noradrenaline in the hypothalamus (Parsons, 1909; Clayden, 1974). It now seems unlikely that they are caused specifically by raised gonadotrophins, because flushes and sweats occur in orchidectomised men, and are indistinguishable from those in women with a low oestrogen level (De Fazio, 1984).

Headaches and weight gain may be due to fluctuating hormonal levels; during ovulation and corpus luteum failure women are likely to be deficient in progesterone but still experience unopposed oestrogen secretion (Brincat, 1988; Table 1) from extraglandular conversion of androgens. This may lead to low blood sugar and fluid retention (hence headache) and consumption of extra food (weight gain). There is also a likely psychological component, since headaches may also be a reaction to stress and weight gain a result of a sedentary lifestyle.

---

1. Hypothalmic-pituitary hyperactivity
(10/15 years before menopause)
Compensates for increased resistance of ovarian follicles and decreased follicular hormone secretion
Evidenced by raised FSH and LH
Pituitary may become exhausted late post menopause

2. Ovulation/corpus luteum failure
Generally more frequent as menopause approaches
Anovulatory cycles or shortened luteal phase
Deficient progesterone and continued unopposed oestrogen secretion
Causes dysfunctional uterine bleeding, endometrial carcinoma

3. Ovarian follicular failure
Failure of follicular development causes reduced oestradiol secretion and cessation of menses
Ovarian stroma remains active; with adrenal cortex, produces androst-enedione and testosterone
Oestrone produced by extra-glandular conversion of androgens is main post-menopausal oestrogen - only 10-14% of post-menopausal women are oestrogen deficient.

Table 1. Endocrine changes in climacteric (Brincat and Studd, 1988).

Vaginal dryness and urinary frequency result from a lack of oestrogen. The mucosal lining of the vagina and urethra have the greatest concentration of oestrogen receptors in the body, and lack of oestrogen leads to the reduction of vaginal secretions. This in turn leads to a reduction in normal vaginal flora, which also reduces vaginal acidity and renders women susceptible to bacterial infection.

Long-term effects include bone loss and increased susceptibility to heart disease. Bone loss (osteoporosis) occurs when new bone formation is outstripped by bone reabsorption; most recent research suggests the decline in the collagenous matrix of bone is the main factor behind this, with reduced mineral content being the second (Brincat and Studd, 1988). Bones become more fragile and likely to fracture, the three most common sites being wrist (Colles fracture), hip (femoral neck) and the vertebral body.

Cardiovascular disease (CVD) includes myocardial infarction, angina and cerebral vascular accident. Premenopausally, ovarian oestrogens seem to offer protection through lipoprotein metabolism. High density lipoproteins (HDL) appear to be cardioprotective, while low density lipoproteins (LDL) are precursive to CVD if normal limits are exceeded; in premenopausal women LDLs are low and HDLs are high compared to those in men. By 70 years, incidence of CVD is equal in men and women.

Psychological symptoms

The most common psychological symptoms cited are depression, irritability, lethargy, forgetfulness and loss of libido. Although there is currently no clear clinical link with menopause and mood stage, Magos (1986) suggests sudden, severe changes in hormone concentration, rather than low levels of oestrogens *per se*, lead to some women becoming vulnerable to low mood. This is supported by the fact that mid-life depression peaks a few years before menopause.

Menorrhagia may lead to anaemia which would add to fatigue and lethargy, while irritability and forgetfulness may be due to disrupted sleep caused by night sweats. Loss of libido may be partly due to vaginal dryness leading to dyspareunia, and also to the exhaustion, induced by continuously broken sleep. These effects may also be experienced because the woman expects to experience them.

Techniques and treatments

The most commonly reported myths about the menopause are that it signals the end of a satisfying sex life, mental breakdown will occur (preceded by irritability etc.), the woman's value to society is at an end, and all these changes will be accompanied by declining health and general disintegration. Nurses can employ a number of techniques and treatments to help women who hold negative beliefs, and who may be experiencing adverse menopausal effects.

One of the worst things about the menopause is the lack of knowledge about what to expect (La Rocco, 1980). The most obvious techniques to counteract this is to educate women about the processes involved. Language must be adapted to suit each client, but the nurse should have detailed awareness of the process.

Briefly, the ovarian (Graafian) follicles begin to fail to ripen, and in an effort to obtain a response, more gonadotrophin is released, shown by increased FSH and LH levels. As the follicles do not develop, plasma oestradiol levels fall, until finally menstruation stops. Levels of FSH and LH peak one to three years post menopause, then begin to tail off. The main oestrogen in postmenopausal women is oestrone, produced by extraglandular conversion of androgens (Table 1). By explaining clearly what happens during the menopause, nurses can do much to reassure women that their symptoms are real, and not in their imagination.

Psychological problems can be discussed, and the possibility raised that other factors may also be playing a part. A woman may, for example, be coping with elderly parents, adolescent children, career, home, financial and social stressors, besides having a partner who may be undergoing his own mid-life crisis and project some of his frustration onto an easily available source. These stressors are not insurmountable, but they may appear so if accepted as a chunk rather than broken down into manageable portions. Counselling techniques involving a systematic approach to problem solving may be most helpful (Dixon and Glover, 1984; Table 2). Other mechanisms that relieve symptoms basically fall into hormonal and non-hormonal categories.

Stage 1.	Problem definition
Stage 2.	Goal selection
Stage 3.	Strategy selection
Stage 4.	Implementation of strategy
Stage 5.	Evaluation

Table 2. A `systematic approach to problem solving (Dixon and Glover, 1984).

Hormonal mechanisms

Hormonal therapy is aimed at relieving both short-and long-term problems. Oestrogen and progestrogen (synthetic progesterone) are given to complement each other; unopposed oestrogen will cause endomentrial hyperplasia which may lead to cancer of the endometrium, but if progestrogen is given for 13 days of each month, this risk no longer exists (Studd and Magos, 1988). Natural oestrogen is used in hormone replacement therapy (HRT) because synthetic oestrogen is not down-graded by the enzymes that act on natural oestrogen, and this leads to metabolic change and increased tendency for the blood to clot. Synthetic oestrogens also have enhanced hepatic potency. Hormones are delivered in tablets, gels, transdermal patches, vaginal creams and implants.

Oral oestrogen　Due to the 'first pass' effect on the liver (Table 3), these must be given at a higher dose relative to the other methods of delivery. They should give relief from most physical effects, but can only develop bone mass if combined with calsitonin (anti-reabsorptive hormone), given in the form of two injections a week (Meschia, 1988). They should, however, help stop further loss of existing bone.

Gels and transdermal patches Gel is applied daily to the skin, and although sticky, it dries quickly. It is probably most acceptable in transdermal patches, worn for 72 hours twice weekly. Skin irritation may be experienced, and the site should be changed frequently to prevent this.

Vaginal creams These contain conjugated oestrogen, and are effective in reducing the effects of vaginal atrophy, but the rate of absorption depends on the medium in which the oestrogen is delivered as well as on the vascularity of the vagina - the greater the vascularity the greater the absorption. It was formerly believed that vaginal creams only had a local effect, but daily application of 1.25mg produces the same plasma level of oestradiol and oestrone as 1.25mg of oral oestrogen (Whitehead, 1978).

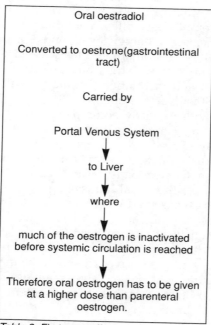

Table 3. First pass effect.

Implants These must be changed twice yearly and give peak delivery of oestradiol at two to three months. Adverse effects of the perimenopause are relieved and increased bone mass can be seen after six months.

Not all women wish to contemplate HRT, and for some it may be contraindicated, such as those who have or have had an oestrogen dependent tumour, liver disease, or sickle cell anaemia. Non-hormonal mechanisms can be offered as an alternative.

Non-hormonal mechanisms
Unlike HRT, which is aimed at relieving all adverse effects simultaneously, non-hormonal methods are directed at relieving individual symptoms. Hot flushes may be controlled by biofeedback training and drug therapy. Biofeedback requires a high level of motivation in both client and nurse, since it involves the client gaining control over an autonomic reaction (the hot flush) which is demonstrated by visual or auditory means. It may take many sessions to learn.

Drug therapy includes clonidine, which blocks the cyclic release of noradrenaline in the hypothalamus (Claydon, 1974); β–blockers such as propranolol, and ethamsylate (used to treat menorrhagia). Tranquillisers seem to have little effect on hot flushes, and add to the lethargy that may already be a subject of complaint.

By controlling vasomotor instability, a good night's sleep is promoted with a subsequent increase in energy levels, and a probable reduction in tiredness and irritability. A woman who feels rested will be in a better position to cope with excessive stress and anxiety. Additional regular practice of relaxation and meditation techniques will further improve her ability to cope with adverse situations.

Vaginal dryness, with its likely accompaniment of dyspareunia and loss of libido, may be helped by the use of a simple water-based lubricant (eg, KY Jelly). This often resolves any loss of libido, but women with psychological disinclination to continue the sexual component of relationships may use the menopause as an excuse. In such cases, clients may need referral for psychosexual counselling.

Consistent aerobic exercise and weight training to increase bone mass before the menopause lessens the risk of later osteoporosis. Diet is also important - postmenopausal women need to ingest at least 50 per cent more calcium than they did premenopausally to remain in calcium balance. When dietary advice is given, it should be mentioned that high levels of fibre in the diet will prevent absorption of most of the calcium ingested; and contrary to popular belief, high protein diets may increase bone loss because the breakdown of protein leads to increased calcium excretion by the kidneys. High intake of caffeine and alcohol, and cigarette smoking also increase the rate of bone loss.

The aetiology of CVD is multifactoral, so other preventive influences appear as helpful as oestrogen replacement. For example, dietary advice (as above) should be given but with the additional suggestion that excessive saturated fats and salt are avoided. Other high risk factors such as lack of exercise, smoking and high levels of stress are all relevant (Haines, 1985). It would be unwise to concentrate on one preventive measure when there are other more obvious causative agents.

A natural event

The menopause is a natural event which may bring with it undesirable consequences. While not denying this 'naturalness' and certainly not regarding it as a disease, we should be able to offer a service that helps women identify their best methods of coping. These may entail medical intervention, counselling or both, but it is up to us to present the menopause as a chance to develop personal potential - so that women may see it as a positive event in their lives.

References

Brincat, M. and Studd, J.W.W. (1988) Menopause - a multisystem disease: In: Stanton, S.L. (Ed.) The Elderly. *Bailliere's Clinical Obstetrics and Gynaecology*, **2**, 290.

Brincat, M., Studd, J.W.W. Stanton, S.L. (Ed.) (1988) Skin and the menopause. *The Menopause*, **8**, 85-101.

Chakravati, S. *et al* (1976) Hormonal profiles after the menopause. *British Medical Journal*, **2**, 784-86.

Claydon, J.R., Bell, J.W., Pollard, P. (1974) Menopausal flushing; double blind trial of a non-normal preparation. *British Medical Journal*, **1**, 409-12.

De Fazio, J. *et al* (1984) Direct action of androgens on hot flushes in a human male, *Maturitas*, 6.

Deutsch, H. (1945) The Psychology of Women. Grune and Stratton, New York.

Dixon, D.N. and Glover, J.A. (1984) Counselling; a Problem Solving Approach. Wiley, New York.

Haines, A.P. (1985) Catching up the Europeans in preventing heart disease. *British Medical Journal*, **291**, 1, 10-13.

Klaus, H. (1974) The menopause in gynaecology: a focus for teaching the comprehensive care of women. *Journal of Medical Education*, **49**, 12, 1186-89.

La Rocco, S.A. and Polit, D.F. (1980) Women's knowledge about the menopause. *Nursing Research*, **29**, 1, 10-13.

Magos, A.L. *et al* (1986) The effects of norechisterone in postmenopausal women on eostrogen replacement therapy: a model for the premenstrual syndrome. *British Journal of Obstetrice and Gynaecology*, **93**, 1290-96.

Magos, A.L. *et al* (1985) Amenorrhoea and endometrial atrophy with continuous oral oestrogen and progestogen therapy in postmenopausal women. *Obstetrics and Gynaecology*, **65**, 496-99.

Neugarten, B. (1980) Middle Age and Aging: a reader in social psychology. University of Chicargo Press, Chicago.

Parsons, A. (1989) Treating the menopausal patient (non-normal therapy) In: The Menopause - a guide for doctors. Scnering Healthcare Ltd, UK.

Studd, J.W.W. and Magos, A. (1988) Oestrogen therapy and endometrial pathology. *The Menopause*, **18**, 197-212.

Weissman, M. (1979) The myth of envolut-ional melancholia. *JAMA*, **242**, 8, 742-44.

Wilson, P.W.F.; Garrison, H.J., Custelli, W.O. (1985) Postmenopausal estrogen use, cigarette smoking and cardio-vascular morbidity in women over 59. *New England Journal of Medicine*, **313**, 1038.

22

A natural setting for personal advice: setting up a GP practice family planning clinic

Val Pretlove, BA (Hons), RGN, RHV, FP Cert
Nurse and Clerical Support Manager for Family Planning, West Berkshire HA; Chair of RCN Family Planning Forum

The increase in family planning consultations currently occurring in GP surgeries, means that practice nurses are inevitably becoming involved in this area of care. Practice nurses are therefore in an ideal position to influence the development of quality family planning services within GP practices. This chapter suggests ways of setting up a family planning clinic, highlighting some of the problems that may be encountered and offering some solutions.

A full service
Family planning is about more than just contraception. It deals with the reproductive health of both men and women, encompasses the whole field of sexuality and fertility and provides excellent opportunities for health screening and health promotion. It deals with an intimate and private area of people's lives and, consequently, requires a high level of sensitivity and expertise, which nurses are often well able to provide.

A family planning service should offer (RCN, 1989):

- **advice and information** on the whole range of contraceptive methods currently available;

- **health screening** eg, breast examination, cervical cytology, testicular examination, blood pressure and weight taking, urinalysis and blood testing for rubella and sickle cell status;

- **health promotion** eg, advice on preconceptual care, smoking, diet, risks of sexually transmitted infections, safer sex and drug or alcohol abuse;

- **specific counselling** for problems associated with unplanned or unwanted pregnancy, subfertility, premenstrual syndrome, menopause and psychosexual problems. In some cases, referral to specialist agencies may be necessary.

Although many family planning consultations are dealt with during normal surgeries, as and when they arise, there are considerable advantages in setting up designated sessions. These allow appropriately trained staff to be involved, provide adequate time for specific needs and assure clients that a specialist service is being offered. An additional advantage is that such sessions can be used to train doctors and nurses.

Essential prerequisites

Definition   A team decision must be made about exactly which services will be offered and by whom, and it is advantageous to have this written down. The clinic may offer a limited contraceptive service, with only pills and diaphragms being made available, or may include the whole range of methods, with the fitting of IUDs, the provision of injectables, emergency contraception and, in some cases, the distribution of condoms. Some practices may offer a more comprehensive service including the teaching of natural family planning and giving psychosexual counselling.

Whatever the level of the service, it should be well advertised in the practice leaflet and the waiting room, so clients know what they can ask for, and it is helpful for reception staff to know exactly what is available.

Training   Before becoming involved in any family planning care, nurses should have successfully completed a recognised basic training course (UKCC, 1984). Currently, these are English and Welsh National Board Course 901, Scottish National Board Family Planning Course or Northern Ireland National Board Family Planning Nurse Course.

The nurse's role

Family planning training courses train nurses to develop their listening, counselling and interpersonal skills, and, together with the sound contraceptive knowledge base they will have acquired, enable them to help clients make their own informed decisions. Teaching clients how to use the chosen contraceptive method is also learned on the course, and plays an important part in encouraging compliance and successful use of the method - many contraceptive failures can be attributed to poor understanding of how to use the method. Having established a good rapport and by being comfortable in the area of sexuality, the nurse may enable clients to express anxieties or raise queries which may seem trivial or embarrassing, but which can cause great distress. Often information or reassurance is all that is required, but nurses may recognise a more serious problem which will need referral for specialist help.

As nurses cannot prescribe, the GP will need to undertake this, and may also wish to examine clients or to take part in the initial consultation. Either the GP or the nurse, or both, may be involved in follow-up visits or screening. In situations where abnormalities or problems present or where specialist advice is needed, it is important a GP is available for consultation. Family planning nurses develop their skills with experience and, at first, may feel tentative and need a clearly defined role. As they develop their expertise, their role will almost certainly change and grow (UKCC, 1984).

Training At the end of the basic family planning course, nurses will be competent to:

- teach the use of diaphragms, but may need more experience before being able to fit them;
- teach women breast self-examination, but not to examine breasts;
- take a cervical smear, but not to do a pelvic-bimanual examination;
- discuss natural family planning but not to teach it in detail.

Both the nurse and the practice need to be aware of these points, and to make appropriate arrangements. Relevant training courses which can meet any outstanding needs are:

- **Marie Curie Breast and Cervical Screening Course** Further information from Marie Curie Memorial Foundation, 28 Belgrave Square, London SW1X 8QG.

- **Teaching Natural Family Planning** Further information from National Association of NFP teachers, Birmingham Maternity Hospital, Edgbaston, Birmingham B15 2TG.

- **ENB Course A08** Clinical nurse specialist in family planning course for nurses with course 901 qualification and experience. Further information from ENB, Tottenham Court Road, London, W1P OHA.

Professional isolation This may be overcome by joining either the Royal College of Nursing Family Planning Forum or the National Association of Family Planning Nurses (NAFPN). Both organisations offer professional support, updating and contact with colleagues, as well as arrangements for insurance. Another useful contact is the local district health authority (DHA) clinic. Links between the two services have proved beneficial to both and some practice nurses find it useful to work on the clinic relief service.

Equipment A range of equipment is required for the successful running of a family planning clinic. Essential items include:

- a comfortable consulting room with a screened area with a couch;
- vaginal examination and swab and smear taking equipment;
- instruments for fitting and checking IUDs if required;

- facilities for sterilising instruments, etc (DoH, 1988; BMA, 1989; Thomlinson, 1991; Tattam, 1991);

- set of caps/diaphragms*;

- samples of all contraceptives for demonstration and teaching purposes*;

- information leaflets*;

- teaching aids such as charts, models, diagrams and leaflets*;

(*These may be purchased by the practice or are often available from pharmaceutical companies.) The Family Planning Association provide an excellent set of methods leaflets. These can be handed to clients, and clearly explain the various contraceptive methods and how they work.

Availability of condoms These are available free in all DHA clinics, but are neither prescribable nor usually available in GP surgeries, and this can cause problems when condoms are either the preferred method of contraception or would be advisable in preventing spread of infection.

Some practices are willing to buy condoms, but the majority are not. Funding can be obtained from some health authorities for this by applying for a grant from the Aids budget holder. Information about this can be found in DoH Circulars EL(90)P/30 and EL(90)MB114. If condoms are to be made available in the practice, it is important clients are taught how to use them properly.

Client difficulties There are problems in providing a service which is flexible and accessible enough to be used by all who need it. Practice nurses need to be aware of the special needs of adolescents and of people with physical or mental disabilities, those who are poorly motivated or from ethnic minorities. Some clients need a great deal of persuasion to take up healthcare, and may find a family planning nurse less threatening than a doctor.

Although clearly defined clinic times may be available, family planning consultation can and should be possible at other times outside these, and special arrangements, including home visits, may need to be made. Young people may fear their confidentiality is at risk if they consult their family doctor, and may find it easier to discuss family planning with a practice nurse instead. DHA young people's advisory services may be more appropriate, however, in such cases and practice nurses should be able to give younger clients information about them. Some people prefer to see a female doctor, but if one is not available in the surgery, the DHA clinic may be a better choice for them.

Having worked in a GP surgery in Reading for 15 years as a family planning nurse, as my expertise has developed, I have found it a fulfilling and rewarding experience. Family planning clinics offer people the opportunity to discuss their contraceptive and related healthcare needs in a relaxed environment which is specifically catered to their needs. Practice nurses are often the ideal professional to offer detailed information to clients on such personal issues as family planning, and can do so in a local setting, offering clients convenience and flexibility.

References
British Medical Association (1989) A Code of Practice for Sterilisation of Instruments and Control of Cross Infection. BMA, London.
DoH (1988) Decontamination of Instruments and Appliances used in the Vagina. EL(88)(MB)/210. HMSO, London.
Royal College of Nursing (1989) Standards of Care: Family Planning Nursing. RCN, London.
Tattam, A. (1991) Unhygienic practices. *Nursing Times,* **87,** 16, 20.
Thomlinson, D. (1991)Everything starts with a risk rate. *Professional Nurse,* **6,** 7, 386-93.
United Kingdom Central Council (1984) Code of Professional Conduct for the Nurse, Midwife and Health Visitor. UKCC, London.

Bibliography
DoH (1990) Handbook of Contraceptive Practice. HMSO, London.
    Current information re contraceptive methods.
Guillebaud, J. (1989) Contraception: Your Questions Answered. Churchill Livingstone, Edinburgh.
    Good contraceptive reference book for health professionals. Deals with problem solving in question and answer form.
Loudon, N.C. (1990) Handbook of Family Planning. Churchill Livingstone, London.
    Good basic textbook for doctors and nurses in family planning practice. It gives background to contraceptive services and clinical procedures.
RCN/Durex (1991) Family Planning Manual for Nurses. RCN/Durex, London.
    A newly published procedure book for nurses giving contraceptive care.
The British Journal of Family Planning, produced by the National Association of Family Planning Doctors, and *Family Planning Today* by the Family Planning Association, provides useful information for healthcare professionals.

Useful addresses
UKCC, 23 Portland Place, London, W1N 3AF.

Family Planning Association, 27/35 Mortimer Street, London W1N 7RJ.

RCN, 20 Cavendish Square, London W1M OAB.

NAFPN, Enterprise House, 4 Chipstead Station Parade, Chipstead, Surrey.

National Association of Family Planning Doctors, 27 Sussex Place, Regents Park, London NW1 4RG.

23

Let them do it for themselves: teaching asthma self-management to children

Sue Richards, SRN, DipHRC, PNT, CertHEd, DipAC
Practice Sister/Regional Asthma Trainer, Penzance, Cornwall

The prevalence of childhood asthma is estimated to be around 11 per cent in the UK (Cochrane and Rees, 1989), making it the most common disease of childhood (Barnes, 1988). It is also the only treatable condition that is increasing in both prevalence and severity in western Europe (Burney, 1986). A number of factors have been suggested as causing this increase, such as increased pollution and increased succeptibility to allergens, but whatever the cause, there is no doubt that nurses are seeing growing numbers of asthmatic children. Successful management of their asthma will not only allow these children to live normal lifestyles, but will also help reduce the number of preventable deaths from asthma – it is estimated that of the approximately 2,000 deaths from asthma each year in the UK, 80-90 per cent are preventable (Barnes, 1988) – and reduce the cost to the NHS.

Too often, the education about management of young children's asthma is aimed at the parent, and fails to actively involve the child. It is important that we learn to educate children about their condition, particularly with recent developments in management and treatment. Peak flow monitors, the simplest and cheapest form of asthma measurement, became available on prescription in 1990, allowing asthma sufferers to objectively monitor their condition, assess the effectiveness of treatment and predict attacks (Andrews, 1991). If the information gained from peak flow monitors is to be used to control asthma, it is important that sufferers themselves learn to use the meters and act upon their results.

Delivery devices

It is vital that children are given the right delivery devices, and this requires assessment of their cognitive skills, as well as their lifestyle and personality. When children start school, it is vital that they can confidently self-administer medication. Few teachers know enough about asthma and its management to take on responsibility for administering a child's treatment, and those who do have the knowledge are unlikely to have the time. A survey of 122 primary school teachers undertaken by the National Asthma Campaign (NAC) in 1990 found that only 5 per cent felt they knew enough about asthma, yet 69 per cent had taught children with asthma. The NAC has responded to the survey by launching a School Asthma Policy and information pack, which schools can adapt to suit their needs. The pack also contains advice in dealing with asthma attacks.

With the situation as it stands currently in schools, it is important that children are taught as early as possible to self-administer treatment. If a parent has taken all this responsibility previously, the need to learn self-administration before starting school can become an additional source of anxiety to that caused by the idea of school itself, and may even precipitate the child's asthma.

Large spacer devices may not be acceptable for schoolchildren, as they are bulky to carry around and all too noticeable for schoolmates, marking the child out as 'different'. For children unable to use a metered dose inhaler (MDI), dry powder devices may be suitable alternatives. The experienced asthma nurse has an important role in closely monitoring children in such transitional periods to ensure the condition is well managed and that the child adjusts as smoothly as possible.

It is important that nurses involved in asthma care have had sufficient training in the disease aetiology and pathology, and its management if they are to be able to assess individuals competently, recommend appropriate devices and have a continuous role in asthma management within the surgery. Recognised asthma training for nurses consists of a distance learning package from the Asthma Training Centre, two day courses at their headquarters in Stratford-upon-Avon, and the ATC/RCGP Diploma in Asthma Care.

Patient education

Patient education is the cornerstone of asthma management, and requires time and patience to ensure that the correct message is being conveyed, and at the appropriate level. This is particularly true in the case of young children if they are to understand their disease and how to manage it. This chapter is concerned with the communication between nurse and patient, and so will not discuss the medical checks and device assessment within an asthma consultation, but will look at the consultation with regard to interpersonal and communication skills.

There are a number of factors nurses need to be aware of in carrying out asthma consultations with young children and their parents. The question of who sits closest to or next to the nurse can say a lot to both child and parent. If the parent is closest, and the child perhaps playing elsewhere in the room, or sitting away from the nurse, this can suggest that the asthma is the parent's responsibility, and that the child does not have an important part to play in the consultation.

Parents often automatically take the leading role in consultations, with the best of intentions, but can usually be persuaded to let their child speak by gently asking them to wait until the child has finished. The same may be true in discussing symptoms – it is often easier in the short term to ask the parent how the child has been, but in the long term this is counterproductive. Even children as young as three or four years should be able to talk a little about how they feel about their asthma and its effect on their playing and socialising. Parents may also try to answer for their children, but again, gently redirecting the question at the child with a question such as 'is that right?' will usually be enough to tell parents that the child is the important person in the consultation. If this fails, it may be necessary to ask the parent if he or she can leave the consulting room for a few minutes. If children are to learn to take control of their own asthma as early as possible, it is vital that all dealings with healthcare professionals tell them that they are important, and give them the confidence to manage their own condition.

Older children

Older children tend to either go along the line of least resistance and simply agree with whatever their parents say, or to argue with everything their parents say. This can obviously cause untold problems in the consultation, but it usually only takes a few minor adjustments to ensure a more meaningful consultation.

Sitting the child nearest to the nurse makes them the focus of the attention, to allows them to feel important to the nurse. It also gives them 'permission' and therefore confidence to speak out and puts value on their needs, feelings, hopes and fears.

The child should be asked how he or she is feeling, whether devices are proving manageable, and to talk about any management problems that may have occurred since the last consultation. The child should be allowed to answer in his or her own words, and given plenty of time to do so. Specific questions, relating to playtime, sports activities, sleeping and other activities will help gain a rounded picture of the child's condition and management, and make them realise they can talk about problems in any area of their life. After the child has had chance to speak, parents should get their turn. They will have much to offer the consultation, and will have their own legitimate worries and questions to attend to, and ensuring they get a chance to speak will avoid antagonism and disagreement.

Structuring the consultation in this way allows everyone concerned to have their say in a useful and meaningful way. Everyone involved should feel they have been listened to, and had their viewpoint acknowledged. If the nurse explains why the consultation is conducted in this way beforehand, 'showdowns' with offended parents, who may not be used to having their child listened to before themselves should be avoided. With time, however, both children and parents will become accustomed to this method of consultation, and easier relationships will develop between child, parent and nurse.

Even very young children are capable of learning about the kinds of things that affect their asthma, and what happens during an attack. Colland (1991) found that children aged eight to 13 responded better to behaviour therapy and training on asthma which came directly from the doctor/nurse than from their parents. Training from the healthcare professionals also resulted in improved management of symptoms and better inhalation technique. If the parents were trained to give the advice, no improvement was found in management, anxiety or any other of the variables studied.

If children with asthma are to grow up managing their asthma in as independent a way as possible, it is vital that asthma nurses support them in gaining this independence. In doing this, nurses must endeavour not to alienate parents, by making it clear that they are still important, and that self-management of asthma is preferable for all concerned.

References
Andrew, L. (1991) Prevention in practice: new developments in asthma management. *Professional Nurse*, **6**, 8, 476-81.
Barnes, G. (1988) Asthma: latest developments in care. *Professional Nurse*, **3**, 9, 364-68.
Burney, P.J.G. (1986) Asthma mortality in England and Wales: evidence for a further increase, 1974-84. *Lancet*, **2**, 8502, 323-26.
Cochrane, G.M. and Rees, P.J. (1989) A Colour Atlas of Asthma. Wolfe, London.
Colland, V. (1990) Study of child asthmatics management and training. *Doctor*, September.

Bibliography
Holmes, B. (1990) Guidelines to asthma care. *Mims*, November.
   This article looks at the guidelines of the British Thoratic Society on asthma management.
Pearson, R. (1990) Asthma Management in Primary Care. Radcliffe Medical Press.
   Up-to-date information on practical asthma management.

Useful address
National Asthma Campaign, 300 Upper Street, London N1 2XX. Tel: 071-226 2260

24

Diabetes: is self-help the answer?

Paul E. Jennings, DM, MRCP
Consultant Physician, York District Hospital

Diabetes mellitus is a chronic disorder and a major health problem affecting two per cent of the population. The condition needs to be fully understood by the patient if good metabolic control is to be achieved. At diagnosis there are major difficulties in educating the patient and relatives about the diabetic life. The major points that need to be covered include:

- An explanation as to what diabetes mellitus is.

- How to control diabetes to enable them to enjoy their life.

- What food should/can they eat?

- What tablets/insulin should they take, including when and how?

- How to recognise and treat hypo- and hyperglycaemic episodes.

- How to monitor their diabetic control.

- Discussion of the later complications of diabetes: nephropathy, neuropathy, retinopathy, and peripheral vascular disease.

Good diabetic control matters

As well as having this initial information, people with diabetes need motivation to maintain good metabolic control (maintaining blood glucose levels between 4-7m mol/l), often at the expense of more frequent hypoglycaemia. Behind this is the increasing awareness that good metabolic control matters as it may prevent some of the later complications of diabetes.

The later complications of diabetes, such as neuropathy, nephropathy, retinopathy and advanced atherosclerosis, account for most of the increased mortality and morbidity of diabetes. It is now generally accepted that the development of these complications is positively associated with the duration of diabetes and poor long-term diabetic control. It has been known for some time that patients with chronic complications have had poorer metabolic control than patients without complications (Pirart, 1978). Only recently, however, have studies started to show that improving metabolic control can prevent the progression of complications (Nyberg, Blohme and Norden, 1987). These studies, based mainly on insulin-dependent patients, have used improved insulin delivery techniques and their main conclusions are applicable to all diabetics, insulin and non-insulin dependent patients alike. The challenge is to improve diabetic control in all patients and thereby prevent a deterioration in quality and length of life. Improvements in insulins and their delivery systems, new oral hypoglycaemic agents, improved dietary practices and better methods of monitoring such as blood glucose monitoring are the improved tools now available to the diabetologist to do this.

The need to educate

Patients' understanding of diabetes and how to control it remain fundamental to treatment, so it is generally accepted that benefits are also obtained from improving a patient's knowledge of diabetes and its treatment (Assal, Muhlhauser, Permet et al, 1985). This is manifest in the increasing development of diabetes educational programmes and the appointment of specialist education nurses, diabetic liaison nurses and diabetic health visitors. The adoption of such modern management techniques can improve diabetic control generally (Barnett, 1985), yet it remains to be shown if this will also prevent the development of complications. The major prerequisite for good metabolic control is the active participation in their own treatment by knowledgeable, committed patients. The aim is for patients to be able to treat themselves safely, maintaining blood sugars as close to the non-diabetic range as possible, and to avoid complications. This day-to-day self-management requires an educated and motivated person if it is to be done consistently and successfully.

Education programmes

One group of highly motivated diabetic patients who have benefitted from educational programmes are pregnant women. In this case the goal is clear, as good control significantly reduces perinatal morbidity and mortality. The pregnant woman will usually perform home blood glucose tests three or four times a day and keep accurately to diet and insulin regimens in the expectation of a healthy baby. The outcome is quite clear for these women and the duration is nine months, but most diabetic patients must be motivated to improve their control for life in the hope that it may reduce the chances of developing renal failure, heart disease or blindness. It has been hoped that improved education of patients will improve their motivation to achieve better control.

Unfortunately, attempts to improve control through formal education programmes have been disappointing. The ideal situation is one-to-one instruction of the patient by an education nurse or clinic doctor since patients differ in the amount of educational information they initially possess. Although this type of instruction is essential at diagnosis, individualised instruction during follow-up is difficult to achieve given the numbers of patients attending clinics, the lack of available clinic space, the need for long-term follow-up and financial constraints. For this reason, a number of different types of group educational programmes have been studied and reported.

Group education Unfortunately, the differing numbers and ages of the patients studied and the forms of evaluation used makes comparisons difficult. Most group studies lack assessment of diabetes knowledge or control, and rely on descriptive evaluation, often concentrating on psychological parameters. One of the earliest large studies described meetings held weekly for one year by a psychologist or physician (Pelser, Groen, Stuyling de Lange et al, 1979). This study of self-selected diabetic patients, including non-insulin dependent diabetics, identified several psychosocial factors that seemed to have an adverse effect on diabetic control. Unfortunately, the study did not formally assess whether the group meetings were beneficial.

An attempt to evaluate psychological and diabetic improvement was made through a study of young inner-city black women (Warren-Boulton, Anderson, Schwartz et al, 1981). Five patients were admitted to the hospital for five days for stabilisation and then studied monthly for 18 months. An improvement in diabetic control was reported, although, because of lack of controls and the small number of subjects, it was not possible to determine which aspect of the education programme was important.

In a review of group therapy in the treatment of diabetes, a study of 14 patients has been reported (Tattersall, McCullock and Aveline, 1981). These were insulin dependent patients attending weekly group meetings. Ten showed a general improvement in their psychological wellbeing, although this was not statistically significant compared with control groups. Diabetic control, however, was unchanged after the group therapy.

Recently, a larger, more ambitious programme has been reported (Bloomgarden, Karmally, Metzger et al, 1987) in which 165 insulin-treated diabetic patients undertook an education programme and were compared with 180 control patients. The education group was invited to attend nine education studies and 56 per cent attended at least seven. Knowledge of diabetes improved in the education group but there was no improvement in diabetic control, patient weight or the use of medical care. The study concluded that "patient education may not be an efficacious therapeutic intervention in most adults with insulin-treated diabetes mellitus".

Self-help groups Although other studies have produced similar disappointing conclusions, some have shown benefits from educational programmes. Most of the successful studies, however, such as that of

Muhlhauser, Jorgens, Berger et al, (1983) have used inpatient education courses. This limits the feasibility of such programmes at present due to financial constraints, so a different approach to the problem of providing educational information and motivation has been tried with success in an inner city area of Birmingham (Jennings, Morgan and Barnett, 1987). This studied the effects of a self-help group for diabetic patients and their relatives. The idea was to test whether information could be usefully and inexpensively shared among diabetic patients if they were in an informal environment. Most, if not all, patients are given some formal education at the diagnosis of their condition and they may also gain further information from a variety of other sources, both within the diabetic clinic and outside, from sources such as books, television and relatives. This information could be utilised and shared with other diabetics.

Self-help group organisation and impact
The study was confined to insulin-dependent diabetics and included a control group who were seen routinely in the diabetic clinic. All those studied were well motivated and were assigned randomly to the self-help group or standard clinic follow-up. The self-help group and their relatives were invited to attend monthly evening meetings away from the hospital. The format was informal, with tea, coffee and biscuits being served throughout the meeting. There was no structured educational input. Topics were chosen by the patients and discussed among themselves. Reducing the total group size was achieved after a general group discussion in which several topics of general (diabetic) interest were proposed; once several topics had been suggested the group divided into smaller groups, each one supported by a member of the diabetic clinic staff. Mixing of age and duration of diabetes was encouraged in the smaller groups, and participants were free to enter as many of the groups during the session as they wished.

The clinic staff present were regular medical and nursing clinic staff and familiar to the patients. They were instructed to provide factual information only upon request, to correct any misconceptions and to involve all members of the group in the discussions to aid the transfer of ideas among the participants. The meetings lasted 60 to 90 minutes and were held for six months. The effect of the meeting was assessed by a questionnaire of diabetic knowledge completed before and after the six-month study period and comparison of glycosylated haemoglobin results (HbA$_1$). Measurement of HbA gives a picture of long-term diabetic control (over the four to six weeks prior to measurement). The questionnaire covered equally six main areas of knowledge: factors influencing control; manifestation of diabetic complications; insulin administration techniques and measures of diabetic control; carbohydrate allowances; causes of complications; and diet. The groups were well attended; 85 per cent of the patients attended all the meetings.

Diabetic knowledge improved significantly as did diabetic control, HbA_1 falling from 12.4 per cent (standard deviation (SD) 2.9 per cent) to 10.3 per cent (SD 2.5 per cent). This improvement in control was significant when compared with the control group whose HbA fell from 11.6 per cent (SD 2.4 per cent) to 11.8 per cent (SD 2.2 per cent) and was maintained for 12 months after the self-help group finished (Table 1). However, there was no significant correlation between the percentage improvement in knowledge and in the HbA_1.

	Before study	After study	12 months later
Control group	11.6 (SD 2.4)	11.8 (SD 2.2)	10.9 (SD 2.3)
Self help group	12.4 (SD 2.9)	10.0 (SD 2.5)	9.9 (SD 2.3)

All figures show HbA_1 (%)
NB Normal levels of HbA_1 in non-diabetic clients range from 4 to 9%

Table 1. Diabetic control of the two groups.

Several other factors were apparent from a further questionnaire sent to patients three months after the study. Over 85 per cent had found the meetings useful and that their knowledge had improved. Only 35 per cent, however, felt their control to have improved, although the biochemical evidence suggested an improvement.

Subgroups
The number of patients who could be catered for in this group seemed initially too large to be educated effectively. The formation of smaller subgroups, through which the participants and staff circulated freely, quickly established an informal atmosphere. Relatives are poorly catered for in most diabetic clinics yet they are often involved in caring for patients with complications both acute (hypoglycaemia) and chronic (blindness, amputations, etc). By joining in the groups they gained information, confidence and support. This exchange of ideas, views and experiences between patients and relatives during the meetings was felt by all participants to provide the major benefit not possible by more didactic teaching methods. Indeed, the exchange of ideas about diet and exercise may have been responsible for the improvement in diabetic control, as insulin adjustments were not undertaken at these group sessions.

Organising self-help groups
The organisation of these large self-help group meetings is minimal, requiring only a suitably sized venue where an informal atmosphere can be established. As some medical information is required by the participants it is recommended that at least one member of the clinic

staff (nurse or doctor) be present at these groups. The group meeting approach may be inappropriate for newly diagnosed patients, who would benefit more from one-to-one educational methods tailored around individual needs. The advantage of the group approach to diabetic therapy is that it is cheap to run, easy to organise and may be effective in improving knowledge and diabetic control. Its one main disadvantage, and that of all other studies, is the need for patients to be sufficiently motivated to attend the initial meeting.

References

Assal, J.P., Muhlhauser, I., Permet, A. et al, (1985) Patient education as the basis for diabetes care in clinical practice and research. *Diabetologia* **28**, 602–13.

Barnett, A.H. (1985) Diabetic control and the effect of changing a diabetic clinic to modern management. *Diabetic Medicine* **2**, 57–58.

Bloomgarden, Z.T., Karmally, W., Metzer, J. et al (1987) Randomised, controlled trial of diabetic paient education education: Improved knowledge without improved metabolic status. *Diabetes Care*, **10**, 263–72.

Jennings, P.E., Morgan, H.C. and Barnett, A.H. (1987) Improved diabetes control and knowledge during a diabetes self-help group. *Diabetes Education*, **13**, 4, 390–93.

Mulhauser, I., Jorgens, V., Berger, M. et al (1983) Bicentric evaluation of a teaching and treatment programme for type 1 (insulin-dependent programme for type 1 (insulin-dependent) diabetic patients: Improvement of metabolic control and other measures of diabetes care for up to 22 months. *Diabetologia*, **25**, 470–76.

Nyberg G., Blohme, G. and Norden, G. (1987) Impact of metabolic control in progression of clinical diabetic nephropathy. *Diabetologia*, **30**, 82–6.

Pelser, H.E., Groen, J.J., Stuyling de Lange, M.J. et al (1979) Experiences in group discussions with diabetic patients. *Psychother Psychosom*, **32**, 257–69.

Pirart, J. (1978) Diabetis mellitus and its degenerative complications: A prospective study of 4,400 patients observed between 1947–1973. *Diabetes Care*, 168–188: 252–630.

Tattersall, R.B., McCullock, D.K. and Aveline, M. (1981) Group therapy in the treatment of diabetes. *Diabetes Care*, **8**, 180–88.

Warren-Boulton, E., Anderson, B.J., Schwartz, N.L. et al (1981)) A group approach to the management of diabetes in adolescents and young adults. *Diabetes Care*, **4**, 620–23.

Loss and Bereavement

25

What comfort for this grief? Coping with perinatal bereavement

Janet Symes, SRN, BA(Hons), CQSW, BAC (Accred.)
Obstetric/Neonatal Counsellor, University College Hospital, London

It is never easy talking about death, but it is particularly difficult to talk about the death of a baby. The subject has often been held taboo, although society may be becoming more open about this as we come to understand how deeply a baby's death affects the parents.

Improved nutrition, living standards and antenatal care have meant that the perinatal mortality rate has been reduced, but this has meant that parents *expect* babies to survive and so bereavement comes as a greater shock. Healthcare staff may also have high expectations of modern medical care and technology, and may find it hard to cope with the death of a baby in their care.

Perinatal death is the ultimate paradox. Birth is often considered the start of life, so death before and around birth confuses life and death together. A sense of unreality often surrounds the event (Lewis, 1989), and it is this sense of unreality that can make the loss especially hard to come to terms with. This chapter aims to identify ways to make the event real for both parents and staff.

Understanding the loss

The classifications of pregnancy loss are confusing and can be contradictory. Perinatal is the term used to cover the time around birth and for one week afterwards, and usually only refers to live births or births after 28 weeks. However, this chapter will use the term perinatal loss to include ectopic pregnancy, miscarriage, therapeutic termination of pregnancy, stillbirth and neonatal death.

A miscarriage is the spontaneous delivery of the baby before 28 weeks, and is common in early pregnancy, occurring in as many as one in five pregnancies. There is no legal obligation to name, register or bury the baby unless born alive, which can increase the sense of unreality. If a baby is born dead after 28 weeks, this is termed a stillbirth and must be registered and buried or cremated. Until relatively recently, however, these babies were also often whisked away and the burial arranged by the hospital without the parents being involved.

An important point to remember about bereavement is that it is often easy to inadvertently make matters worse - careless talk can hurt. Bereaved parents often remember the exact words used to break the news. They have few memories to cherish, no baby to look forward to, so are very sensitive, and what staff say can be tremendously important. Perinatal bereavement can be one of the hardest areas of healthcare to work in as so many hopes are invested in the new baby. Women may become pregnant for a variety of reasons, not just because they want a child, but also to keep a marriage together; to give another child a brother or sister; to try for a baby of the opposite sex to one(s) already in the family; to prove fertility and functioning of the body; to make up for the loss of someone else - so it can be truly devastating for this baby to die.

Perinatal death is also hard to accept because it is so unexpected, with rarely any warning such as an illness. The mother may come in for a routine antenatal check expecting good news, so bad news will be even more devastating. Parents expect many tests, such as ultrasound scanning, to be routine and often do not realise they are checking for abnormalities. Healthcare staff are, in some sense, responsible for this misunderstanding, perhaps because we do not like to consider the possibility that something may be wrong or are concerned that a forewarning increases anxiety when, of course, all is usually well. Some National Childbirth Trust antenatal groups are now including discussions on perinatal loss to balance the high expectations.

Telling parents
So what can we say to parents, shocked and grieving over the loss of their baby ? There aren't, unfortunately, any magic sentences that make it easy, although I can suggest some that should *never* be said. These include:

"She/he was so young you never really got to know her/him!", "Don't worry, you can always have another.", "At least you have other children.", "It was for the best" (especially if the baby was malformed).

These all discount the importance of the loss to the parents. A midwife was recently heard commenting to some parents in a neonatal unit after one of their triplets had died, "well three would have been an awful lot of work, wouldn't it." By saying this, the midwife was denying the parents their right to grieve because their baby had died. Parents will not forget their baby, but hopefully will adjust to the loss in time. Do not say "I understand how you feel" because you don't - even people who have had a similar experience will respond in their own unique way. It is also inappropriate to talk about one's own experiences. Parents need our support and should not have to worry about staff's problems - this is their time. This does not mean staff should not show their emotions, many parents are comforted by knowing that staff care and can cry too. You can start the sentence with "I'm sorry", even though it may sound trite, it will mean a lot if said with feelings.

Parents always appreciate honesty, and it is best to be frank about what has happened. Try not to use medical jargon, and be particularly careful to avoid the terms 'missed or spontaneous abortion'. Although technically correct, it can be very distressing for parents because they imply an intention to abort. Terms such as 'fetus' or 'products of conception' depersonalise the event and create a barrier between staff and parents. True, parents may cry at the word 'baby', but they are crying inside anyway. Be guided by the words the parents themselves use. Even if their baby was born dead, it was not a stranger to them: there were physical and emotional changes during the pregnancy, plans for names, nurseries etc - parents do not plan which nursery they are going to take their 'product of conception' to. Try also to ascertain a diagnosis as soon as possible. It is not unheard of for mothers, when no fetal heart beat has been heard, to have to wait until their next antenatal visit for an ultrasound scan before a diagnosis is made. Imagine waiting days to find out if your husband or wife was still alive.

When breaking the news of a baby's death, try to tell both the parents together. Obviously, not all fathers are or can be present, and the mother has to be told alone. However, if the father (or another family member) is present, it is not acceptable to tell him first and then make him tell the mother. White *et al* (1984) note the importance of marital support, and a meeting with both parents can be used to give permission for the father to openly grieve, mourn and cry. It may sound odd to say 'give permission' but, in fact, it helps some parents to be told there is nothing shameful about an adult, man or woman, crying. If possible, allow the father to stay with his partner in the hospital.

Reactions

Parents' reactions to being told of their baby's death are unique to them, and none will be textbook cases. It can be useful to bear in mind the phases of mourning - 'shock', 'searching', 'denial', 'anger', and 'resolution' (Parkes, 1972) - but as guidelines only. The initial shock can make it hard for parents to take in much information, and they often only clearly remember the sentence telling them their baby is dead, and forget the explanation which followed. Patience is therefore needed when repeating information later, if required. Guilt is a common reaction, and parents may ceaselessly go over what has happened, trying to see if it could have been prevented. While a certain amount of guilt is a normal part of grieving, excessive self-persecution can hinder parents from coming to terms with their baby's death.

Anger is often directed at hospital staff, and it is sometimes difficult not to become defensive and alienate the parents. Anger is also often directed at the spouse, and can lead to misunderstandings and arguments.

Staff reactions   Healthcare staff must acknowledge the importance of

the loss for the parents - it may be the first major loss they ha
experienced. Although a miscarriage is a relatively routine medic
occurrence, it can be a significant trauma for those involved (Friedma
1989). It can also be very frightening, and women have said they fe
they were going to bleed to death. Healthcare staff also need
acknowledge how they see the loss. The need to give advice ar
prescription for care may stem more from our own need to be able to 'c
something'. Staff may need to question why bedrest for a threatene
miscarriage is recommended - no study shows that complete bedre
significantly decreases the chances of a miscarriage, and it can be ve
difficult to maintain at home, which may increase the mother's feelin
of guilt. We need to be honest with ourselves about for whose benefit v
are suggesting these things. Similarly, are prescriptions for sleepir
tablets or bromocriptine (used to suppress lactation) made because tl
mother requested them or because we cannot bear to witness such gri
and try to hide it away?

Future pregnancies

A three month wait is often advised and felt to be sufficient for paren
before starting their next pregnancy, why is this suggestion mad
Healthcare staff may feel that another baby will help the recovery aft
the death of their first one, but to mourn 'successfully' requires time ar
space (Bourne and Lewis, 1984). Furthermore, if a woman conceiv
three months after her baby's death, and carries to term, her next bat
will be born at the anniversary of the previous baby's death.

Parents may well have complex reactions to their next baby. It w
often be not only a time of joy and probably worry, (especially when tl
baby reaches the age at which the first baby died), but may also evol
feelings of guilt at enjoying this baby, resentment that the first baby
not alive, sadness and possibly confused feelings of a replacement.
subsequent pregnancy will arouse considerable anxiety, and anger ma
well be taken out on staff. Some Stillbirth and Neonatal Death Socie
(SANDS) groups are now encouraging parents to tell the obstetric tea
what happened to their first baby and explain how they feel; continui
of the carers would also help tremendously, so that they are not asked
repeat this numerous times.

Specific difficulties

After an ectopic pregnancy, the mother may be made to feel she shoul
be grateful to be alive. However she has lost not only her baby, but als
possibly a part of herself (her fallopian tube), and her future fertilit
may be affected. It can seem a contradiction to want and grieve for
baby that nearly killed her. Likewise, after a termination for fet
malformation, the contradiction between wanting, and possibl
planning, this baby and the termination is often difficult to come
terms with, and the parents may need permission to grieve - they chos

the termination and yet will be feeling terribly sad (Lloyd and Laurence, 1985). We need to be particularly sensitive, supportive and non-judgemental towards parents who have made this very difficult decision so as not to increase any feelings of guilt and isolation.

Practical care

Healthcare staff also need to be sensitive to differences in race, culture and religion. Many people have strong views about what should be done after a death, but we must not assume that, for example, all Jewish families will want the same care. The best way to ensure parents' wishes are adhered to is to simply ask if there is anything specific they would like done or help with.

To help overcome the sense of unreality at the time of death and to give some memories to hold onto, many hospitals now encourage the parents to see and hold their baby (Cathcart, 1988). This idea needs to be gently introduced to the parents, especially if early in their pregnancy and their wishes must be respected. 'Parents must see their baby' should not become the new dogma.

Photographs of the baby can be taken and ultrasound pictures retrieved to give to the parents to remember him or her by. Other mementoes such as a lock of hair, name band or cot card can be kept, and these are especially important if there are twins or multiple births. Try to have a photograph of the babies together to confirm it was a multiple pregnancy, and to help avoid confusion if one survives. These parents may also need permission to grieve, and should not be made to feel grateful for their surviving infant (Bryan, 1983).

Funeral or memorial

A ceremony, whether legal or private, also helps the mourning process, enabling many parents to feel they have done something for their baby. If the parents wish, staff who were closely involved in the care of the baby also often gain comfort from attending the funeral or memorial service. It is useful to find out what services are available in your hospital and community. Many hospitals now have a bereavement officer who can help parents with these practical arrangements.

No member of staff who is involved with bereaved parents can be unmoved, whatever their training or experience, and staff support groups can be a valuable means of helping staff share with each other their feelings about a bereavement. A working party is also useful to look at how bereavement is dealt with in a hospital. Several books are available on the subject, and study days are a good opportunity to share skills and gain support.

We need to think about and let ourselves feel what the death of a baby, before or after birth, means to us and how it reminds us of losses we have had. It is natural to want to avoid looking at painful issues, yet by facing them straight on we can learn more about ourselves and how to help others better. This increased understanding will help to mitigate feelings of inadequacy, concerns of over-identification, fear of or vulnerability to the pain and worry of being overwhelmed by the grief. If we can share our feelings of sadness, anger and a sense of failure or futility with colleagues, we can then support each other, and so be more able to help parents.

References
Bourne, S. and Lewis, E. (1984) Pregnancy after stillbirth or neonatal death. *Lancet*, **1**, 31-33.

Bryan, E.M. (1983) The loss of a twin. *Maternal and Child Health*, May, 201-6.

Cathcart, F. (1988) Seeing the body after death. *British Medical Journal*, **297**, 997-98.

Friedman, T. (1989) Women's experiences of general practitioner management of miscarriage. *J. R. Coll. GPs*, **39**, 456-58.

Lloyd, J. and Laurence, K.M. (1985) Sequelae and support after termination of pregnancy for fetal malformation. *British Medical Journal*, **290**, 907-9.

Parkes, C.M. (1972) Bereavement. Studies of Grief in Adult Life. Tavistock, London.

White, M.P., Reynolds, B., Evans, T.J. (1984) Handling of death in special care nurseries and parental grief. *British Medical Journal*, **289**, 167-9.

Self-help/support groups
Still Birth and Neonatal Death Society (SANDS),
28 Portland Place, London, W1N 4DE. Tel: 071-436 5881.
(SANDS publish guidelines for professionals, price £12.50.)

Support after Termination for Abnormality (SAFTA),
29-30 Soho Square, London, W1V 6JB. Tel: 071-439 6124.

Miscarriage Association,
PO Box 24, Ossett, West Yorkshire, WF5 9XG. Tel: 0924-200799.

National Childbirth Trust (NCT),
Alexander House, Oldham Terrace, Acton, London, W3. Tel: 081-992 8637.

Twins and Multiple Births Association (TAMBA),
Bevearement Coordinator
PO Box 30, Little Sutton, South Wirral, L66 1TH. Tel. 051-348 0020.

26

Bereavement: the needs of the patient's family

Jenny Penson, MA, SRN, HVCert, Cert Ed, RNT
Senior Lecturer in Nursing Studies, Dorset Insitute of Higher Education

Through this chapter bereaved people are referred to as "family" or "relatives" for ease of comprehension. Terms such as "key people" or "significant others", while rather unwieldy, may more accurately describe the grieving person who is, for example, a life-long friend.

"Bereavement" means "to be robbed of something valued" – this definition seems particularly helpful as it indicates that this someone or something has been wrongly or forcibly taken from you. A key concept to understanding bereavement is that of loss. As Caplan (1964) and others have suggested, the grief experienced after losing someone close to you may be similar to the emotions felt after other types of loss, life transitions such as redundancy, divorce, failing an important exam or losing a much loved pet. As nurses we become aware of the emotions that patients experience after operations such as mastectomy, amputation of a limb or the loss of body image caused by suffering from a disfiguring disease.

When people are bereaved they suffer not only the loss of a person but also a substantial part of themselves, because everything they have shared with that person cannot be repeated with anyone else. The bereavement experience, therefore, is one of strong, violent and sometimes overwhelming reactions. These feelings actually begin from the moment the relative is told that the patient will not recover, referred to by Lindemann (1944) as "anticipatory grief".

The patient

Kubler Ross (1970), states: "We cannot help the terminally ill patient in a really meaningful way if we do not include his family." She determined that family members undergo stages of adjustment similar to the five phases she described for dying patients – denial, anger, bargaining, depression and acceptance as they come to terms with the reality of terminal illness in the family. She advocates that when there is time to do so, the family should be encouraged to express grief as much as possible prior to the death of a loved one which serves to alleviate, to some extent, the pain that is felt afterwards. If members of a family can share these emotions they will gradually face the reality of the impending separation and come to an acceptance of it together.

Unresolved family stress can significantly affect the outcome of the patient's illness, so the care of the family is part of the total care of the patient. It is also about understanding him as a member of the family group, and being aware that he and his family are not separate entities. Each constantly influences the other, thus affecting the health and happiness of both. It is possible that nursing actions may affect the long-term adjustment of the bereaved relatives after the death of the patient.

Molter (1979) studied family needs as they identified them, and looked at whether these were being met, and if so, by whom. The results showed that relatives could identify their needs during an intensive phase of hospitalisation. Their universal and strongest need was for hope. Nurses can go some way towards meeting this need by helping to set short-term goals for the patient. A weekend at home, a visit from a favourite friend, planning something special to enjoy together all helps to relieve that sense of helplessness which is often felt. They also go some way towards providing good memories to look back on. Reassurance that the patient will not be allowed to suffer pain or great distress, that someone will be with them when they die, and that support is available after the death if they need it, are all significant to those for whom no hope of an ultimate recovery can be given.

Hampe (1975) also found that spouses believed that the nurse's primary responsibility was to the patient and therefore they would be too busy to help relatives. One of the principal needs she identified from her study was for the family to be able to visit the dying patient at any time and for as long as they wished. They also wanted prompt help with the physical care and a demonstration of friendliness and concern in their relationship with the nurse.

My own experience indicates that encouraging involvement of the family in the care of the patient may minimise feelings of guilt during bereavement. There is a sense of not having failed when one was needed and the satisfaction of having done something tangible to give comfort and show love.

Hospital or home care?

This must be borne in mind when discussing the pros and cons of hospital versus home care. Where dying at home is possible because both the patient and their relatives want it, and there are enough resources available when needed, the family are likely to feel a sense of achievement, of not having failed the patient. On the other hand, relatives do derive comfort from the security of constant professional expertise and the knowledge that any emergency will be dealt with by a 24-hour service. However, they still need to feel involved and should be encouraged to give to the patient in any way they can. This might range from helping with nursing care to arranging photos and flowers or bringing in special food or drink that the patient may ask for which the hospital cannot supply.

To tell or not to tell

Whether or not to tell the patient of his diagnosis and prognosis is a dilemma which causes much distress to family, patients and nurses. Sometimes relatives are advised by doctors and/or nurses not to be truthful with the patient and this can create a barrier between them, described by Solzhenitsyn (1971) as "a wall of silence" which separates them.

There is an obvious conflict in many relatives' minds between the idea of the patient's right to autonomy to knowing the truth if he wishes it, and the idea of paternalism, having the right to withhold it on the grounds of protecting the patient and giving him hope. Relatives will often say such things as "it will be too much for him", "he will give up", "I know he won't be able to stand it", "he will be frightened". These sort of statements may well be true but they may also reflect the relatives' own fears.

The cue to how much information is given should lie with the patient and the nurse's role with the relatives is often to explain to and sustain them during that gradual realisation that comes to most patients near the end. This may or may not be expressed and shared. However, when a patient and family can openly discuss their situation together, their relationship can be deepened and this can give great comfort to the bereaved person afterwards. It also creates a basis of honesty and trust which facilitates the relationship between patient, family and carers. Ann Oakley (1985) described when her father, Richard Titmuss, was dying: "You said things you never would have said had you not known you were dying – and that is how I knew you were."

That families fail to share their feelings openly with one another when faced with terminal illness may be due to the defence of denial and also a function of experience. Although we, the health workers, have been enlightened about combating this so-called conspiracy of silence which surrounds the topic of death, it is also possible that some families have been over-exposed to that viewpoint. As Bowen, (1978) points out, in spite of whatever attitudinal change that may have taken place the "basic problem is an emotional one and a change in the rules does not automatically change the emotional reactivity."

Support

So, should staff be so involved as to sit and weep with the relatives? Is this what sharing and support is about? Kubler Ross, (1974), suggests that we ask ourselves whether we would judge someone who cared enough to cry for us. "A display of emotions on the part of the therapist is like drugs, the right amount of medicine at the right time can work wonders. Too much is unhealthy – and too little is tragic."

It has been suggested that nurses are in a prime position to meet the family needs through active listening and supporting. They found that relatives wanted support but they tended to feel they should not burden the "too busy" nurses with their problems. It is important, therefore, that a sense of availability is conveyed to families so that they will not feel guilty when sharing fears and worries with the nurse. Families usually appreciate information and explanation about nursing procedures, tests, treatments, medications. This helps them to feel they are part of the life of the patient and increases feelings of control, which can enable them to cope more realistically and effectively with the immediate future.

Relatives who feel that they have not been "told enough" are suffering from a lack of sustained professional interest. Effective nursing care is *planned* care and relatives can and should be involved in this. Short-term objectives for the patient such as an improved night's sleep, can be explained to relatives and are positive indicators that there are always things which can be done to improve the quality of life for the patient.

There is often an accompanying aspiration or, for many people, a desperate need to find that the experience of grieving does have some meaning. This may lead to a turning or returning towards religion, or other philosophies of living. The nurse can often meet this need with tact and sensitivity by introducing the hospital chaplain or family priest at an appropriate moment. Their availability to families as well as patients gives comfort, and helps them to explore their own beliefs and what they mean.

Physical fitness is related to the ability to cope with stress and measures to maintain health may be more acceptable to the family if they are seen in terms of enabling them to support and be with the dying patient. They also serve to reinforce the message that the grieving relative *is* an important individual whose needs are also the nurse's concern. Simple relaxation techniques to promote sleep and encouragement to eat regularly are all part of this care.

Interpersonal skills

It is important, therefore, for nurses to develop interpersonal skills to enable them to meet the needs of the patient's family. The creation of a trusting relationship, the ability to give information in a clear and sympathetic manner, the ability to listen actively to their concerns and to help them to clarify problems and options all involve skills which can be learned and practised.

As Frederick and Frederick (1986) point out, although there is a great deal of controversy surrounding anticipatory grief, it appears that it may be a way of doing some of the work of mourning before the death occurs. In this way, it may soften the impact of the actual death on the bereaved.

The nurse is in a unique position, being in constant contact with the family. Her attention to their needs may have long-term beneficial effects on their adjustment to bereavement and is likely to enhance the quality of their remaining time with the dying patient.

References

Bowen, M. (1978) Family reactions to death. In: Family Therapy and Clinical Practice. Aronson, New York.

Caplan, G. (1964) Principles of Preventive Psychiatry. Basic Books, New York.

Frederick, J.F. and Frederick, N.J. (1985) The hospice experience: possible effects in altering the biochemistry of bereavement. *Hospice Journal*, 1, 3, 81-89.

Hampe, S. (1975) Needs of the grieving spouse in a hospital setting. *Nursing Research*, 24, 20.

Kubler-Ross, E. (1970) On Death and Dying. Tavistock, London.

Kubler-Ross, E. (1974) Questions and Answers on Death and Dying. Macmillan, London.

Lindemann, E. (1944) Symptomatology and management of acute grief. *American Journal of Psychiatry*, 101, 141-149.

Molter, N.C. (1979) Needs of critically ill patients: a descriptive study. *Nursing Research*, 8, 2.

Oakley, A. (1985) Taking it Like a Woman. Penguin, London.

Solzhenitsyn, A. (1971) Cancer Ward. Penguin, London.

Ward, A.W.M. (1976) Mortality of bereavement. *British Medical Journal*, 11, 700-102.

Bibliography

Penson, J. (1990) Bereavement: A Guide For Nurses. Harper Collins, London.

27

Helping clients to come to terms with loss

Teresa Lombardi, BEd(Hons), RGN, RSCN, RNT, Cert Ed, Dip Counselling
Director, Professional Development, West Sussex College of Nursing and Midwifery

Working with terminally ill people, although rewarding and challenging, is far from easy, for a variety of reasons. It is impossible to identify a 'right and wrong' way of communicating with them, as each client has individual needs and ways of expressing him or herself. Similarly, each situation is different, and as nurses we bring our own individual attitudes, values, beliefs, experiences and skills into them. We also bring our feelings of anxiety and helplessness and our need to 'make it better' for patients or clients, which it is not always possible to do.

Witnessing strong emotions in others and learning to cope with and accept them may remind us of our own areas of difficulty and losses, whether real or feared. This can make us vulnerable to feelings of anxiety, inadequacy and pain. If we are not sufficiently aware of our own values, beliefs and areas of 'unfinished business', it may affect the way we relate to our clients and hinder the development of the qualities of warmth, acceptance, genuineness, empathy and flexibility that are so essential when working with this client group. Finally difficulties arise because ultimately 'effective helping' requires a degree of self confidence and courage and it is often easier to 'opt out' and avoid the situation. This is a normal coping strategy that we all need to do when we are vulnerable. We must care for ourselves as nurses or we will not be free to effectively care for others.

Tasks of mourning

Although each client and situation is different, there are certain principles that can be followed to make our helping skills more effective. It may be useful to consider these within the framework of the four tasks of mourning (Worden, 1983).

When clients are informed of their situation they often feel a sense of disbelief, that 'it is not really happening'. During this first stage the nurse's prime aim is to help the client become aware and accept that the situation is real, it is happening and is not a figment of the imagination. This is essential, as only when reality is accepted can the client progress and experience the pain of grief, ultimately moving through to resolution. One of the best ways to help clients accept their loss is to encourage them to talk. Many clients mentally relive where they were when they first heard of their diagnosis, what happened and who said what. They may need to talk through this again and again, over weeks or even months. While family and friends may grow tired and even impatient the effective nurse is a patient listener who encourages the clients to talk.

Acknowledging grief

The second task of mourning is to acknowledge and experience the pain of grief. Feelings such as anger, guilt and sadness may not be acceptable to either family or friends or to clients themselves. They may therefore try to suppress or even deny their pain in order to avoid burdening, distressing or embarrassing their loved ones, while other clients may think they are 'going mad'. During this stage clients need to be helped to give themselves 'permission' to be angry or sad, or to cry, and must be given opportunity to talk through their guilt and unburden themselves. A nurse's quiet acceptance and acknowledgement of the pain of grief will facilitate this difficult task, which means that clients are not left to carry the burden of their pain with them into the next stage of their lives.

Adjustment

The third task of mourning is that of adjusting to the loss, real or impending. Essentially the nurse helps clients to identify problems and then to explore alternative ways of dealing with them. For example, this may mean identifying short term goals, of looking at today and next week rather than next month or next year. This is an active stage and may involve adopting and coming to terms with a new role or learning new skills such as coping with a prosthesis.

The final stage of mourning involves withdrawing emotional energy from the loss and reinvesting it in another relationship or diverting it to other channels. At this point the intense pain of grief diminishes and although clients will still experience a sense of sadness they will be able to channel their emotions into living and dealing with their lives today.

Skills for effective helping

Effective helping can be viewed as a problem solving activity. Most nurses use a variety of skills throughout the helping process and although there is no standard classification of such skills, for convenience they can be divided into two main stages.

Stage one — attending Effective helpers are those who can establish a caring, non threatening relationship with their clients. Many nurses begin this relationship with an advantage in that the client's trust is already invested in them because of the nurturing nature of the nursing role. Trust will also develop if the nurse can be open and honest — relationships bound by any degree of mutual pretence will lead to feelings of insecurity and non-acceptance in clients (Glaser and Strauss, 1965), who will then be more likely to withdraw into their lonely worlds.

The first contact between nurse and client is crucial in developing and maintaining a warm trusting relationship. The client will have doubts and fears, and some problems will seem too large, too overwhelming or too unique to share. He may ask himself, ''Can I really trust this person?'', ''Is she really interested in me?'' ''Does she have the time for me?'' Answers to such questions will be provided not merely by words but by other more subtle and powerful means of communication. The physical setting, the way the nurse greets the client and her gestures and tone of voice can all convey sensitivity and consideration.

Observing and reacting

From the first meeting nurse and client will engage in the process of observing and reacting to the other. Success in helping depends upon the client's perception of the nurse's manner and behaviour. He will look for, and must experience, empathy, respect and sensitivity. Being with, attending to and listening are supportive and comforting behaviours which convey respect and concern for the client.

At this stage an opening statement such as, ''I wonder what worries you have about your illness?'' may provide the necessary invitation for the client to take the lead and talk freely while the nurse 'attends'. This involves 'being with' the client physically and psychologically. Body communication, posture, degree of relaxation and eye contact indicate interest in and attention to the client. Attending behaviour encourages the trust that is so necessary for promoting exploration and will also help the nurse listen more effectively.

Listening is an active, complex process and perhaps the most important of all helping skills. It involves first observing and interpreting the client's non-verbal behaviour and then listening to and interpreting his verbal messages. During the process of listening, the skill of reflection can be used by the nurse to sensitively communicate to the client her understanding of his concerns. It is an empathetic response that involves restating in fresh words the client's core feelings. For example:

Client: ''I'm bewildered, there's so much to take in and consider, and so many different doctors each with their own ideas.''

Nurse: ''It all seems so confusing, even overwhelming and almost out of your control.''

Client: ''Yes, that's it, it feels like that.''

An accurate reflection, while not halting the flow of talk can help clarify and bring less obvious feelings into the client's awareness so that they can be 'owned' and acknowledged. Reflection also increases the degree of trust which will ultimately facilitate further exploration.

Stage two — responding This stage of helping involves maintaining the good relationship developed in the first stage and taking the process further by helping the client explore, clarify and define his problem or area of concern. Responding skills help the client progress through the stages of mourning, the appropriate and effective ones at this stage are those which enable the client to extend and develop his understanding of himself and his difficulties.

Effective helping will be determined by the nurse's ability to respond accurately to the needs and cues provided by the client. This 'staying with the client' demonstrates empathy and acceptance. To achieve this the nurse needs to avoid directing and leading, eg "I don't think you should be spending so much time talking about your illness."; reassuring, eg "That's a common problem, but you'll be alright."; advising, eg "I wouldn't tell your family about this;" or not accepting the client's feelings and hiding behind the professional facade, eg "Your depression will pass, it's just part of the body's response to your treatment."

Staying with the client may also mean staying silent if he needs time to gather thoughts and feelings together. Although there are many different meanings for a silence, it is often a productive time and it is helpful if the nurse simply waits quietly until the client is ready to go on. This is perhaps a very difficult strategy to adopt as we are used to commenting on, advising or teaching.

Other skills

Other responding skills which will help exploration and clarification are probing, questioning and summarising. Prompts and probes are verbal tactics which help clients talk about themselves and define their problems more concretely. A prompt may be a head nod or a simple "Aha" or "I see" while a probe may take the form of a statement, eg "When you were told you had cancer you said you were both relieved and depressed. I'm wondering how you've been since then."

The careful use of questions can also help focus and clarify. These should be open questions, usually beginning with 'how', 'what' or 'who', which leave the respondent free to answer as he wishes, eg "Can you explain what you mean?", or "What was it about your treatment session today that was so upsetting?". Asking too many questions, however, may make the client feel interrogated, anxious and insecure, which will interfere with the rapport between nurse and client. Questions which begin with 'why', such as, "Why did you feel like that?" are also unhelpful, as they lead the client to search for intellectual explanations to justify his feelings.

Summarising

Summarising is the process of tying together all that has been communicated during part or all of a helping session. It can also be a natural means of finishing the session or beginning a new one. This then paves the way for the client to commit himself to further exploration and to developing awareness. Thus, with continuing emotional support the client, finding and utilising his own inner resources, moves on with hope to another day.

These strategies have been identified to help the nurse care for clients who are experiencing loss, but it should be remembered that the nurse has to deal with her own personal feelings of grief in response to the client's situation. In addition she may be constrained by fears that she will make the situation worse for the client through lack of skill. Only the client can judge what is helpful and is likely to seek a nurse who can support, comfort and care, and is herself — a real person with strengths and weaknesses like anyone else.

References
Glaser, B. and Strauss, A. (1965) Awareness of Dying. Aldine, Chicago.
Worden, W.J. (1983) Grief Counselling and Grief Therapy. Tavistock Publications, London.

Bibliography
Brammer, L. M. (1979) The Helping Relationship Process and Skills. Prentice-Hall, New Jersey.
   Provides more in-depth discussion of the issues raised in this paper.
Egan, G. (1982) The Skilled Helper Model, Skills and Methods for Effective Helping. Brooks Cole Publishing Company, California.
   Describes in detail the skills and methods needed for effective helping.
Munro, E. A., Nanthei, R. J., Small, J.J. (1983) Counselling: A Skills Approach. Methuen, New Zealand.
   A clearly-written text with some very practical exercises and examples of helping skills.
Nelson-Jones, R. (1983) Practical Counselling Skills. Holt, Rinehart and Winston, London.
   Applies the theory of counselling in a very practical way using exercises to aid skill development and case studies as examples.

Psychotherapy

28

What is psychotherapy?

Brendan McMahon, BA, SRN, RMN, Cert Dynamic Psychotherapy
Clinical Nurse Specialist in Dynamic Psychotherapy, Southern Derbyshire Health Authority

There are many different kinds of psychotherapy. Although the term can be used to describe approaches based on behavioural or systems theory, dynamic psychotherapy, with which this article is mainly concerned, owes its inspiration to the Freudian theory and practice of psychoanalysis. Dynamic psychotherapy can be applied in an individual one-to-one setting, in groups, families, or in working with couples.

Analytic theory and practice

Psychotherapy is "essentially a conversation which involves listening to and talking with those in trouble with the aim of helping them understand and resolve their predicament" (Brown and Pedder, 1979). During his time with Charcot, the great French neurologist, Freud had become fascinated by the use of hypnosis as a form of treatment for hysteria (Breuer and Freud, 1895). After returning to Vienna, however, he soon abandoned hypnosis in favour of free association – encouraging the patient to talk about whatever comes into his or her head. The importance of this technical innovation, which is still utilised in dynamic psychotherapy, cannot be overstated: for the first time in the long history of the doctor/patient relationship, responsibility for what happened between them was ceded by the doctor to the patient. Freud's observations of Charcot's work on hypnosis had led him to conclude that hysterical symptoms were the product of unconscious mental processes and, since in free association patients inevitably express, often in symbolic form or through the retelling of dreams, the internal conflicts of which they are consciously unaware, then the use of the free association technique might be the most effective way of eliciting such unconscious material. By connecting unconscious conflict with current life experience and showing how the one can affect the other, the analyst/therapist can enable the client to achieve greater self-understanding and freedom of action.

Psychotherapy and the patient

Relatively few nurses are trained analysts or therapists and it will not, except in certain specialised settings, be appropriate for them to make in-depth interpretation, but the free association model is still relevant to nursing practice. All too often we get agendas for our patients, on the basis of what we think they are thinking and feeling: all too often we 'do things' to patients rather than allowing them to be. We need to learn when and how to be silent so our patients have room to express the anxieties of which they may be only dimly aware. In this way nurse and patient can cease to be object and subject, active and passive, and are freed to become human beings occupying the same therapeutic space. In practical terms this means instituting a change in the quality of the time we spend with patients, so that the burden of our expectations is lifted from their shoulders. When we are admitting a patient to our ward or preparing a patient for surgery, we need to allow time, in the midst of the necessary clerical and technical tasks, for the patient to be and to express him- or herself.

Of course, it is not enough in psychotherapy to connect current problems with past events in the hope that this will in itself produce dramatic symptomatic improvement. There are two reasons for this. First, we all tend to resist painful self-knowledge or insight, and are inclined to maintain our view of ourselves and our way of relating to others, however pathological these might seem to an outsider. We have a vested interest in remaining as we are. Our psychological defences against pain, however inadequate and ultimately self-defeating they may be, at least provide us with a way of coping, of making our lives to some extent predictable and, therefore, manageable. The psyche is innately conservative and the thought of relinquishing or even modifying our defences can seem to many of us a terrifying leap into the unknown.

Second, insights, newly acquired truths about the self, need to be integrated – to be accepted on an emotional level and so absorbed into the personality. It is not enough merely to accede to an insight into the self, as one might accede to an emotionally neutral intellectual proposition. There is a world of difference between saying "Yes, I now realise that I both love and hate my mother" and saying "Yes, I now realise that a millimetre is equivalent to 0.04 inches" but the first statement can be said in the same manner as the second, so as to drain it of all emotional meaning. For this process of integration to take place, the underlying conflict must be 'worked through' – be relived and resolved in the context of the relationship with the therapist. This is often a lengthy and painful process, and it leads us to consider the crucial factor of the transference.

The transference
The term 'transference' is used to denote those feelings and attitudes experienced by the client with regard to the therapist which cannot be accounted for in terms of the reality of their relationship – feelings and attitudes which relate to other important figures in the client's life particularly his parents. Initially Freud regarded these angry or affectionate phenomena as a block to therapy, but later he realised that on the contrary, they offered a unique opportunity to get in touch with the client's repressed, 'forgotten' experience of those early relationship

in which psychological and emotional conflicts frequently have their roots. Through the transference these troubled early relationships can be re-experienced, interpreted and worked through.

Mr Anderson presented for therapy in a depressed state, which seemed to be connected with the recent break-up of his marriage. Over time, it emerged that this event had reactivated childhood conflicts connected with his mother who, for reasons of her own, had been unable to respond to him in a consistent and loving way. This had made him grow up in constant fear of rejection and led to him adopting a stance towards women which alternated between dependence and possessiveness, which inevitably brought about the rejection he feared. By exploring these conflicts in therapy he was gradually enabled to come to terms with his sense of inner despair and begin to relate to women in more realistic and creative ways. This was accomplished through the female therapist's focus on the transference – Mr Anderson's feelings 'about' her which actually related to his mother.

Resolving inner conflict is a task none of us ever entirely completes. If it is to be at least partially accomplished in therapy, the therapist must respond to the client's communication in an empathic, non-judgemental way, so that a trusting relationship can develop. Only thus will the client become able to confront the pain and begin to seek his or her own solutions to overcome it.

Nurse/patient relationships

Transference is *not* an esoteric concept, only of use in the rarefied atmosphere of the psychotherapist's consulting room – it is a part of everyday life, as is its counterpart 'countertransference'. In the psychoanalytic setting, this is the "analyst's transference on his patient . . . by extension, the analyst's emotional attitude towards his patient, including his response to specific items of the patient's behaviour" (Rycroft, 1972). These twin concepts are particularly relevant to nursing. The patient is, by definition, in a dependent position, while the nurse is, by definition, in a position to minister to his or her needs, so the relationship between them will inevitably evoke the mother/child relationship. This is often a benign process, at other times less so. It can, for instance, lead to the patient's anxious attachment to the nurse, or a short-lived but painful 'falling in love'. It can also lead, on the part of the patient, to hostility, and resistance to treatment. Understanding the importance of transference can help the nurse respond to such situations with understanding and sympathy. Countertransference is equally important. We have all encountered patients for whom we feel an inexplicable dislike, and with whom we find it difficult to work, and this is clearly a block to the establishment of a genuinely therapeutic relationship, whether in a general or a psychiatric setting. At such times the notion of countertransference can help us examine ourselves and our own past and current relationships. If, in the course of such self-examination, we can begin to understand why we experience such hostility towards the patient, we are well on the way to freeing ourselves of it, or at least containing it. We will also have made a step forward in our own personal growth.

Therapy and the therapist

'Psychotherapy' in the general sense of offering support and the opportunity to express feelings and share problems, is as old as the human race. Dynamic psychotherapy however, offers more than this. In one sense it is tougher – it requires clients to take responsibility for their own life and to make their own decisions, to confront painful truths about themselves and their relationships. It focuses on clients' internal world, their unconscious motives, conflicts and defences, and on the therapeutic relationship itself. Its purpose is not to offer superficial reassurance or transitory comfort but, through interpretation and working through, to facilitate personal change and help clients move in the direction of more creative interpersonal relationships on the one hand and greater intrapersonal integration on the other: in later articles we will look in more detail at how these tasks are accomplished.

To perform the task effectively the therapist needs a sound theoretical knowledge of psychodynamic processes, the nature of unconscious conflict and motivation, defence mechanisms, psychological development and psychic structure, as well as interpersonal and family dynamics. The ability to form a relationship of mutual trust, in which the therapist is attuned to clients' feelings while remaining sufficiently detached to work with them is essential. The therapist must have the skill to confront, clarify and interpret clients' communications as and when appropriate, and the wisdom to know when to remain silent and be sufficiently mature to recognise his or her own areas of personal difficulty and emotional needs, and the strength to prevent them impinging on clients, who have enough problems of their own. Although this paragon does not, to my knowledge, exist, it does represent the ideal towards which everyone engaged in psychotherapy should be striving.

Use of psychotherapy

Regrettably, although the effectiveness of psychotherapy is now well established, and client demand (and satisfaction) is high, the provision of psychotherapy services in very patchy. Whether a particular client receives psychotherapy or not is as much or more a matter of where he or she happens to live as an accurate assessment of need. It is also a matter of the attitude of the assessor/referrer, who will not refer for therapy unless he or she can recognise its value as a treatment option. Nurses can help to change these attitudes by arguing the case for psychotherapeutic input where this is appropriate and available. Where it is not available they should be arguing for its provision: their patients deserve no less.

References

Brever, J. and Freud, S. (1895) Studies on Hysteria. Standard Edition of the Complete Psychological Works of S. Freud (1955). Hogarth Press, London.

Brown, D. and Pedder, J. (1979) Introduction to Psychotherapy. Tavistock Publications, London.

Rycroft, C. (1968) A Critical Dictionary of Psychoanalysis. Penguin Books (1972) Harmondsworth.

29

Psychoanalysis and psychotherapy?

Brendan McMahon, BA, SRN, RMN, Cert Dynamic Psychotherapy
Clinical Nurse Specialist in Dynamic Psychotherapy, Southern Derbyshire Health Authority

In the previous chapter (McMahon, 1990) we looked at some of the theoretical concepts and technical innovations introduced by Freud. We will consider now psychoanalytic ideas and skills in more detail, and look at some of the ways they have contributed to what is now known as dynamic or analytic psychotherapy.

Typically, analysts see their patients individually four or five times a week, in 50 minute sessions, over a period of some years. Patients may or may not be asked to lie on a couch, but all analysts adopt an emotionally detached attitude, attempting to become a 'blank screen' on which patients can project their unconscious fears and fantasies. The aim is to bring patients' unconscious conflicts into consciousness through the use of interpretation, and analysts mainly confine their work to neurotic patients, though an increasing number are beginning to work with borderline and even psychotic clients.

Analytic therapists see their patients once or twice a week over a shorter period of time, and where appropriate they may offer a specific number of sessions, say 20 or 30. These therapists do not use a couch, and though they are careful not become embroiled in their clients' emotional difficulties, in general they adopt a freer, more active role than analysts would find appropriate. Analytic therapists also take on patients with a wide variety of problems. Both analysts and analytic psychotherapists endeavour to use their relationships with their patients to promote constructive personal change.

Psychosexual development

Psychoanalysis is both a body of theory and a technical procedure. The Freudian view of psychosexual development is not only central to psychoanalytic theory: it also underpins the practice of psychoanalysis and analytic therapy. In Freud's view there is a form of mental energy known as libido, which is present from birth and which attaches itself to different objects at different stages of development (Freud, 1905). In the first year of life libido centres on the mouth, which, through suckling, is both the principal source of pleasure for the baby and the focus of his or her total experience. This period is known as the oral stage. From age one to three years the focus shifts to the anus, as the child discovers the pleasure of defaecation and of being able to withold faeces. For the first time the child becomes aware of an ability to exert some control over him- or herself and the environment. This anal stage is succeeded by the oedipal phase of libidinal development (age three to five years), which is characterised by attachment to the parent of the opposite sex and hostility to the parent of the same sex. In this phase children become very interested in their own and others' genitalia – libido centres on the genital area. The phase is named after King Oedipus, a figure in Greek myth who inadvertently killed his father and married his mother. It is followed by the latency period, in which sexual interest lies dormant only to be reawakened at puberty, which constitutes the beginning of the genital stage of healthy adult sexuality.

Freud's model of development is of more than academic interest – it provides a way of thinking about the genesis of psychiatric disorder. It seems likely, for instance, that conditions such as personality disorder and psychosis have their origins in the earliest developmental stage, and neurotic illnesses can be traced back to difficulties encountered later. This has important implications for clinical work. If a therapist can see that a particular client's presenting problem is rooted in, for instance, the oedipal phase, the focus of therapy will be upon the client's conflicted feelings about his or her parents, which should be brought into consciousness and resolved. If the presenting problem has its basis in some disturbance which occurred during the anal stage of development, the therapist will work with anxieties connected with autonomy, loss of control and so on. This is, of course, a highly simplistic account of Freud's theory of development, and many later thinkers, particularly Melanie Klein and the other British object relations theorists, have questioned aspects of it. The point I wish to emphasise here is that development is a crucial issue for psychoanalysis and analytic psychotherapy. They are *dynamic* forms of treatment – concerned with personal growth, both in theory and in practice.

Resolving conflict

The idea that psychological problems in adult life can be caused by conflict originating in childhood does not in itself take us very far. The problem remains of how the conflict is to be brought into consciousness, worked through and resolved. This leads us to transference.

Transference is a blanket term used to describe feelings and attitudes experienced by one person towards another, which cannot be accounted for in terms of their actual relationship – feelings and attitudes which in fact relate to other important figures in the person's life, particularly his or her parents. Many nurses will recognise this phenomenon in their patients. Initially Freud regarded these angry, affectionate or ambivalent reactions as a block to therapy, but later he recognised that they offer a unique opportunity to get in touch with patients' repressed 'forgotten' memories of early relationships. Depression or difficulty in forming relationships, for example, may stem from unsatisfactory mothering, and if the patient's original feelings about this can be re-experienced through the transference, he or she can be helped to understand and work through them, and so become free of their noxious influence. Most nurses will not wish to work with transference in this way, nor is it desirable that they should. As a theoretical concept though, transference is an invaluable tool in helping us understand our patients and our relationship with them.

Transference is only a part of the story, however. Although as nurses we are not generally encouraged to examine any feelings our patients may arouse in us, such feelings can enrich our understanding of them – and of ourselves – enormously, and in psychotherapy this is particularly important. The term used to describe these feelings is countertransference. The countertransference can and should be understood as a form of communication: of course, it can only be regarded in this way if therapists are clear that their feelings towards their patients do not stem from their own neurotic conflicts or personal circumstances at the time. Once they are sure about this they are free to regard their feelings in the session as a statement issued by their patients. For example, a therapist who feels depressed for no personal reason may regard this as an expression of the patient's despair. One who is being drawn into a hostile, critical position may think the patient is recreating an earlier relationship with a parent through the therapist. In either case the therapist's perception of what is going on can be shared with the client, thereby helping him or her to release blocked emotions and begin to come to terms with the problems.

In the limited scope of this chapter it has not been possible to give more than a brief account of what psychotherapists do and why they do it, but I hope enough has been said to stimulate interest and raise questions about the relevance of psychotherapeutic theory and practice for nurses. The next chapter will consider the individual within the family context, what can go wrong and what psychotherapy has to offer.

Reference
Freud, S. (1905) Three Essays on the Theory of Sexuality. Standard edition of the Complete Psychological Works of Sigmund Freud. Hogarth Press and The Institute of Psychoanalysis, London.

30
Helping families towards open communication

Brendan McMahon, BA, SRN, RMN, Cert Dynamic Psychotherapy
Clinical Nurse Specialist in Dynamic Psychotherapy, Southern Derbyshire Health Authority

Most of us come from a family. This is so obvious we sometimes forget it, and that is why it is important to remind ourselves of what the family is and what it does.

Our family gives us crucial emotional support and the opportunity to grow and learn, particularly about relationships. It is within the family that we learn to share, cooperate, and strike a balance between our own needs and the needs of others. The family provides us with role models: our fathers and mothers give us our first and most powerful impression of what it means to be a man or woman, and we use these impressions to develop our own sense of ourselves as we grow. The family prepares us to take our place in the wider society by the inculcation of appropriate attitudes, sets of behaviour and a sense of responsibility. It gives us the existential security which can only come from a personal, meaningful connection with history. As a family member, we know we are a part of something which existed before we were born and that, in our turn, we have the capacity to pass that something on to future generations. At the most basic level the family provides us with the material necessities without which life cannot be sustained, food, shelter and protection from physical danger.

Healthy family

The above is one definition of the functions of a 'healthy' family, though there are others, and this area is not free from controversy (Textor, 1989). In some respects it is, of course, a somewhat idealistic concept – no-one is perfect, and every family has its problems and its own inevitable conflicts. Sometimes families fail to perform one or more of their basic functions adequately: in recent years we have all become more aware of the prevalence of child abuse, for instance, and on a wider social context, concern has been expressed about the long-term consequences for local communities in which traditional family structures have broken down (Murray, 1989). At the less extreme end of the spectrum there are many families which do not meet their full potential – families which are characterised by unclear roles, rigid rules, the inability to express feelings, lack of warmth, or a culture of threat and recrimination. Such families often produce misery or even illness in one or more of their members – the actual 'symptoms' may include alcoholism, drug abuse, depression, truancy, anxiety and many more – and are thus brought to the attention of the helping professions. Most families, of course, are doing the best they can in circumstances which are often difficult, and the problems they encounter are rarely the result of deliberate malice. It is also worth remembering that all families have much in common. Virginia Satir writes:-

"In all families every person has a feeling of worth, positive or negative: the question is which is it?

"Every person communicates: the question is how, and what happens as a result?

"Every person follows rules: the question is, what kind, and how well do they work for him?

"Every person is linked to society: the question is how, and what are the results?" (Satir, 1972).

Types of family therapist
Family therapists tend to belong to one of three subgroups:-

The conductors   See their role as being to re-educate the family in more healthy and creative attitudes. These therapists will openly confront the pathological functioning of the family. This group includes such workers as Ackerman, Virginia Satir and Salvador Minuchin.

The reactor-analysts   Use their own emotional response (counter-transference) as a means of understanding and changing the family pathology, according to psychoanalytic precepts.

The systems purists   Such as Jay Haley, who endeavour to change the ground rules of relationships within the family (including, while therapy lasts, the therapist him- or herself), to promote constructive change (Beels and Ferber, 1976).

Within this broad framework family therapists do, of course, develop their own unique styles.

Where such a service is available as a local resource, a troubled family might find themselves referred to a family therapist who is qualified, as a result of specialist training and extensive supervised experience to undertake this type of work. The therapist will use the assessment interview to gain a sense of how the family functions as a system. He or she might ask individuals to draw up a geneogram (family tree) to compare the ways in which each member sees the family and their place in it, and to discover whether particular roles and expectations are passed from generation to generation and have thus become embedded in the family culture. Family members often have quite different perceptions of the family to which they belong, and sharing these perceptions can in itself promote mutual understanding and change.

Family therapists pay close attention to the power structure within the family, perceptions and expectations of the self and others, and patterns of communication. They take note of evasiveness and double messages, speaking for others, giving orders, the suppression of negative feelings, blaming, sarcasm, and deliberate attempts to lower the self-esteem of others, and are alert for family secrets, taboos and collusions, scapegoating, and the making of unjustified assumptions about the feelings, motives and behaviour of others. They try to gain an understanding of the boundaries between individual members and between the family and the outside world. If these boundaries are too flexible (a mother, for instance, may put her teenage son into the role of 'man of the house', which makes him feel intolerably anxious and also undermines the father's self-esteem), or too rigid, (where, for instance, the father has to be strong and decisive at all times, to the detriment of his own emotional needs) then families can run into trouble. All these negative mechanisms can stifle both the individual growth of family members and the collective efforts of the family to realise its full potential. On the basis of their understanding of the family system, and assessment of the family's capacity and willingness to change, therapists construct a strategy for therapeutic intervention which will modify the systems in such a way that individual and family needs can more effectively be met (Ogden and Zevin, 1976).

Careful structure

Family therapy must be carefully structured. Many therapists aim to facilitate change in a short space of time, sometimes as little as three to six sessions, though others continue therapy over a longer period, and boundaries of time and length of treatment need to be clearly established at the outset. For families with poor boundaries, this is often a useful learning experience in itself. Therapists sometimes make use of live supervision, and the implications of this also need to be spelled out to the client family. Under this arrangement another therapist will watch the therapy sessions on a video or by means of a special screen, and will be available for consultation by the family therapist, who will either leave the room for that purpose or speak to the supervisor by telephone. The supervisor, who is not working directly with the family, can often notice significant aspects of family interaction which the therapist misses. The question of who to include in the client family is an interesting one – sometimes it is appropriate to include grandparents or other relatives, as well as the core family, or even a non-family member, such as a lodger or close friend, if they are thought to be an important part of the family system in its widest sense. Appointment letters are addressed to 'The Smith Family' rather than to 'Mr Smith' or 'Miss Smith' or the presenting patient. The response to the letter, and the choice of who attends the assessment interview, will provide important information about the family, who makes decisions and who is included or excluded.

Within the sessions, therapists act as a model of clear and honest communication for the family to follow. They attempt to clarify (by, for instance, restating, summarising and paraphrasing) family communication, observe accurately how family members interact and share their observations with the family to promote change. They adopt a non-judgemental stance and foster a culture of understanding rather than one based on blame, guilt and recrimination, and encourage the sharing of secrets and clarification of roles, along with the exploration of expectations – what does the father expect of the mother and vice-versa? How is an adolescent son to be allowed to develop greater independence? Therapists help the family to acknowledge its assets as well as its deficits, and promote self-esteem and mutual gratification, and help the family to understand how it takes decisions and where authority does and does not reside, and to modify these processes where appropriate. Is the father burdened with responsibilities which his wife would, in fact, be prepared to share? Could growing children be given some say in the making of decisions without presenting too much threat to parental authority? Although therapists must avoid identifying with one family member to the detriment of others, they may on occasion side with one or another family member in order to help the family resolve a particular conflict. They will comment openly on the way in which the family affects them, thus modelling more open communication, and will stress the positive aspects of conflictual relationships which, to the family, may seem entirely negative, for example: "It sounds like a positive sign that you want to live a more independent life now you're 16, and it's also good that your father cares so much about you that he worries when you're late home."

Therapists take an active role in directing the family to make positive changes, and sometimes this takes the form of the paradoxical injunction. They might say: "I hear you saying that every time Mr Jones comes home from work the two of you have an argument. This happens so regularly that it must be important for you, so I want you to continue doing it." This often has the effect of stopping the undesirable behaviour. The logic behind this seems to be that therapists "encourage and label behaviour that is already going on at the direction of the family's rule-keepers, thus making the momentary leadership of the group explicit and breaking its power" (Haley, 1963). This is a sophisticated technique which should not lightly be attempted.

The above is an eclectic and to that extent unsatisfactory account of what family therapists actually do. It is also, of course, hopelessly condensed, and the reader is referred to the list of references for several more detailed descriptions of family therapy practice.

Although it has not been possible to explore the topic here, some knowledge of the concepts involved in family therapy would be usefu to all nurses in every setting. After all, patients are family members, and we cannot fully understand their difficulties unless we take this into account. Introductory courses, as well as longer term specialist training courses are available at The Institute of Family Therapy in London and a

The Scottish Institute of Human Relations, and at a number of regional centres. Further information is obtainable from the Association of Family Therapy, which is based in Cardiff.

References
Beels, C.C. and Ferber, A. (1976) Family Therapy: A View. Family Process 9 In: Skynner, R. One Flesh, Separate Persons: Principles of Marital and Family Psychotherapy. Constable, London.
Haley, J. (1963) Strategies of Psychotherapy. Grune and Stratton, New York.
Murray, C. (1989) Underclass: a disaster in the making. *Sunday Times*, November 26.
Ogden, G. and Zevin, A. (1976) When a Family Needs Therapy. Beacon Press, Boston, Mass.
Satir, v. (1972) Peoplemaking. Science and Behaviour Books Inc, Palo Alto.
Skynner, R. (1976) One Flesh, Separate Persons: Principles of Family and Marital Psychotherapy. Constable and Co. Ltd, London.
Textor, M. (1989) The healthy family, *Journal of Family Therapy*, 59-75.

Useful addresses
Association of Family Therapy, 83 the Hawthorns, Hollybush Road, Cyncoed, Cardiff.
Institute of Family Therapy, 43 New Cavendish Street, London W1.
Scottish Institute of Human Relations, 56 Albany Street, Edinburgh.

31

Group psychotherapy: a route to personal insight

Brendan McMahon, BA, SRN, RMN, Cert Dynamic Psychotherapy
Clinical Nurse Specialist in Dynamic Psychotherapy, Southern Derbyshire Health Authority

There are many different kinds of group therapy, from the mundane but useful psychiatric community meeting to the more exotic and sinister erhardt seminar training. Gestalt, Rogerian encounter, psychodrama and creative therapy groups all have a useful part to play. This chapter will concentrate on the group analytic approach, since it is, in my view, the one which addresses itself most directly to the dynamics of the group process.

> "It would be quite impossible for obvious reasons for the group therapist to base his procedure in a group situation on free association as understood in the individual sense. The relationship which now develops is that of a complex and mutual interaction between members. Only the therapist maintains the analytic attitude and detachment and can see the inner mechanism of this interaction, the unconscious dynamics. It would be quite impossible for him to follow each individual separately at the same time. He focuses on the total interactional field, on the matrix in which unconscious reactions meet. His background is always, and should consciously be, the group as a whole. Conflicts are now dynamically displayed in the group and yet they are . . . not less intra-psychic for that reason" (Foulkes and Anthony, 1957).

What then is group analysis, how does it differ from individual analysis or analytic therapy, and what do therapist and clients actually do together?

Analytic group psychotherapy

Classically, the analytic group has eight to 10 members, one therapist or two cotherapists, and meets once or twice a week. It is either 'closed' with a fixed membership and predetermined termination date or 'slow' open', in which case no closure date is set and new members replace those who leave over time. Ideally, group members are unknown to each other outside the group, and members are expected to regard the group as confidential. As in individual therapy the therapist will allow the group to talk about whatever it wishes to discuss without taking a directive role, confining him- or herself to commenting on the material the group brings along. This mode of therapy is widely practised in a modified form in psychiatric hospitals and outpatient clinics.

Group psychotherapy is truly group-centred and does not simply constitute psychotherapy in a group setting (a sort of watered-down psychoanalysis). It aims to achieve personal change for each individual group member by addressing the group process rather than each individual member's conflicts in turn. For example, we would say something like "it seems to me that the group is rather anxious about the fact that a new member will be joining us soon", rather than, "you look pretty anxious today, John, and I wonder if this is because of the new group member?"

We do not cease to be ourselves when we enter a therapy group, and our way of responding to others is an integral part of ourselves. Other group members, including the therapist, can help us to understand how we respond to others and why, and we can use that understanding to move towards a more authentic and creative way of relating to other people both within and outside of the group. One case history provides an illustration of this. Peter has always felt threatened by women as a result of his relationship with his mother. His way of dealing with this feeling was to attempt to dominate women, which inevitably led to a string of broken relationships, leaving him feeling hurt and angry. When this pattern asserted itself in group psychotherapy, Peter was confronted by group members and, although hurt, he began to realise how his behaviour affected women. With the group's help he came to understand why he was behaving as he did, modified his perception of women, and acquired the capacity to relate to women (first within the group and then outside it) in a more appropriate way. The need to dominate gradually evaporated as he became more able to share his vulnerability and receive the support and affection he had really wanted.

To attempt to work with each individual separately and at the same time is to attempt the impossible. The therapist, however, will often be under pressure to do this for a number of reasons:

• Individual clients' unresolved dependency needs; their transference to the therapist and unwillingness to share him or her with others; a desire for an exclusive relationship with the therapist.
• The occasional desire of the group to avoid facing up to its conflicts by focusing on the problems of one individual. The helplessness of the group, (its 'badness' or 'sickness') can be projected onto one individual with other group members rallying round manically trying

to help and, of course, failing. This sometimes expresses itself as 'spot-lighting' or 'taking turns': "We talked about John last week so we must talk about Lucy today". This is generally a denial, as well as a covert expression of the competitiveness which is the real problem facing the group at this point, and it is the therapist's task to bring the group back to its concealed focal conflict.

• The countertransference of the therapist – feelings about a particular group member – can lead him or her to lose a group perspective and engage in fruitless individual work. The therapist may be pushed into this by overidentification with a particular client, by a desire to be seen as effective and compassionate, or a fear of some current group conflict which has a personal significance he or she cannot deal with.

The therapist under pressure

It is not as easy for most of us to maintain a focus on the 'total interactional field' as it was for Foulkes. One reason is that group transactions are particularly rich and complex and are thus rarely susceptible to only one interpretation. Which particular strand of meaning do I, the therapist, decide to pick up at this precise point? How long do I allow the group to struggle with its current problem in the hope that it will arrive at its own resolution? This, of course, assumes I have a choice. I might not have the foggiest idea what is going on, and that presents me with the twin dilemmas of trying to understand my lack of understanding, and of trying to use my lack of understanding constructively. Am I confident enough and sufficiently in touch with my own 'internal supervisor' (in Patrick Casement's useful phrase), to counter group pressure to interpret or not to interpret?

Confronting group resistance is qualitatively different from confronting individual resistance, particularly for group therapists working alone. A group may unconsciously diverge from its stated objective, and attempt to avoid insight and change. This situation produces a clash of interests for the therapist, whose role is to promote insight and change but who is also, in some senses, a member of the group whose assumptions must be challenged.

To return to our hypothetical group: the imminent arrival of a new member arouses all sorts of anxieties to do with competitiveness, self-exposure and confidentiality. The group's response is to resort to manic flight, telling jokes and amusing anecdotes and, apparently, having a good time. The therapist must shift the focus back to the underlying anxieties and so cast him- or herself in the role of spoilsport. Much of the pressure facing therapists stems from this dichotomy which is central to their role. Therapists must be members of their groups, committed to their continuation and effective functioning as well as being fully attuned to their emotional and interpersonal process. At the same time, they must remain sufficiently detached to reflect on the process and share their reflections with the groups in useful ways.

From time to time the group will exploit this dichotomy to prevent change from taking place, or to avoid facing up to painful realities. Members will do this by either attempting to suck the therapist into the group process, and so prevent him or her from thinking, or by attempting to split the therapist from the group process by marginalising him or her, disregarding interventions, or responding to them with puzzled incomprehension. This can cause therapists to doubt their own sanity at times.

Foulkes emphasised the value of group members' own interventions and interactions, rather than those of the therapist, and also stressed the importance of careful selection to avoid a situation where a particular group member is in an obvious minority position in terms of age, background, sex, presenting problem or ethnic origin. Although often difficult to achieve, this reduces the potential for scapegoating and increases that for interpersonal learning. Scapegoating is the process whereby the group avoids facing up to its problems by blaming one individual for everything that is going wrong. Sometimes clients offer themselves up as scapegoats to punish themselves and collude with the group's avoidance. It is, of course, the therapist's function to interpret what is going on and so enable the group to face up to its collective dilemmas. In Foulkes's view it is the therapist's duty to establish and maintain a group culture in which members can share feelings in an atmosphere of mutual understanding, and experiment freely with different modes of interaction. The passive Lucy can allow herself to be angry without provoking rejection, and Peter can allow himself to be vulnerable without being destroyed.

Levels of meaning

When the group comes together, individuals arrive in ones and twos to share a particular physical and emotional space. Initially there is some desultory conversation on general topics such as the weather, traffic holdups and world affairs. There is then a pause, often precipitated by the arrival of the therapist, and it feels as though the real business of the group has begun. The group does not necessarily begin by overtly addressing its most pressing current preoccupations and the pre-group discussion about the dreadful state the country is in may continue. In the light of recent group events, the therapist may understand this as expressive of anxiety about the group disintegrating, the effect of new group members or about his or her concern or lack of concern. The therapist therefore assumes that communication is taking place on at least two levels – the overt and the covert even though the group doesn't necessarily share this assumption. Whitaker and Lieberman (1965) discuss this concept in the context of the focal conflict model: "We assume that a subsurface level exists in all groups in which the manifest content is itself relatively coherent and internally consistent. When a group is talking about something, one might assume that this is all that is happening . . . yet, even when the group situation consists of a conversation which is coherent in itself, we assume that another level of meaning also exists for, even in such a group, breaks and shifts occur in the topic under discussion. There are reversals and non-verbal accompaniments, suggesting that to assume that only a conversation is going on is to miss an important aspect of the situation . . . even in non-therapeutic groups one can observe the same phenomenon!".

Similarly, Ezriel (1950) writes: "it is one of the essential assumptions for psychoanalytic work with groups that, whatever the manifest content may be, there always develops rapidly an underlying common group problem, a common group tension of which the group is not aware but which determines its behaviour".

It is, in fact, possible to see this underlying group tension manifest itself. Often a group will start haltingly with different group members attempting to start a conversation which does not catch on. Different topics will be tried until one is found which reflects the group's current preoccupation. It is at precisely this point that the individual pathologies of group members intersect and can be addressed collectively through the therapist's interpretation. The therapist's function is to be alert for the manifestation of hidden conflict and to translate it from the symbolic language it is expressed in to a form of words the group can understand. The group can begin to explore and resolve its conflict on the basis of its new understanding. Where Id was Ego shall be.

It has not been possible, given the scope of these chapters, to do more than provide a sketchy survey of psychotherapeutic theory and practice. I hope, however, enough has been said to point the way forward for those nurses who wish to develop their knowledge and skills in this creative field.

Long and short courses in group analytic psychotherapy are available at the Institute of Group Analysis in London, and at regional centres in Birmingham, Manchester and Cambridge.

References
Ezriel, H. (1950) A psychoanalytic approach to group treatment. *British Journal of Medical Psychology.*
Foulkes, K. and Anthony, E. J. (1957) Psychotherapy – The Analytic Approach. Penguin, Harmondsworth.
Whitaker, D.S. and Lieberman, M. (1965) Psychotherapy Through the Group Process. Tavistock Publications, London.

Bibliography
Karnac, A. (1984) Therapeutic Group Analysis. Allen and Unwin, London
de Mare, P. (1983) The Evolution of Group Analysis. Routledge and Kegan Paul, London.
    These two books provide an introduction to development and practice of group analysis.
Storr, A. (1979) The Art of Psychotherapy. Secker and Warburg, London.
    Good introduction to psychotherapy generally.

Whiteley, J.S. and Gordon, J. (1979) Group Approaches in Psychiatry. Routledge and Kegan Paul, London.
Different applications of groupwork in clinical practice.
Wright, H. (1989) Groupwork: Perspectives and Practice. Scutari Press, Harrow.

Useful address
Institute of Group Analysis, 1 Daleham Gardens, London NW3 5BY.

32
Rooting for the source of anxiety: child psychotherapy at work

Dorothy Judd, BA, Dip. Art Ther., Cert. Ed., MACP

Principal Child Psychotherapist, Oncology Department, Middlesex Hospital, London and Visiting Teacher, Tavistock Clinic, London

Child psychotherapy aims to help children, even very young children, to rework unresolved emotional conflicts. All children experience conflict, anxiety, and trauma in response to their families and the world around them, as well as inner struggles over growing up and coping with aggression, frustration, separation and loss. This is often felt at an unconscious or fantasy level, and may be expressed through play.

Objectives of child psychotherapy

Child psychotherapists help children who have been subjected to adverse experiences or show emotional difficulties to share and explore aspects of their unconscious internal world. The child's mood, play, drawings, body-language and speech are carefully observed and experienced by the therapist, while any anxieties which may interfere with the child's development (often originating in early experiences) are directed towards the therapist, as are positive or loving feelings. This phenomenon, called transference, is one of the central forces in any therapeutic relationship with both children and adults. Indeed, the safe and sequestered nature of the setting, the regularity of the sessions, and the therapist's interpretations of the transference of feelings make it an intrinsic 'tool' of the treatment.

Clearly the 'vehicles' of communication children use are usually very different from those of adults, so the technique, equipment and setting for child psychotherapy also differ. However, child psychotherapist whose qualifications are recognised by the NHS work on psychoanalytic lines, and their theoretical framework is basically that of psychoanalytic psychotherapists working with adults. Child psychotherapists can be Kleinian, Freudian, or Jungian, or a combination of these 'schools' depending on their training, and will have to undergo personal psychoanalysis. In work with adults, it is generally the 'child within the adult' that is identified for treatment; with children, the young child or baby part of the self is often more accessible. Children can, however, be haughtily indignant when their 'baby feelings' or 'baby needs' are addressed, especially when they are consciously struggling to be more grown-up and to resist regressive pulls towards earlier infancy and dependence. These earlier phases of development, though, may not have been adequately worked through.

Children of course, unlike adults, do not volunteer for treatment, nor do they necessarily acknowledge the need. Adolescents generally need to be prepared to attend and to allow the process to begin, while younger children have less choice in this matter. Carers are usually responsible for initiating an assessment, bringing the child to the sessions and supporting the treatment, even in the face of resistance. However, children generally enjoy and value the experience of being really listened to and made sense of, and often do not want sessions to end.

Child psychotherapy in practice

One case study illustrates the benefits of child psychotherapy. In a psychotherapy session, Paul, aged 14, complained about his school bag being full of holes. He had come for weekly psychotherapy since his disclosure to the child psychotherapist five months previously that his mother and older brothers had been beating him. This was investigated and validated by social services, and Paul was taken into care. He had originally been brought to child guidance by his mother, at the suggestion of their GP, for his persistent stealing at school - of which his mother felt ashamed. In the initial meetings Paul's mother spoke for him, and relentlessly accused him, but was unable to consider the problem itself. The child psychotherapist arranged a few exploratory meetings with Paul on his own, while a colleague met with his mother.

In the two individual sessions, the child psychotherapist paid attention to this little boy (he was very undersized and immature): to his withdrawn and miserable manner, his silences, and the implications of his behaviour and difficult history (he was sent to live abroad with his grandparents for most of his life, and his father had died of drug-addiction one year previously). In the second meeting, feeling safe enough to risk the consequences and threats from his mother, he had asked if he could go and live in a children's home, and then talked about the beatings which he had kept hidden from all outsiders for two years.

In the light of follow-up long-term work, Paul's reference to the tattered bag was his way of talking about feeling maltreated and unsafe, showing how he was unable to hold onto his thoughts properly when he did not feel safely held in his mother's, or indeed anyone's mind. As his placement was still with a short-term foster mother, he found the uncertainty, upheavals and far-reaching implications hard to bear. The psychotherapy aimed to give Paul the opportunity to work through some of these feelings of distress. His anger was at times redirected onto the therapist, expressed partly by tearing up an appointment letter. He felt confused, guilty, uncertain, as well as, at times, a sense of loss.

Many of Paul's communications were non-verbal, indirect, or

symbolic. His reference, for example, to the bag full of holes was a symbolic expression of his feelings about himself and his mother, and were re-experienced with the therapist. With skilful listening, experience, and attention to her own emotional responses to the child, the therapist was gradually able to make sense of Paul's underlying feelings and feed them back to him in a way he could understand and hold inside himself. In time, Paul felt less like an inadequate and neglected 'bag full of holes' as he built up a sense of the therapist's ability to hold onto him in her mind over a period of time. He no longer needed to express his distress through the presenting symptom of stealing.

When do children need psychotherapy?

The kinds of problems children may demonstrate and which can be helpfully analysed within the safety of a therapeutic setting include: enuresis, encopresis, eating disorders, depression, sleep disturbances, over-clinging behaviour, aggression, school phobia, stealing, withdrawn behaviour, excessive masturbation, obsessional behaviour, poor ability to socialise, impaired learning or under-achievement, pseudo-maturity, fears, phobias, confusional states, being accident-prone, excessive escapes to a fantasy world and hyperactivity. The impact of chronic illness or physical or mental handicap, and the ways these affect their caregivers are probably further adequate reasons for the emotional understanding child psychotherapists can offer. Other adverse life events, such as lengthy hospitalisation, the death of someone close, lengthy separations, a seriously ill sibling or emotional environmental deprivation and abuse are pointers where, upon assessment, psychotherapy might be considered advisable.

Child psychotherapy, however, can only be carried out if the child's carers and support system (parents, foster parents or residential social workers) support the treatment. Generally, it is desirable that they participate in the treatment programme, perhaps by regularly seeing another professional who liaises with the child's therapist. If this is not possible, it can be all too easy for parents to undermine their child's treatment, however unintentionally, due to unacknowledged envy of the treatment the child is receiving. The minimum involvement with the carers would be regular review meetings with the child psychotherapist.

The child is viewed as a part of a wider unit. The option of family therapy may be ruled out if initial explorations reveal emotional difficulties in the child's own right or if significant family members are unavailable. However, the continual inter-relatedness and evolution of child and family or carers has to be facilitated alongside the child's development within the therapeutic relationship, so child psychotherapy is rarely carried out in isolation. While the detailed interaction must be confidential to facilitate trust and uncover layers with which other relationships need not concern themselves, the child needs to feel assured that the various adults in his or her life are working together.

Some treatments can be completed within a few weeks, if the problem is not deeply entrenched, but programmes usually last from at least a year up to several years. Frequency varies from regular once-weekly sessions to five times a week, and depends on availability of treatment, practical arrangements, the nature of the problem, and the child's ability to 'hold on' between sessions. For example, Emma, aged four, experienced the gaps between her weekly therapy sessions as an unbearable repetition of the feeling of being 'dropped' by previous foster placements which had broken down. When the therapy was increased to twice weekly sessions, Emma could begin to sustain hopefulness not only that there would be future sessions, but also that her therapist could bear and survive her aggressive attacks.

Improvements and developments in any therapy need to be consolidated, and this is done by repeating, for example, the experience of holiday breaks. This may arouse feelings of intolerable frustration, rage, manic defences, denial, sadness or loss. Time after time these reactions are re-experienced and brought to a level where they can be thought about and learnt from, so their sway over the child lessens. In this way, children gradually relinquish their need to excessively control the world or flee from it in their imagination, and take the often painful steps towards valuing the important people in their lives, accepting their dependence, and managing their infantile feelings.

Where is child psychotherapy practised?

Child psychotherapy is mainly practised in child guidance clinics, funded by either the health service, social services, education department or by a combination of these. Occasionally it is funded by a charity, or by the relatively recently created Child Psychotherapy Trust, which aims to promote the availability of child psychotherapy in the NHS. The service is also available in some hospitals or hospital child psychiatry departments as well as in some health centres, schools and counselling services. Some child psychotherapists work part-time in private practice.

Child psychotherapists also consult to other professionals who deal with children, such as nurses, hospital doctors, health visitors, nursery officers, child minders, teachers, GPs and social workers. Referrals come from all these professions, as well as from parents themselves. Consultative work is often preventive: problems can be dealt with before they become entrenched, or adults can simply be helped to think about management issues. This can be more effective and wide-reaching than when child psychotherapy is chosen as a 'last resort'.

Child psychotherapists also run small therapy groups for children of different ages and with different problems, such as adolescents, children who have been sexually abused and mothers and toddlers with eating problems. Group therapy is ideal for problems which can be shared with peers and, above all, are more rapidly unearthed in a group situation, where they can then be 'held' and interpreted by the group therapist.

In the hospital setting, child psychotherapists either work with children who have been referred to child psychiatry (with a similar population to child guidance clinics), or with children on the ward. This would include a wide range of situations, such as road traffic accident victims, cases of non-accidental injury, anorexia, attempted overdose cases, surgical and chronic conditions as well as children facing life-threatening illness. The aim is to address the children's concerns by offering anything from emotional 'first aid' to long-term intensive psychotherapy. It is well-documented that children tend to avoid expressing their anxieties to their parents for fear of upsetting them, and that parents similarly 'protect' their children by trying to be cheerful and avoiding the more serious implications of illness (Bluebond-Langner, 1978). This is where child psychotherapists (with the permission of the parents and, ideally, in conjunction with other members of a psychosocial team) help children to express their worries (Judd, 1989). Psychotherapy for children with cancer has been found to markedly decrease the frequency and severity of their emotional problems (Watson, 1983).

Working with parents

An important part of a child psychotherapist's work is with parents: not only regular reviews of the therapy and discussion of the parents' view of the child, but also work with parents in their own right. Pregnant women and mothers of very young babies may be in special need of a child psychotherapist's experience and understanding. Sarah, for example, a woman in her late twenties, sought help when she was experiencing negative feelings towards her unborn 'alien' baby and the changes to her body. Psychotherapy enabled her to understand how the unborn baby was imbued with her feelings of herself as an unwanted and unloved child. By the time of the birth, Sarah felt positive about her baby, and was able to mother him well, while continuing over several years to work in her therapy on her own 'infantile' feelings of worthlessness. In this way baby Ben was spared from having many of his mother's problems heaped upon him from birth, on top of the inevitable struggles of normal development.

There is a great need for the availability of child psychotherapy to spread beyond London. It is a cost-effective way of keeping children out of care, delinquency, and ultimately even prison or psychiatric hospital. Our children's future and accordingly that of the country as a whole would benefit if more services were available.

References
Bergmann, T. (1965) *Children in the Hospital*. International University Press, New York.
Judd, D. (1989) *Give Sorrow Words – Working with a Dying Child*. Free Association Books, London.
Watson, M. (1983) Psychological intervention with cancer patients: a review. *Psychological Medicine*, **13**, 839–46.

Bibliography

Bluebond-Langner, M. (1978) *The Private Worlds of Dying Children*. Princeton University Press, New Jersey.
Illustrates clearly the way mutual protectiveness prevents patients and carers from communicating openly.
Boston, M. and Szur, R. (Eds) (1983) *Psychotherapy with Severely Deprived Children*. Routledge and Kegan Paul, London.
Demonstrates how children previously considered unsuitable for psychotherapy have the capacity to respond to treatment.
Daws, D. and Boston, M. (Eds) (1977) *The Child Psychotherapist and Problems of Young People*. Wildwood House, London.
A clear exposition, suitable for the lay reader, of many applications of child psychotherapy.

For more information and video contact:
The Child Psychotherapy Trust,
c/o TIHR,
Tavistock Centre,
120 Belsize Lane,
London NW3 5BA.
Tel: 071-433 3867.

Careers leaflet available from:
The Association of Child Psychotherapists,
Burgh House,
New End Square,
London NW3 1LT.
Tel: 071-794 8881.

33

Can a nurse be a therapist? Running an anxiety management group

Geraldine E. Harrison, RGN, RMN, DipDMT
Part time Staff Nurse, Queen Mary's Hospital, Roehampton and Freelance Dance Movement Therapist

Anxiety is a common problem - about 82 per cent of psychiatric consultations in general practice involve anxiety and worry, and one in 20 are referred for specialist attention (McPherson,1980). Anxiety management would, therefore, be valuable in any psychiatric setting, but clinical psychologists are in short supply and are not always available to give this therapy. Their skills can, however, be shared or 'given away' (Carr, 1987), and non-psychologists can be taught behavioural psychotherapy (Ayllon and Michael, 1959; Yule, 1978). Since anxiety management training (AMT) has been shown to be effective in reducing anxiety (Woodward and Jones, 1980; Jannour et al, 1982; Barlow et al, 1984), it was decided that a nurse should be given the skills needed to run such a group with the support of a psychologist in a day hospital.

Rationale

Lang (1968) and Rachman (1977) argue that treatment for anxiety should follow the systems model of fear: autonomic, behavioural and cognitive, and this is the basis for the AMT course. A general explanation of anxiety phenomenon is outlined in the first session, and relaxation skills are taught early in the course. Weekes (1984) states how "understanding (anxiety) in itself releases some tension", while relaxation is directly antagonistic to anxiety (Wolpe, 1966). The methods of relaxation used in the course are those of Jacobson (1938) and Benson (1977). The Jacobson method requires the individual to recognise the presence of muscular contraction, and then to relax it, and is done with all of the muscle-groups of the body. Benson relaxation involves the 'relaxation response', and is more akin to meditation. Breathing control is addressed next, as this can play an important part in both the development and management of anxiety (Clark et al, 1985).

Thought challenging is also outlined in the AMT. Stress-prone people are apt to engage in thinking errors such as polarisation (black and white reasoning) and to over-emphasise the most negative possibilities in a given situation - catastrophic thinking (Beck, 1984). Having 'caught' these automatic thoughts, clients can question their validity and appraise them in a more rational and realistic way.

1. Introduction)	
2. Relaxation) Autonomic	
3. Breathing Control)	
4. Graded Practice)	
5. Problem Solving) Behavioural	
6. Thought Management - Cognitive	
7. Assertiveness	
8. Coping in the Long Term	

Table 1. Areas covered each week in the course.

Michenbaum (1985) defines assertiveness training as "behavioural rehearsal, role playing, and modelling". Stressful interactions are anticipated, and different ways of coping rehearsed. Powell (1987) recognises that clients value meeting others with similar problems, and the group itself is a vital part of the treatment process (Eayrs *et al*, 1984).

Weekly format of the group

Anxiety and mood rating These scores are collected each week, using Beck Anxiety Checklist (BAC, unpublished) and mood ratings (BDI) (Beck, 1967). The mood rating questionnaire is included because clients often have a concurrent affective disorder.

Individual review of progress This often refers to the use of diaries, and can highlight previously unnoticed problems (one client, for example, was able to show that her anxiety levels were high when she was with her daughter). The use of coping methods taught in the session are reinforced, and clients' use of strategies supervised. Socratic questioning, which models self-questioning, is used by the leader, as "...a single question may simultaneously attempt to draw the patient's attention to a particular area, assess his responses to this new subject of inquiry, obtain direct information..., generate methods for solving problems..., and...raise thoughts in the patient's mind regarding previously distorted conclusions" (Beck, 1987).

Teaching This is primarily a didactic group.

Tea-break A tea-break is planned each week, when the therapist(s) withdraw, allowing a debriefing. Yalom (1975) says this plays an important role in the therapy process because members are "helped to experience themselves as autonomous, responsible and resourceful adults who, though they may profit from the therapists expertise, are nevertheless able to control emotions, to pursue the primary task of the group, and to integrate their experience."

Practical sessions These include questions and feedback.

Homework setting This includes keeping diaries, and practising skills. Clients need a clear explanation of what to do, and the rationale must be explained with homework set up as an information-giving exercise, providing motivation to complete the work (Beck, 1979). An information sheet is given out after each session (Kennerley, 1990).

Week 1: introduction
Teaching points This session introduces several key concepts:
- The course involves self-management of anxiety by regular practice of coping skills. Its aim is not to 'cure', but to present coping methods.
- Anxiety is normal, but problem anxiety occurs when it is out of proportion to the situation and/or goes on too long.
- An outline of the biological responses during anxiety is given.
- The symptoms of anxiety are covered, as is adaptive and maladaptive coping.
- The role of stimulants in maintaining/causing anxiety, and how hunger can mimic an anxiety state is discussed.

Methods used Some of the session involves straightforward information being given by the therapist, but other methods are also used. A brainstorm technique is used to encourage group participation in generating:
1. Symptoms of anxiety - grouped by the therapist into three lists: somatic (or physical); behavioural and cognitive (or thoughts).
2. Coping methods - divided into two lists: adaptive (good) and maladaptive (bad).

Discussion is used, and there are several interludes for this. Initially, group members introduce themselves, clear guidelines are given to keep anxiety low and the leader goes first. The group discusses how anxiety can be a friend (for example, when running away from an attacker or to spur one on to revise for an exam), and finally focuses on contributory factors such as poor memory, family arguments, staying in, lack of social life, tiredness, poor performance at work and lack of enjoyment.

Group members are encouraged to sample decaffeinated products, and both caffeinated and decaffeinated drinks are on offer.

Homework setting
1. Read information sheet.
2. Keep a diary of the use of stimulants and anxiety.

Week 2: relaxation
Teaching points The vicious cycle of anxiety is introduced, whereby muscles tense and other unpleasant bodily symptoms ensue during anxiety, and these in turn can cause further anxiety.

Relaxation is shown to be effective in controlling body tension, and the principles and methods of Jacobson and Bensons' relaxation techniques are covered. Applied relaxation is also explained; this entails shortening the method (once fully learnt) and using the sequence at different times, places and positions. This acquisition of a portable skill - being able to relax in a range of environments - is required for real life coping. Finally, the role of exercise in the management of anxiety is outlined.

Methods used The second week involves more practical work. Each group member shades in the areas where they feel tension on a diagram of a human figure. This can be done in pairs, and is then viewed by the whole group to discuss similarities and differences; the leader also fills in areas of the human figure to reinforce that anxiety is a normal human phenomenon. The leader explains the Jacobson and Benson methods of relaxation, and the room is dimmed, the chairs turned away from the circle and both methods tried, with feedback invited after each.

Homework setting
1. Anxiety diary.
2. Relaxation practice, with a tape recording and information handout providing instructions. Clients are asked to practise relaxation exercises twice daily, if possible.

Week 3: breathing control
Teaching points The concept that breathing can play an important part in the development and management of anxiety is introduced. Hyperventilation is defined, and the consequences of reduced blood carbon dioxide explained. The principles and method for emergency control of breathing are also outlined using a paper bag, as are those for controlled breathing.

Methods used Practical demonstration is featured, and at the beginning of the session, group members count their breathing over one minute. Clients usually achieve 20-30 breaths per minute and not the desired eight to 12, thus demonstrating their over-breathing.

A forced hyperventilation exercise follows, the subject stands panting or over-breathing for one minute, sits down and then rates him or herself on the BAC. This exercise can be repeated later, making use of a paper bag and/or controlled breathing until the symptoms abate. It can also be performed by the therapist, a volunteer or as pair work. The leader demonstrates how to use a paper bag for emergency control of anxiety, and the group is taken through the controlled breathing exercise technique.

Homework setting
1. Diary of anxiety.
2. Continue to practise relaxation skills.
3. Practise controlled breathing. Dots are given to each group member to stick on their watches, acting as a cue or reminder to check breathing patterns. As the dot catches the eye, clients can register their breathing and adopt controlled breathing, if needed. The dots can also be used as a cue to relax, (dropping the shoulders, for example), and emergency control of breathing is also practised.

Week 4: graded practice
Teaching points It is explained that avoidance maintains anxiety, by stopping clients learning that it is safe for them to do the things they avoid. The principles and methods of graded practice are detailed, or the fear is faced one step at a time.

Methods used A real or imagined difficulty is used to script graded practice techniques for a situation which is being avoided. This method is modelled by the therapist, and the group divides into pairs to script their own graded practice for a situation they would avoid in real life. This work is supervised by the therapist(s).

It is important that the subject - not the therapist - primarily dictates the next step in graded practice; targets should seem manageable to clients, and a collaborative stance is aimed for.

Homework setting
1. Anxiety diary.
2. Relaxation and breathing skills - continued practice.
3. Start step one of planned graded practice - the handout recaps principles and method, and in weeks five to eight, group members can seek supervision with their graded practice programme.

Week 5: problem-solving
Teaching points The principles and methods of problem-solving and decision making are itemised and a blue-printing strategy introduced establishing contingency plans for the worst that can happen.

Methods used The problem-solving process is modelled by the therapist using a real or imagined problem. Everyone joins in brainstorming session for possible solutions. Group members then work in pairs applying the problem-solving process to real life problems supervised by the therapist.

Homework setting
1. Practise relaxation and breathing control.
2. Continue graded practice.

3. Put into practice intentions from problem-solving exercise.
4. Practise this skill, and read handout.
5. Anxiety diary: a record of thought/images experienced during anxiety.

Week 6: thought management

Teaching points The focus is now placed on the management of thoughts or cognitions during anxiety, and the link between thoughts and emotion is explained. The vicious cycle, where worrying thoughts can fuel anxiety is introduced, and both the principles and methods of distraction technique and thought-challenging are covered.

Methods used Group members are asked to generate examples of how to distract themselves when they feel anxious, and thought-challenging is modelled using several examples of worrying thoughts.

Pair-work involves scripting thought challenging statements from the group members' diaries, and the 'listener' can facilitate or prompt and then swap roles. This exercise is supervised by the therapist(s), and a discussion follows on the best technique for certain situations.

Homework setting

1. Read this week's information handout.
2. Use distraction.
4. Fill in "thought challenge" in thought diary.
5. Homework from previous weeks repeated.

Week 7: being assertive

Teaching points Clients are taught that anxiety creates not only avoidance but loss of confidence and that the assertive approach may, therefore, mean they suffer less stress or tension in the long run and develop more self-confidence. The concept of a continuum is presented, which consists of: passive; assertive; aggressive/manipulative (Bond, 1986). Behaviours associated with these headings are outlined, and the components of an assertive response are covered: explanation; feelings; needs and consequences.

Methods used The group brainstorms typical characteristics (including non-verbal signs and speech content) of the three groups.

A game or exercise is proposed where clients practise saying 'no' to a request. Each group member is asked to do an outrageous favour, and their brief is to refuse; the responses are slotted into 'passive' or 'assertive' categories. Group members then ask favours of the therapist, whose answers are labelled by the group. Examples of an assertive response, including explanation and feelings, are modelled. After tea, group members work in pairs to script an assertive solution to a problem, or to role-play imagined or real scenarios where assertiveness may be called for.

Homework setting
1. Read this week's handout.
2. Script an assertive solution to a problem and test skills if situation arises.
3. Homework from previous weeks repeated.

Week 8: coping in the long term

Tasks/teaching points   This meeting takes place after a two-week gap, to help prepare group members for separation from the group and therapist. The skills and strategies learnt on the course are summed up and shown to apply to real-life coping. Members are told that if their work and practice continues, the benefits will show - the choice is theirs. Setbacks are likely, but constitute a learning experience as well as a cue for better planning next time.

Reassurance is mentioned at this stage. This ultimately, means avoiding uncertainty, and repeatedly seeking reassurance is an unhelpful coping strategy - the aim should be to reassure oneself. Finally, farewells and good wishes are exchanged.

Methods used   The group generate their own tips, for example useful skills learned in the sessions or a more personal maxim. A discussion ensues about the value of reassurance and, finally, about how it feels to say goodbye.

Homework setting
1. Keep working - practice improves skills.
2. Read self-help texts (a list is given).
3. Make a summary diary of progress with the following headings: relaxation and breathing; graded practice; problem solving and decision making; thought management; assertiveness.

Follow-up

A follow-up meeting takes place three months after the course, and reminders and questionnaires are posted two weeks beforehand. The questionnaires used are BDI and BAC, and a group evaluation form is also given, so that clients can rate the usefulness of items such as the relaxation tape, handouts and green spots.

At the meeting, clients report outstanding events since the last meeting, and review their progress under the five headings mentioned above. Further supervision may be sought and points clarified, and encouragement is given to keep working.

The group evaluation forms are scanned to see what clients found most and least helpful, and BDI and BAC scores plotted on a graph to show improvement or decline. A written report is compiled for the case notes, and one is sent to the referring agent. Feedback received from the clinical psychologist supervising the AMT suggests that nurses can operate as therapists for clients with anxiety, given the correct training and supervision. However, it is naive to consider running such groups alone - clinical psychologists are experts in anxiety management, and their help should always be sought.

Running an AMT is a thorough test of understanding anxiety management using the psychological model, as well as of one's own teaching and group skills. The leader's role is to inform, direct, facilitate and reinforce. The treatment package is evaluated using weekly questionnaires, and scores demonstrate whether the treatment works. These skills can boost professional development, and the strategies can also be used by the group leader to reduce his or her own anxiety!

References
Beck, A.T. (1967) Depression. Harper and Row, London .
Beck, A.T. *et al* (1979) Cognitive Therapy of Depression. John Wiley and Sons, Chichester.
Benson, H. (1977) The Relaxation Response. Collins, London.
Bond, M. (1986) Stress and Self Awareness: A Guide for Nurses. Heinemann, Oxford.
Butler, G. (1985) Managing Anxiety. University Department of Psychiatry, Oxford.
Carr, J. (1987) Giving away the behavioural approach. *Behavioural Psychotherapy Journal*, **16**, 2, 78-84.
Catalan, J. and Gath, D.H. (1985) Benzodiazepines in general practice: time for decision. *BMJ*, **290**, 1374-75.
Clarke, D.M., Salkovski P.M. and Chalkley, A.G. (1985) Respiratory control as a treatment for panic attacks. *Journal of Behaviour Ther. and Exp. Psychi.*, **16**, 23-30.
Douglas, A.R. Lindsay, W.R. Brooks, D.N.(1986) The three systems model of fear and anxiety: Implications for assessment of social anxiety. *Behavioural Psychotherapy Journal*, **15**, 181-87.
Hambly, K. (1983) Overcoming Tension. Sheldon Press, London.
Jacobson, E. (1938) Progressive Relaxation. University of Chicago Press, USA.
Kennerley H. (1990) Managing Anxiety: A Training Manual. Oxford University Press, Oxford.
Kennerley, H. and Marzillier, J. (1988) Can General Practitioners Manage Anxiety. Division of Clinical Psychology. Division of Clinical Psychology, Forum No. 14.
Marks, I. (1981) Cure and Care of Neuroses. Wiley, Chichester.
Marks, I. (1985) Controlled trial of psychiatric nurse therapists in primary care? *BMJ*, **290**, 1181-84.
Menchenbaum, D. (1985) Stress Inoculation Training. Pergamon Press, Oxford.
Powell, T.J. (1986) Anxiety management groups in clinical practice: A preliminary report. *Behavioural Psychotherapy Journal*, **15**, 181-87.
Weekes, C. (1984) More Help for your Nerves. Angus and Robertson, London.
Wolpe, J. and Lazarus, A. A. (1966) Behaviour Therapy Techniques. Pergamon Press, Oxford.
Yalom, I.D. (1975) The Theory and Practice of Group Psychotherapy. Basic Books Inc, London and New York.

Note: The author was invited by a clinical psychologist to join an anxiety management training (AMT) group, which ran as an eight week course at the day hospital where she worked. She attended the first session as a learner, the second as cotherapist and progressed to leader. The psychologist attended four sessions, and was available for supervision.

Referrals came from the wards, out-patient department and the day hospital itself. A selection procedure was completed by the clinical psychologist, and no more than 10 clients attended one course; the groups met weekly.

Index